writing skills for the

GRE and GMAT

tests

THOMSON

PETERSON'S

Australia • Canada • Mexico • Singapore • Spain • United Kingdom • United States

About The Thomson Corporation and Peterson's

With revenues of US$7.2 billion, The Thomson Corporation (www.thomson.com) is a leading global provider of integrated information solutions for business, education, and professional customers. Its Learning businesses and brands (www.thomsonlearning.com) serve the needs of individuals, learning institutions, and corporations with products and services for both traditional and distributed learning.

Peterson's, part of The Thomson Corporation, is one of the nation's most respected providers of lifelong learning online resources, software, reference guides, and books. The Education Supersite^{SM} at www.petersons.com—the Internet's most heavily traveled education resource—has searchable databases and interactive tools for contacting U.S.-accredited institutions and programs. In addition, Peterson's serves more than 105 million education consumers annually.

For more information, contact Peterson's, 2000 Lenox Drive, Lawrenceville, NJ 08648; 800-338-3282; or find us on the World Wide Web at www.petersons.com/about.

ISBN 0-7689-1094-3

Printed in the United States of America

10 9 8 7 6 5 4 3 2 1   04 03 02

CONTENTS

Introduction

GET READY FOR GRE OR GMAT ANALYTICAL WRITING

Graduate admissions officials are increasingly relying on GRE and GMAT essay scores to predict graduate-level academic performance and, in turn, to make admissions choices among similarly qualified applicants. The point is clear: You'd better take the essay portion of your exam seriously! Fortunately, you've come to the right place. This book will give you the competitive edge you need to gain admission to your first-choice graduate program or B-school.

All GMAT test takers and, beginning in October 2002, all GRE test takers, will need to compose two essays as part of their testing experience. The following two essay tasks, while quite distinct from each other in terms of material, are essentially the same on the GRE as on the GMAT:

> **Present Your Perspective on an Issue (GRE)** or **Analysis of an Issue (GMAT):** In this type of essay, you'll adopt a position on a given issue of broad intellectual interest and support that position with reasons and/or examples *(45-minute time limit on the GRE; 30-minute time limit on the GMAT)*.

> **Analyze an Argument (GRE)** or **Analysis of an Argument (GMAT):** In this type of essay, you'll analyze a paragraph-length argument and point out and discuss problems with its line of reasoning, adequacy and use of evidence, and internal logic *(30-minute time limit on both exams)*.

During your GRE or GMAT tests (both of which are now administered only by computer), the computerized testing system will randomly select your essay questions from its large database —or "pool"—of official questions. The test maker, Educational Testing Service (ETS), has revealed its complete pool of essay questions—250 altogether—for each of the two exams, which will help you be prepared for what you will see on the test.

ESSAY-PHOBIC? YOU'RE NOT ALONE!

Okay, you've committed yourself to taking the GRE (or GMAT). Perhaps you've already bought one of those big, thick test-prep books to help you get ready for your exam. But if you're like most test takers, you've put off any earnest attempt to prepare for the two essays, focusing instead on the exam's multiple-choice sections. Why do so many test takers neglect Analytical Writing when it comes to GRE and GMAT prep? Probably for one or more of the following reasons:

- *The task is intimidating because there's no room for guesswork.* During the exam's multiple-choice sections, you can score points by making lucky, random guesses and by making so-called "educated" guesses (by eliminating some answer choices). But it's impossible to fake your way through the essay sections.

- *Scoring the essays is so subjective.* It's difficult to know what the readers will reward you for and where you stand in relation to other test takers—or so you think.

- *Writing essays is such hard work.* Organizing and composing an essay inherently requires far more activity, both mentally and physically, than analyzing and answering a multiple-choice question.

- *There are so many possible essay questions but so little time to get ready for them.* Since ETS has pre-disclosed all of the questions, you might feel you're at a competitive disadvantage unless you're ready for each and every one of them. And given a pool of 250 questions, who has the time, let alone the brain power, to get ready for every single one? Not you—so you wonder why you should even bother trying.

Take heart: Nearly all your peers experience similar insecurities about the GRE or GMAT writing tasks. And by picking up this book, you've taken an important first step toward overcoming your anxiety!

SOME TESTING TERMINOLOGY YOU SHOULD KNOW

Throughout this book, I refer to various acronyms and other terms that test makers use and you should know. This first one is for GRE as well as GMAT test takers:

ETS This is the nonprofit organization that creates the GRE and GMAT tests, administers the exams, and reports exam scores to the graduate schools. ETS also conducts ongoing research projects aimed at improving its tests.

GRE TERMINOLOGY

GRE General Test or **GRE** *(Graduate Record Exam)*. Sitting for this exam is a prerequisite for admission to many college and university graduate programs (Masters and Ph.D.). The GRE is designed to measure a broad range of verbal, quantitative, and analytical writing abilities. Remember, the exam is offered only by computer now (except in some remote locations outside the U.S.).

NOTE: Do not confuse the GRE General Test with the GRE *subject tests*. Each subject test is designed to gauge the test taker's knowledge of one particular academic field. GRE subject tests are administered separately from the GRE General Test.

Analytical Writing section. This is the section of the GRE that includes the two writing tasks. This test section is new on the GRE as of October 2002.

GRE Writing Assessment. This is a stand-alone test that is identical to the Analytical Writing section of the new GRE. ETS began administering the GRE Writing Assessment in fall 1999 and will continue to do so through December 2002. On January 1, 2003, ETS will discontinue the stand-alone GRE Writing Assessment.

Present Your Perspective on an Issue. This is the name of one of the two writing tasks on the Analytical Writing section of the GRE. Throughout this book, I refer to it by the single word "Issue" (using an uppercase "I").

Analyze an Argument. This is the name of the other writing task on the Analytical Writing section of the GRE. Throughout this book, I refer to it by the single word "Argument" (using an uppercase "A").

GMAT TERMINOLOGY

GMAT CAT (*Graduate Management Admission Test, Computer-Adaptive Test*). Sitting for this exam is a prerequisite for matriculation at most graduate business schools (MBA programs). The GMAT is designed to measure a broad range of verbal, quantitative, and analytical writing abilities. Since the GMAT is offered only by computer now (except in some remote locations outside the U.S.), the acronym "GMAT" is synonymous with "GMAT CAT."

GMAC (*Graduate Management Admission Council*). This policy-making organization guides business schools in establishing their admission requirements and guidelines. GMAC also confers with ETS about possible refinements in the GMAT and about possible changes in policies and procedures with respect to GMAT evaluation and score reporting. GMAC is primarily comprised of administrators from various graduate management schools.

AWA (*Analytical Writing Assessment*). This is the term that GMAC and ETS use in referring to the two GMAT essay sections as a unit and to the single score that ETS awards for both essays.

Analysis of an Issue. This is the name of one of the two GMAT essay tasks. Throughout this book, I refer to it by the single word "Issue" (using an uppercase "I").

Analysis of an Argument. This is the name of the other GMAT essay tasks. Throughout this book, I refer to it by the single word "Argument" (using an uppercase "A").

THE OFFICIAL "POOLS" OF GRE AND GMAT ESSAY QUESTIONS

During your GRE (or GMAT) sitting, the computerized testing system will randomly select your Issue and Argument questions from a large database, or "pool." (You won't know beforehand which particular questions the testing system will present to you.) ETS has predisclosed its complete pool of essay questions for each of the two exams. To get the greatest possible benefit from this book, especially from the sample essays in Parts 5–8, you should obtain your official list. They're available on line, and the GMAT list is also available in print. (For details, see below.)

THE POOL OF GRE ESSAY QUESTIONS

The official list (pool) of GRE Analytical Writing questions currently consists of 125 Issues and 125 Arguments. Here are three different ways to obtain the complete list:

- View the list, free of charge and without registration, at the official GRE Web site (www.gre.org). Follow the link to the description of the GRE General Test, then locate the description of the Analytical Writing section. There, you'll find separate links to the list of Issues and list of Arguments.

- Link directly to the Issue and Argument lists from my GRE Analytical Writing Web site (www.west.net/~stewart/grewa).

- The two lists *might* be available from ETS in printed form. For the latest information, check my update page at this book's Web site (www.west.net/~stewart/ws).

THE POOL OF GMAT ESSAY QUESTIONS

The official list (pool) of GMAT essay questions (for the admissions year 2001-02) consists of 125 Issues and 125 Arguments. Here are three different ways to obtain the list:

- Download the list, free of charge and without registration, from the GMAC's official GMAT Web site (www.mba.com). The list is available only as a PDF (portable document format) file, not as an

HTML file (Web page). A single file contains all 125 Arguments and 125 Issues. The file is 38 pages in length; you'll find the Arguments on pages 1-25 and the Issues on pages 26-38.

> **NOTE:** To view the PDF file, you'll need Adobe's *Acrobat Reader* software. In all likelihood, *Acrobat Reader* is already installed on your computer. If it isn't, you'll find instructions for downloading and installing it when you come across the PDF file at the official GMAT Web site.

- Download the PDF file described above via my GMAT Analytical Writing Web site (www.west.net/~stewart/awa).

- ETS publishes the GMAT essay questions in a printed publication: *The Official Guide for GMAT Review* ($19.95). The questions are *not* published in the official *GMAT Information Bulletin* (free from ETS).

WHAT YOU'LL LEARN FROM THIS BOOK

This book is designed as a stand-alone resource for GRE and GMAT essay preparation. In Parts 1-4, you'll learn how to brainstorm, organize, and compose your best possible GRE or GMAT essays—all within the constraints of the exam's testing environment. Then, in Parts 5-8, you'll learn how to apply what you read in Parts 1-4, by studying model responses to a variety of Issues and Arguments from the official pools.

PART 1

Part 1 is the primer, where you'll familiarize yourself with both essay sections (Issue and Argument). In Part 1, you'll learn:

- Ground rules for the two essay sections

- About typical Issues and Arguments

- About the Writing Assessment computer interface

- What to expect of the exam's special word processor

- How your essays are scored, evaluated, and reported

At the end of Part 1, you'll perform two diagnostic writing tasks under simulated exam conditions. You'll then score your own essay by using the official scoring criteria and by comparing your essays with scored essays composed by other test takers.

PARTS 2 AND 3

Parts 2 and 3 provide the basic training you need to score your best on the Issue essay and Argument essay, respectively. These two parts walk you, step-by-step, through the process of:

- Analyzing the Issue (or Argument), to ensure your ideas are the type that the readers reward with a top score

- Outlining and organizing your essay to achieve a cohesive product in which your ideas flow logically and coherently from one to the next

- Allocating your time to ensure a good balance between depth and breadth, so that you don't end up with a truncated essay, a rough-draft, or an outline-only essay

Part 2 also provides brainstorming suggestions and resources for the Issue essay to help ensure that you're not caught without anything to say about the issue at hand. Part 3 also goes into great depth about the various logical fallacies and other reasoning problems that the test makers build into GRE and GMAT Arguments and that you must recognize in order to score high on your Argument essay. You'll learn how to discuss each type of problem in an articulate manner, thereby leaving a distinctly positive impression on the reader.

PART 4

In scoring your essays, GRE and GMAT readers take into account not just your ideas but also how effectively your words, phrases, and sentences communicate those ideas. To ensure yourself a top score, you should strive to demonstrate the following to the reader:

- An appropriately mature writing style

- Good control of the elements of standard written English (grammar, sentence construction, and sentence sense)

- A solid command of the English language through proper diction (word choice and usage) and idioms

Part 4 contains a style guide, a grammar review, and vocabulary, usage, and idiom tips to help you accomplish everything in the above list.

PARTS 5, 6, 7, AND 8

Parts 5–8 contain responses to some of the Issues and Arguments from the official GRE and GMAT pools. (Parts 5 and 6 are for GRE test takers only; Parts 7 and 8 are for GMAT test takers only.) As you read these essays, keep in mind they were not composed under timed conditions. Also, I did quite a bit of fine-tuning to make them better models for you to study. So don't be concerned if your essays aren't as polished as mine. Be realistic about what *you* can produce under exam conditions.

How to Use the Essays in Parts 5–8

My essays are intended to provide you with substantive, organizational, and style ideas for composing your essays. There's nothing wrong with borrowing ideas, reasons, and transitional phrases from my samples and incorporating them into your own practice essays until they naturally become part of your arsenal. Rest assured: many test takers will use similar ideas, arguments, and phrases. Do try, however, to include your own *examples*, especially in your Issue essay, and be sure that in both essays you express your ideas *in your own words*.

How *Not* to Use the Essays in Parts 5–8

Whatever you do, do *not* try to memorize my essays. Why not? The total number of questions in the official pool is more than six times the number I provide in this book. So, even if you memorize all forty of my GRE (or GMAT) essays, odds are that the computerized testing system will deal you an unfamiliar hand. Besides, GRE and GMAT readers will have access to this book, and they'll be on the lookout for plagiarism.

Matching the Essays to the Questions in the Official Pool

You'll notice that the essays in Parts 5–8 are *not* accompanied by the questions themselves. ETS does not permit me to reprint its official exam questions. Therefore, for your reference, in the first paragraph of each essay, I recapitulate the Issue or Argument at hand.

Nevertheless, if you have access to the official pool, you should by all means consult the actual questions to which my essays respond. To match an essay to its question, refer to the essay's number, which corresponds to its position in the official pool (at the time this book goes to print). For example, an essay that is labeled "Issue No. 13" would correspond to the thirteenth Issue in the official list. (The questions in the official lists are not numbered, so you should generate a printout of the lists, then number the questions on your printout.)

> **NOTE:** From time to time, the test makers might change the sequence of questions in a pool or remove or add questions. Be sure to check my update page at www.west.net/~stewart/ws for the latest information.

ADDITIONAL RESOURCES FOR GRE AND GMAT ANALYTICAL WRITING

Although this book is your best single resource for GRE and GMAT essay preparation, it should not necessarily be your only resource. If you have more time to get ready for your exam, supplement this book with one of my other two Analytical Writing test-prep books (both published by Peterson's):

GRE—Answers to the Real Essay Questions. This book contains my essays for all 250 official GRE questions (125 Issues, 125 Arguments). More information is available at the book's Internet Edition (www.west.net/~stewart/grewa).

GMAT CAT—Answers to the Real Essay Questions. The book's second edition contains model essays for 230 official GMAT questions (115 Issues, 115 Arguments). More information is available at the book's Internet Edition (www.west.net/~stewart/awa).

ICONIC SYMBOLS USED IN THIS BOOK

Throughout this book, you'll encounter the following symbols:

▮▮▮ denotes material that applies only to the GRE

▮▮▮▮ denotes material that applies only to the GMAT

ABOUT THE AUTHOR

Mark Alan Stewart (B.A., Economics, J.D., University of California at Los Angeles) is an attorney and one of today's preeminent authorities and top-selling authors on the subject of graduate-level entrance exams. For more than a decade, Mr. Stewart served as a consultant to schools in the University of California and California State University systems in graduate-level entrance exam programs. His books on GMAT, LSAT, and GRE preparation continue to be top-sellers among aspiring business, law, and graduate students. His other book-length publications for graduate-level admissions include *GRE-LSAT-GMAT-MCAT Reading Comprehension Workbook, GMAT CAT—Answers to the Real Essay Questions, Teach Yourself the GMAT CAT in 24 Hours, Teach Yourself the GRE in 24 Hours, 30 Days to the LSAT, 30 Days to the GMAT CAT, GRE-LSAT Logic Workbook, GRE—Answers to the Real Essay Questions,* and *Perfect Personal Statements—Law, Business, Medical, Graduate School* (all published by Peterson's).

Part 1

ALL THE FACTS ABOUT GRE AND GMAT ANALYTICAL WRITING

Here, in Part 1, you'll familiarize yourself with both of the GRE and GMAT writing tasks. At the end of Part 1, you'll perform two diagnostic writing tasks under simulated exam conditions, and then you'll score your own essays using the official scoring criteria.

GRE AND GMAT ANALYTICAL WRITING—AT A GLANCE

WHAT'S COVERED

Present Your Perspective on an Issue (GRE) or **Analysis of an Issue (GMAT)**
In this essay, you adopt a position on a given issue of broad intellectual interest and support that position with reasons and/or examples.

Analyze an Argument (GRE) or **Analysis of an Argument (GMAT)**
In this essay, you analyze a paragraph-length argument, pointing out and discussing problems with its line of reasoning, adequacy and use of evidence, and internal logic.

ESSAY TOPIC SELECTION

The computerized testing system will select your topics randomly from its large pool of Issue statements and Arguments.

GRE
The system will present *two* Issue topics, *one* of which you'll choose for your Issue writing task. However, you won't have a choice when it comes to the Argument task; the system will randomly select only one Argument to which you must respond.

GMAT
The system will present to you one Issue statement and one Argument to which you must respond. You won't be able to select among choices.

Time Allowed

GRE

45 minutes for the Issue writing task

30 minutes for the Argument writing task

GMAT

30 minutes for the Issue writing task

30 minutes for the Argument writing task

Ground Rules

1. No break is provided between the two writing tasks.

2. The testing system does not allow you to spend more than 45 minutes (GRE) or 30 minutes (GMAT) on the Issue writing task, nor does it allow you to spend more than 30 minutes on the Argument writing task.

3. The testing system does not allow you to return to the first writing task once you've moved on to the second task. But if you've finished the first one early, you can proceed immediately to the second one at your option.

4. Scratch paper and pencils are provided (just as for the multiple-choice sections).

5. The testing system might present the two tasks to you in either order.

6. On the GMAT, you must use the word processor built into the testing system to compose your essays. On the GRE, you can either use the testing system's built-in word processor or submit your responses in handwritten form.

7. The testing system imposes no word limit on either response. (The only limitation on length is the practical limitation associated with your time limit.)

Skills Tested

Content

Your ability to present cogent, persuasive, and relevant ideas and arguments through sound reasoning and relevant supporting examples

Organization

Your ability to present your ideas in an organized and cohesive fashion

Language

Your control of the English language as demonstrated by your vocabulary, use of idioms, and diction (word choice and usage)

Mechanics

Your facility with the conventions of standard written English, including grammar and syntax (sentence structure)

> **NOTE:** Your essays won't be evaluated based on spelling and punctuation, unless you make many such errors and they interfere with your ability to communicate your ideas effectively. (The built-in word processor does not include either a spell-checker or a grammar-checker.)

SCORING SYSTEM

Each of your two essays is evaluated on a scale of 0–6 (0, 1, 2, 3, 4, 5, or 6), 6 being the highest possible score, based on the skill areas listed above. You'll receive a single Analytical Writing score, which is an average of the individual scores.

THE ISSUE WRITING TASK

The Issue task is designed to test your ability to present a position on an issue effectively and persuasively. Your task is to analyze the statement presented, considering various perspectives, and to develop your own position on the issue raised by the statement. In scoring your Issue essay, the reader will consider how effectively you:

- Recognize and deal with the complexities and implications of the issue

- Organize, develop, and express your ideas

- Support your ideas (with reasons and examples)

- Control the elements of standard written English

> **NOTE:** For the Issue writing task, there is no "correct" or "best" answer or perspective on an Issue. In other words, what's important is how effectively you present and support your position, not *what* your position is.

What GRE and GMAT Issues Look Like

Your GRE or GMAT Issue will consist of two elements:

- A brief *directive* (description of your task)

- A 1-2 sentence *statement* of opinion on an issue

The statement will appear as a quotation (in quotation marks). On the GRE, the directive *precedes* the topic; on the GMAT, it *follows* the topic. Here are two samples that are *similar* to Issues in the official pools (although you won't encounter either one on your exam):

■■| A Typical GRE Issue

Present your perspective on the following issue; use relevant reasons and/or examples to support you viewpoint.

"In order to achieve greatness in a particular field—whether it be in the arts, sciences, or politics—any individual must challenge tradition and the conventional wisdom of the time."

■■|| A Typical GMAT Issue

"No business should sacrifice the quality of its products or services for the sake of maximizing profits."

In your view, how accurate is the foregoing statement? Use reasons and/or examples from your experience, observation, and/or reading to explain your viewpoint.

The GRE Issue Directive

The directive for every GRE Issue in the official pool is exactly the same (essentially as indicated above).

The GMAT Issue Directive

The directives for the Issues in the official GMAT pool are all similar, yet they are not all exactly the same. All but a handful of Issues in the pool include essentially one of the following directives:

- Discuss the extent to which you agree or disagree with this statement

- Assess the accuracy of this statement

- Explain the meaning of this quotation (or statement)

The first directive listed appears most frequently. But remember: Regardless of the particular directive, your task is essentially the same for any one of the pool's Issues—take a position on the Issue and support that position with reasons and/or examples.

12

NOTE: Directives for approximately ten Issues in the GMAT pool are more idiosyncratic and specific to the statement given. Be on the lookout for them in the official pool, and if the testing system deals you one of these, be sure that your essay responds specifically to that directive.

TYPES OF ISSUES IN THE OFFICIAL POOLS

GRE and GMAT Issue statements are designed to cover a broad spectrum of issues of intellectual interest and with which college and graduate-level students often deal.

Common Themes Among GRE Issues

The topics in the official GRE Issue pool share many common themes. Although each Issue statement in the pool is unique, the basic themes cover a lot of common ground. Here's a list of themes that cover most of the statements in the pool (listed here in no particular order):

- Conformity and tradition versus individuality and innovation

- Practicality and utility versus creativity and personal enrichment

- The importance of cultural identity (customs, rituals, and ideals)

- Keys to individual success and progress

- Keys to societal progress and how we define it

- How we obtain or advance knowledge and what constitutes knowledge or advancement of knowledge

- The objectives and methods of formal education

- The value of studying history

- The impact of technology on society and on individuals

- The sorts of people society considers heroes or great leaders

- The function and value of art and science (for individuals and for society)

- The proper role of government, business, and individuals in ensuring the well-being of society

Considered collectively, the GRE Issue topics involve virtually all areas of mainstream academic inquiry—including sociology, anthropology, history, education, law and government, political science, economics, philosophy, the physical and behavioral sciences, the fine arts, and the performing arts.

Some GRE Issue statements focus on one particular area. Others are cross-disciplinary in nature, embracing two or more areas. The sample you encountered earlier is one example of a cross-disciplinary Issue. Here's another simulated cross-disciplinary statement. This one embraces the arts and the sciences as well as raising certain philosophical issues about the nature of truth and knowledge:

> "The objective of science is largely opposed to that of art; while science seeks to discover truths, art seeks to obscure them."

Here's another simulated cross-disciplinary Issue statement. This one embraces a variety of other areas, including public policy, government, international politics, and business:

> "The only way to ensure that our natural environment will be protected and preserved is through government penalties and other regulatory measures. No society can rely on the voluntary efforts of its individuals and private businesses to achieve these objectives."

Keep in mind: The GRE testing system will present *two* Issues to you, and you'll select either one for your writing task. Moreover, the system's algorithm for selecting topics is designed to present two Issue statements that differ from each other in terms of area of focus. These features help ensure that no test taker, regardless of undergraduate curriculum, is at an unfair disadvantage when it comes to the Issue writing task.

Common Themes Among GMAT Issues

Although each statement in the official GMAT pool is distinct, many of the statements cover similar thematic ground. I've categorized the statements below according to theme, from more common to less common (understandably, more topics involve business issues than any other type):

- Business—organizational structure/behavior, management
- Culture and social mores, attitudes, values
- Business productivity, efficiency, and teamwork
- Business—labor and employment issues
- Education—its overall role and objectives
- Government's role in ensuring the welfare of its citizens
- Technology and its impact on business and society
- Keys to individual success
- Business—its overall role and objectives in society
- Business ethics
- Personal qualities and values

- Government's role in regulating business, commerce, speech

- "Global village" issues

- Bureaucracy and "the system"

- Business—advertising and marketing

- Learning lessons from history

- Individual power and influence

These categories are not mutually exclusive; in other words, many Issues can fall into more than one category. The sample Issue you encountered earlier involves two of the categories listed above: business ethics and the objectives of business. Here it is again:

"No business should sacrifice the quality of its products or services for the sake of maximizing profits."

Here are two more simulated statements that embrace more than one thematic area. The first involves cultural norms and values as well as business advertising, while the second embraces three areas—the role of education, the role of government, and cultural values:

"In today's advertising-oriented society, most people, ironically, are happier when they have fewer goods and services from which to choose."

"It is up to parents and educators, not government, to instill in young people a nation's most cherished values."

OFFICIAL DIRECTIONS AND GUIDELINES FOR THE ISSUE WRITING TASK

During your pre-test computer tutorial (before you begin the timed test), the testing system will review the directions for each exam section. For the Issue writing task, the system will present to you one "screen" of directions and guidelines specific to the Issue task. The screen will describe the task in general and indicate the four general scoring criteria. Here's essentially what you'll see on this screen:

This writing task is designed to test your ability to present a position on an issue effectively and persuasively. Your task is to analyze the issue presented, considering various perspectives, and to develop your own position on the issue. In scoring your Issue essay, readers will consider how effectively you:

- Recognize and deal with the complexities and implications of the issue

- Organize, develop, and express your ideas

- Support your ideas (with reasons and examples)

- Control the elements of standard written English

The screen will also indicate rules and guidelines for the Issue writing task. Here's essentially what you'll see further down the screen:

- Your time limit is 45 minutes (30 minutes on the GMAT).

- Writing on any topic other than the one presented is unacceptable.

- The topic will appear as a brief statement on an issue of general interest.

- You are free to accept, reject, or qualify the statement.

- You should support your perspective with reasons and/or examples from such sources as your experience, observation, reading, and academic studies.

- You should take a few minutes to plan your response before you begin typing.

- You should leave time to reread your response and make any revisions you think are needed.

NOTE: You can access these directions and guidelines at any time during the Issue writing task by clicking on the HELP/ DIRECTIONS button.

THE ARGUMENT WRITING TASK

The Argument writing task is designed to test your critical-reasoning skills as well as your writing skills. Your task is to critique the stated Argument in terms of its cogency (logical soundness) and in terms of the strength of the evidence offered in support of the argument. In scoring your Argument essay, GRE and GMAT readers will consider how effectively you:

- Identify and analyze the key elements of the argument

- Organize, develop, and express your critique

- Support your ideas (with reasons and examples)

- Control the elements of standard written English

WHAT GRE AND GMAT ARGUMENTS LOOK LIKE

Your GRE or GMAT Argument will consist of two elements:

- A paragraph-length *passage* (which presents the argument itself)

- A brief *directive* (description of your task)

The Passage

The Argument will indicate its hypothetical source (e.g., a memo, editorial, advertisement, or speech) and then provide the argument itself—as a quoted passage from the source. Here are two sample Arguments, both of which are *similar* to the ones in the official pools (although you won't encounter either one on your exam). The first sample is more typical in length of a GMAT Argument, while the second (and longer) one is more typical in length of a GRE Argument:

▪▪‖ A Typical GMAT Argument

The following appeared in a regional business magazine:

> "Yoga Essentials, a small retail store located in the town of Mountcrest, has remained in business for about a decade without advertising in Mountcrest's local newspaper. Now Yoga Essentials is offering franchise opportunities in other areas. In the nearby town of Lakeview, there is an even greater number of yoga studios and health clubs than in Mountcrest. Thus, a Yoga Essentials franchise in Lakeview would surely be a profitable investment."

▪‖ A Typical GRE Argument

The following is taken from an editorial appearing in a local newspaper:

> "An increasing percentage of new graduates from this state's colleges and universities are finding jobs in other states. If this trend continues, this state will soon face a crisis in which the size of its workforce will be insufficient to replace current workers as they retire. Consider Giant Industries, the state's largest private business, where the average production worker is now 42 years old. Recently, Giant's revenue from the sale of textiles and paper, which together account for the majority of Giant's manufacturing business, has declined significantly. In order to prevent a decline in this state's overall economy, businesses in the state should favor recent college graduates over other job applicants when hiring new employees."

The Directive

On the GRE, the directive immediately *precedes* the passage and is the same for every Argument in the official GRE pool. The directive is essentially as follows:

Discuss how well reasoned you find the argument below.

On the GMAT, a more detailed directive immediately follows the passage and is the same for every Argument in the official GMAT pool. The directive is essentially as follows:

> Discuss how well reasoned you find this argument. In your discussion, be sure to analyze the line of reasoning and the use of evidence in the argument. For example, you may need to consider what questionable assumptions underlie the thinking and what alternative explanations or counterexamples might weaken the conclusion. You can also discuss what sort of evidence would strengthen or refute the argument, what changes in the argument would make it more logically sound, and what, if anything, would help you better evaluate its conclusion.

OFFICIAL DIRECTIONS AND GUIDELINES FOR THE ARGUMENT WRITING TASK

During your pre-test computer tutorial (before you begin the timed test), the testing system will provide directions for all exam sections, in turn. For the Argument writing task, the system will present to you *two* "screens" of directions and guidelines specific to that task.

> **NOTE:** You can access these directions and guidelines at any time during the Argument writing task by clicking on the HELP/DIRECTIONS button.

Screen 1 (General Guidelines and Suggestions)

The first screen will describe the task in general and indicate the four general scoring criteria. Here's essentially what you'll see on the screen:

> This writing task is designed to test your critical-reasoning skills as well as your writing skills. Your task is to critique the stated argument in terms of its logical soundness and in terms of the strength of the evidence offered in support of the argument. In scoring your Argument essay, the reader will consider how effectively you:
>
> - Identify and analyze the key elements of the argument
>
> - Organize, develop, and express your critique
>
> - Support your ideas (with reasons and examples)
>
> - Control the elements of standard written English

The screen will then indicate rules and guidelines for the Argument writing task. Here's essentially what you'll see further down the screen:

- Your time limit is 30 minutes.

- You must critique the logical soundness of the argument presented.

- A critique of any other argument is unacceptable.

- You should take a few minutes to plan your response before you begin typing.

- You should develop your ideas fully and organize them in a coherent manner.

- You should leave time to reread your response and make any revisions you think are needed.

Screen 2 (Specific Guidelines for Critiquing the Argument)

The second screen will indicate specific guidelines for critiquing the Argument. Here's essentially what you'll see on the screen:

- You are not being asked to agree or disagree with any of the statements in the argument.

- You should analyze the argument's line of reasoning.

- You should consider questionable assumptions underlying the argument.

- You should consider the extent to which the evidence presented supports the argument's conclusion.

- You may discuss what additional evidence would help strengthen or refute the argument.

- You may discuss what additional information, if any, would help you to evaluate the argument's conclusion.

THE ARGUMENT WRITING TASK IS VERY DIFFERENT FROM THE ISSUE WRITING TASK

Do not confuse the Argument writing task with the Issue task. Although both are designed to measure your general analytic and writing skills, that's where the similarity ends.

For the Argument Task, Your "Perspective" Doesn't Matter—At All!

The Argument section is not the place to present your own opinions about an issue that the Argument might involve. Your analysis must focus strictly on the Argument's logical features and on its evidence. Consider, for example, the second of the two Arguments you encountered a few pages back (about Giant Industries). An Issue topic involving the economic and employment trends cited in the Argument might call for you to present various viewpoints about who should take responsibility for ensuring full employment or equal job opportunities. But such viewpoints are irrelevant to the Argument task, in which you must focus strictly on the internal cogency (logical soundness) of the Argument.

For the Argument Task, Your Specific Analysis Does Matter—A Lot!

In your Issue essay, you are free to accept, reject, or qualify the statement at hand; there is no "correct" or "best" response. On the other hand, in designing the Arguments, the test maker makes sure to incorporate into each one certain reasoning problems (fallacies and other flaws) for you to identify and address in your essay. That's what the Argument writing task is all about. Should you fail to identify and address these built-in problems, you won't attain a high score.

A typical GRE or GMAT Argument will contain at least three or four discrete reasoning flaws. Here's a list of the ones that appear most frequently in the official GRE and GMAT Arguments:

- Confusing a cause-and-effect relationship with a mere correlation or temporal sequence

- Drawing a weak analogy between two things

- Relying on a potentially unrepresentative statistical sample

- Relying on potentially tainted results from a survey or poll

- Assuming that a certain condition is necessary and/or sufficient for a certain outcome

- Assuming that characteristics of a group apply to each group member (or vice versa)

- Assuming that all things remain unchanged over time

Be forewarned: Not all GRE and GMAT Arguments are created equal. In some of them, the logical flaws seem to jump off the page (or screen) at you, one at a time, while in others, the flaws are intertwined or hidden from clear view, making it especially challenging to extract, separate, and organize them. And there are no guarantees that the test will deal you a favorable hand. But who said life is fair? At least you have this book to help even the playing field.

NOTE: In Part 3, you'll learn to recognize and handle each of the flaws listed above and others as well.

THE ANALYTICAL WRITING COMPUTER INTERFACE

The Analytical Writing computer interface has a lot in common with the interface for the multiple-choice sections of the GRE and GMAT. At the top of the screen, you'll see:

- The time remaining (in minutes) for the current writing task
- The name of the test
- The task number (either 1 or 2)

At the bottom of the screen, you'll see:

- A QUIT TEST button (to stop and cancel your test)
- An EXIT SECTION button (to move ahead to the second writing task or to the other exam sections if you've completed the second task)
- A TIME button (to display time remaining to the nearest second)
- A HELP button (to display directions for using the word processor and the toolbar buttons and for responding to the writing topics)
- A NEXT button (to proceed to the second writing task if you've completed the first one before the allotted time)

Don't worry: to prevent you from unintentionally quitting the test or exiting a section, the test will prompt you to confirm these actions.

THE ANALYTICAL WRITING COMPUTER TUTORIAL

Before you begin the first section of your timed GRE or GMAT, the testing system will lead you through a series of multi-section tutorials for the various exam sections. The Analytical Writing tutorial consists of several sections, each of which leads you through a series of screens. During the tutorial, you'll learn:

- How to use the mouse
- How to scroll the screen display up and down
- How to use the toolbar buttons (at the bottom of the screen)
- How to use the built-in word processor

You won't have the option of skipping any section or any screen, and the system will require you to demonstrate competence in using the various computerized features before you can begin the actual test. You can also practice using the word processor, at your option, before beginning the timed test.

FEATURES AND LIMITATIONS OF THE WORD PROCESSOR

Built into the Analytical Writing testing system is a bare-bones word processor. It lacks many of the sophisticated features of its commercial counterparts to eliminate any advantage test takers who use certain software might hold over other test takers. Here's a look at the features and limitations of the testing system's word processor.

Navigation and Editing—Available Keyboard Commands

Here are the navigational and editing keys available in the testing system's built-in word processor:

Backspace	removes the character to the left of the cursor.
Delete	removes the character to the right of the cursor.
Home	moves the cursor to the beginning of the line.
End	moves the cursor to the end of the line.
Arrow Keys	move the cursor up, down, left, or right.
Enter	inserts a paragraph break (starts a new line).
Page Up	moves the cursor up one page (screen).
Page Down	moves the cursor down one page (screen).

Common Keyboard Commands Not Available

Certain often-used features of standard word-processing programs are not available in the testing system's word processor. For example, no keyboard commands are available for:

TAB—disabled (does not function)
Beginning/end of paragraph (not available)
Beginning/end of document (not available)

NOTE: Since TAB is disabled, signify a new paragraph with an extra line break (hit the "Enter" key twice).

Mouse-Driven Editing Functions

Cut, Paste, and Undo

In addition to editing keys, the testing system's word processor includes mouse-driven CUT (but not "copy"), PASTE, and UNDO. To cut text, select the text you wish to cut with your mouse. To paste, position the mouse pointer at the desired insertion spot, then click your mouse. Drag-and-drop cut-and-paste is not available. Also, the GRE word processor stores only your *most recent* cut, paste, or undo.

NOTE: The testing system's word processor does not include a COPY function. (The test maker wants to dissuade test takers from using shortcuts to compose lengthy essays and to ensure fairness to GRE test takers who submit handwritten responses.) If you want to copy certain text, first cut the text, and immediately paste it back in the same position; then move the cursor and paste the same text elsewhere in your document as needed.

The Vertical Scroll Bar

Once you key in 10 lines or so, you'll have to scroll to view your entire response. If you don't know how to scroll, the computer tutorial preceding the test will show you how. For the Argument task, a vertical scroll bar will also appear to the right of the topic itself. Be sure to scroll all the way down to make sure that you've read the entire Argument.

Fonts, Attributes, Hyphenation, and Special Characters

The testing system's word processor does not allow you to choose typeface or point size. Automatic hyphenation is not available. Attributes such as bold, italics, and underlining are not available, nor are special characters that do not appear on a standard computer keyboard.

Substitutes for Attributes and Special Characters

As for words you would otherwise italicize or underline (such as titles or foreign words), it's okay to leave them as is, just as I did in my essays in Parts 5–8. To signify an em-dash, use either two hyphens (—) or one hyphen with a space both before and after it (-).

Spell-Checking and Grammar-Checking

The testing system's word processor does not include either a spell-checking or grammar-checking function.

Opting to Submit Handwritten Responses (GRE Only)

Although GMAT test takers must compose their essays on a word-processor, GRE test takers may elect to submit handwritten responses instead. GRE readers are not predisposed to award different scores (either higher or lower) for handwritten essays. If you're not sure which means you would be more comfortable with, use a word processor for at least two practice essays, then try handwriting two essays. Also consider the following:

- If you're an especially slow typist, handwriting your essays may actually be more efficient.

- If your handwriting borders on illegible, you should word-process your essays. Remember: During the timed exam, you'll need to write quickly, and your penmanship might suffer.

- With the word processor, you'll have a far easier time revising an essay and correcting errors. (If you have difficulty organizing or expressing your ideas without "tweaking" your first draft, you're better off word-processing your essays.)

- You elect to submit handwritten essays at the time you *register* (make an appointment) for the GRE General Test. Otherwise, you must word-process your essays.

- If you submit handwritten essays, scoring your essays and reporting *any* GRE scores to you or to the schools may take up to *six weeks* (rather than 10–15 days if you word-process your essays).

If you decide to submit handwritten GRE essays, keep in mind these procedural points:

- For each writing task, the testing supervisor will provide a special lined paper for writing your essays. The supervisor will also supply scratch paper.

- To write your essays, you'll use the black pen provided to you at the testing center.

- For each writing task, the supervisor will personally inform you when your time limit has expired.

ESSAY EVALUATION AND SCORING

Shortly after the exam, both of your essays will be evaluated, and one single Analytical Writing score (not two separate scores) on a scale from 0 to 6 will be awarded and then reported to you and to the schools to which you have directed your score report. This section explains the evaluation, scoring, and reporting process.

> **NOTE:** Some of the details differ according to the exam (GRE or GMAT), so focus on those that apply to you.

EVALUATION BY GRE AND GMAT READERS

Within a short time after the test (10–15 days), your two Analytical Writing essays will be evaluated by "readers"—college and university faculty members that ETS commissions and trains specifically for this purpose. GRE and GMAT readers are drawn from various academic areas—most from the fields of English and Communications.

For the GRE, two readers will read and score your Issue essay, and two different readers will read and score your Argument essay. For either essay, if the two readers' scores differ by more than one point, an additional, very experienced reader will read that essay and adjudicate the discrepancy.

For the GMAT, one reader will read and score your Issue essay, and another reader will read and score your Argument essay. In addition, a computerized rating system called *E-Rater* will score each essay. For either essay, if the human reader's score differs from E-Rater's score by more than one point, an additional, very experienced human reader will read and score that essay (and your final score will average the two human readers' scores for that essay).

Each reader evaluates your writing independently, and no reader is informed of any other's evaluation. All readers employ the same so-called "holistic" grading method, by which the reader assigns a single score from 0 to 6 (0, 1, 2, 3, 4, 5, or 6) based on the *overall quality* of your writing. In other words, instead of awarding separate sub-scores for content, organization, writing style, use of language, and mechanics, the reader will consider how effective your essay is *as a whole*—accounting for all these factors (but see the note below).

> **NOTE:** Readers are instructed to focus *primarily* on your ideas and analytic logic and on how well you've organized your thoughts. The readers will consider your use of language and your writing mechanics only to the extent that they impede the clarity of your writing—in order to ensure fairness toward ESL (English as a second language) test takers.

SCORING CRITERIA

GRE and GMAT readers follow the same official scoring criteria. All readers are trained by ETS in applying these scoring criteria. Here are the essential requirements for top-scoring "6" essays (notice that you can attain a top score of 6 even if your essays contain minor errors in grammar, word usage, spelling, and punctuation)

The Issue Writing Task—Requirements for a Score of 6 (Outstanding)

- The essay develops a position on the issue through the use of incisive reasons and persuasive examples.

- The essay's ideas are conveyed clearly and articulately.

- The essay maintains proper focus on the issue and is well organized.

- The essay demonstrates proficiency, fluency, and maturity in its use of sentence structure, vocabulary, and idiom.

- The essay demonstrates an excellent command of the elements of standard written English, including grammar, word usage, spelling, and punctuation—but may contain minor flaws in these areas.

The Argument Writing Task—Requirements for a Score of 6 (Outstanding)

- The essay identifies the key features of the argument and analyzes each one in a thoughtful manner.

- The essay supports each point of critique with insightful reasons and examples.

- The essay develops its ideas in a clear, organized manner, with appropriate transitions to help connect ideas.

- The essay demonstrates proficiency, fluency, and maturity in its use of sentence structure, vocabulary, and idiom.

- The essay demonstrates an excellent command of the elements of standard written English, including grammar, word usage, spelling, and punctuation—but may contain minor flaws in these areas.

The criteria for lower scores are the same as the ones suggested above; the only difference is that the standard for quality decreases for successively lower scores.

> **NOTE:** The ETS scoring criteria for all six score levels are published in the official GRE and GMAT bulletins as well as directly at the official GRE and GMAT Web sites.

COMPUTERIZED RATING OF GMAT ESSAYS

While two human readers evaluate your GMAT essays (one reader per essay), a computer program called *E-Rater* will evaluate your essays for grammar, syntax (sentence structure), repetitiveness (overuse of the same phrases), sentence length, and spelling. In many respects, E-Rater is similar to the grammar- and spell-checkers built into popular word-processing programs such as Word and WordPerfect. However, E-Rater is custom-designed for ETS to weigh certain criteria more heavily than other criteria. For instance, very little weight is given to minor mechanical errors (e.g., in punctuation and spelling). Also, E-Rater overlooks so-called "gray" areas of grammar (e.g., use of the passive voice) and flags certain problems (e.g., repetitiveness) that off-the-shelf checkers might not. Of course, E-Rater is only useful to a point. It cannot evaluate your ideas or how persuasively you've presented and supported those ideas. That's what human readers are for.

> **NOTE:** According to the testing service, the human readers' and E-Rater's combined evaluation takes into account more than 50 structural and linguistic criteria altogether.

CALCULATION OF YOUR ANALYTICAL WRITING SCORE

As noted earlier, your final Analytical Writing score is an average based on the readers' individual scores (and, for the GMAT, E-Rater's score as well). Average scores falling midway between half-point intervals are rounded up.

Computation of GRE Analytical Writing Scores

Here are the *specific* steps involved in calculating your GRE Analytical Writing score:

1. Two readers will read and score your Issue essay, and two different readers will read and score your Argument essay. Each reader will award a single score on a scale of 0–6 in whole-point intervals (6 is highest).

2. For each essay, in the event of a score discrepancy greater than one point, a third, very experienced reader will read the essay and adjudicate the discrepancy (i.e., determine your final score for that essay).

3. For each essay, your final score is the average of the scores awarded by the two readers (or the adjudicated score awarded by the third reader).

4. Your final Analytical Writing score is the average of your final scores for each essay; scores are rounded *up* to the nearest half-point.

Here's an example showing how the GRE essay-scoring system works:

5	Reader A's evaluation of the Issue essay
4	Reader B's evaluation of the Issue essay
4.5	Final score for the Issue essay

3	Reader C's evaluation of the Argument essay
5	Reader D's evaluation of the Argument essay
4	Reader E's adjudicated score
4	Final score for the Argument essay

4.5	*Final Analytical Writing score*

NOTE: In this example, the average of the two final scores (4.25) has been rounded up to the nearest half-point interval (4.5).

Computation of GMAT Analytical Writing Scores

Here are the specific steps involved in calculating your GMAT Analytical Writing score:

1. One human reader will read and score your Issue essay, and a different human reader will read and score your Argument essay. Each reader will award a single score on a scale of 0–6 in whole-point intervals (6 is highest).

2. E-Rater will also evaluate and award a score of 0–6 for each essay.

3. For either essay if the human reader's score differs from E-Rater's score by more than one point, then a second human reader will read and score the essay (and E-Rater's score for that essay will be disregarded).

4. For each essay, your final score is the average of the scores awarded by the human reader and E-Rater (or by the second human reader).

5. Your final Analytical Writing score is the average of your two final scores for your individual essays; scores are rounded up to the nearest half-point.

Here's an example showing how the GMAT essay-scoring system works:

4 Reader A's evaluation of the Issue essay
2 E-Rater's evaluation of the Issue essay
3 Reader B's evaluation of the Issue essay
3.5 Final score for the Issue essay

3 Reader C's evaluation of the Argument essay
3 E-Rater's evaluation of the Argument essay
3 Final score for the Argument essay

3.5 Final Analytical Writing score

NOTE: In this example, a second human reader evaluated the Issue essay, and the average of the two final scores (3.25) has been rounded up (to 3.5).

YOUR PERCENTILE RANKING

Just as for each multiple-choice section of the GRE and GMAT, you'll receive a percentile rank, from 0–99 percent, for your performance in Analytical Writing. A percentile rank of 60 percent, for example, indicates that you scored higher than 60 percent of all other test takers (and lower than 40 percent of all other test takers). Percentile ranks reflect your performance relative to the entire GRE or GMAT test-taking population over a multi-year period, not just those test takers responding to the same essay topics as you.

SCORE REPORTING AND USE OF SCORES

Once your final Analytical Writing score is determined, the testing service will report it to you and to the schools to which you have directed your score report, that in turn use them in making the final admissions decision.

REPORTING OF SCORES TO TEST TAKERS AND TO THE SCHOOLS

Ten–fifteen days after your test, ETS will mail to you an official score report for your GRE or GMAT. The report will include your Analytical Writing score as well as your percentile ranking for Analytical Writing. At the same time, ETS will mail a score report to each school you've designated to receive your score report. (ETS does not report percentile rankings to the schools.) Beginning in July 2003, score reports will also include your essay *responses*.

NOTE: GRE test takers who submit handwritten essays should not expect score report until six weeks after the test.

HOW THE SCHOOLS USE ANALYTICAL WRITING SCORES

Each graduate department or B-school will determine for itself how much weight to place on Analytical Writing scores relative to scores for the multiple-choice sections as well as to other admission criteria (GRE subject-test scores, GPA, personal statements, recommendation letters, work, and other experience, etc.). An admissions committee might use Analytical Writing scores as a preliminary screen for all applicants; more likely, however, a committee will use Analytical Writing scores to decide among similarly qualified candidates. Contact the individual academic departments or B-schools for their particular policies.

ANALYTICAL WRITING—DIAGNOSTIC TEST

To determine your natural strengths and weaknesses when it comes to Analytical Writing and to get the most out of Parts 2–4 of this book, respond to the simulated Issue statement and Argument provided below. In preparing, composing, and evaluating your responses, follow these steps:

1. Before you begin each writing task, review the relevant directions and guidelines you encountered earlier in Part 1.

2. Use scratch paper for taking notes and planning your response.

3. Limit your use of word-processing features to the ones available during the actual test. (GRE test takers may elect to provide handwritten responses instead.)

4. When you've finished, score your essays according to official criteria.

NOTE: Earlier in Part 1, indicated the criteria for top scoring essays. To help you further in evaluating and scoring your diagnostic essays, at this book's Internet supplement (www.west.net/~stewart/ws), I've provided sample benchmark responses for the same Issue and Argument as well as links to the test maker's official scoring criteria for each score level (0–6).

WRITING TASK NO. 1 (YOUR PERSPECTIVE ON AN ISSUE)

Time limit: 45 Minutes (GRE) or 30 minutes (GMAT)

"Leisure time is becoming an increasingly rare commodity, largely because technology has failed to achieve its goal of improving our efficiency in our daily pursuits."

Discuss the extent to which you agree or disagree with the foregoing statement. Support your perspective using reasons and/or examples from your experience, observation, reading, or academic studies.

WRITING TASK NO. 2 (YOUR ANALYSIS OF AN ARGUMENT)

Time limit: 30 Minutes

The following appeared in an advertisement for United Motors trucks:

"Last year, the local television-news program *In Focus* reported in its annual car-and-truck safety survey that over the course of the last ten years, United Motors vehicles were involved in at least 30 percent fewer fatal accidents to drivers than vehicles built by any other single manufacturer. Now United is developing a one-of-a-kind computerized crash warning system for all its trucks. Clearly, anyone concerned with safety who is in the market for a new truck this year should buy a United Motors truck."

Discuss how well reasoned you find this argument. In your discussion, be sure to analyze the line of reasoning and the use of evidence in the argument. For example, you may need to consider what questionable assumptions underlie the thinking and what alternative explanations or counterexamples might weaken the conclusion. You can also discuss what sort of evidence would strengthen or refute the argument, what changes in the argument would make it more logically sound, and what, if anything, would help you better evaluate its conclusion.

Part 2

HOW TO COMPOSE A HIGH-SCORING ISSUE ESSAY

Here, in Part 2, you'll learn all you need to score your best on your GRE or GMAT Issue essay. At the end of Part 2, you'll put into practice what you've learned through a series of skill-building exercises.

For a high-scoring Issue essay, you need to accomplish these three basic tasks:

1. Recognize and deal with the complexities and implications of the Issue

2. Organize, develop, and express your ideas in a coherent and persuasive manner

3. Support your ideas with sound reasons and relevant examples

> **NOTE:** You'll also need to demonstrate adequate control of the elements of standard written English (grammar, syntax, and usage). You'll focus on that task later, in Part 4.

To make sure you accomplish all three tasks within your time limit (45 minutes for the GRE, 30 minutes for GMAT), follow this 8-step approach (suggested times are parenthesized):

8 STEPS TO THE ISSUE WRITING TASK

Plan your essay (5 min.)

1. Read the statement with an eye for its complexity and implications. (1 min.)

2. Brainstorm for "Pros" and "Cons." (2 min.)

3. Decide on a tentative position, then organize your ideas. (2 min.)

Compose your essay (GRE: 30 min., GMAT: 20 min.)

4. Compose a brief introductory paragraph. (GRE: 3 min., GMAT: 2 min.)

5. Compose the body of your response. (GRE: 23 min., GMAT: 15 min.)

6. Compose a brief concluding or summary paragraph. (GRE: 4 min., GMAT: 3 min.)

Refine your essay (GRE: 10 min., GMAT: 5 min.)

7. Review and revise for coherence and balance (GRE: 6 min., GMAT: 3 min.)

8. Proofread for significant mechanical problems (GRE: 4 min., GMAT: 2 min.)

> **NOTE:** The suggested time limits for each step are merely guidelines, not hard-and-fast rules. As you practice composing your own Issue essays under timed conditions, start with my guidelines, then develop a pace that works best for you personally.

In the following pages, I'll walk you through each step in turn, applying each one to the following two simulated Issue statements:

Issue Statement 1

"The best way to ensure protection and preservation of our natural environment is through government regulatory measures. We cannot rely on the voluntary efforts of individuals and private businesses to achieve these objectives."

Issue Statement 2

"Large businesses should focus on teamwork as the primary means of achieving success."

1. READ THE STATEMENT WITH AN EYE FOR ITS COMPLEXITY AND IMPLICATIONS

Read the statement carefully, noting ways in which it might be possible to:

*   *Qualify it*—if it seems convincing only to a certain extent or in certain cases;

*   *Break it apart* into two distinct claims, either of which you may or may not agree with; and

*   *Apply it* to various areas or examples that lend varying degrees of support to the statement.

Look especially for key words such as *and*, *only*, *must*, *all*, and *should*. Words like these suggest ways that you can show an Issue's complexities or implications. Jot down your ideas on your scratch paper (shorthand form is okay).

> **NOTE:** Later in Part 2, you'll examine in greater detail the ways in which you can analyze an Issue statement. I'll identify additional patterns you should look for in a statement.

Here are the two simulated Issue statements again. This time, I've underlined some key words in each one:

Issue Statement 1

"The <u>best</u> way to ensure protection and preservation of our natural environment is through government regulatory measures. We <u>cannot</u> rely on the voluntary efforts of individuals <u>and</u> private businesses to achieve these objectives."

Issue Statement 2

"Large businesses <u>should</u> focus on teamwork as the <u>primary</u> means of achieving success."

2. BRAINSTORM FOR "PROS" AND "CONS"

According to the official directions for both exams, you should support your perspective with *reasons* and/or *examples* from your academic or other reading, your experience, or your observations. During step 2, try to conjure up at least a few *reasons* both for and against the statement's position as well as some *examples* supporting each side of the issue. Jot down any idea you can think of, even if it seems far-fetched, trite, insupportable, or unconvincing at the moment. As you compose your essay, it might occur to you how to transform one of your weaker ideas into a strong one. During step 2, don't filter your ideas! Let them all flow onto your scratch paper. (You'll sort through them during step 3.)

In jotting down your ideas, you might try creating two columns, one for points that support the statement (your PRO column) and the other for opposing points (your CON column). If you're not sure whether a particular reason or example supports or weakens the statement, jot it down below the columns in the center.

Here's what my notes for the two simulated Issues look like after a few minutes of brainstorming (I jotted them down simply in the order they occurred to me):

Notes (Issue 1)

PRO

- self-interest rules ind. & bus.
    - e.g. auto emissions
    - but nations too
- environ problems too widespread for ind. & bus.
    - but nations must cooperate

CON

- lawmakers pander
    - but accountable to voters
- enforcement problems
    - e.g. bus. relocate
- bureaucratic problems
    - e.g. delays
    - e.g. compromises
    - e.g. admin. expense
    - but must put up with problems to save environ.

Notes (Issue 2)

PRO

- division of labor requires coop.
- coworker conflict
    - nothing gets done
    - attrition
- football team/military analogy?

CON

- innovative product
    - but R&D requ. coop.
- CEO vision (e.g. Apple)
    - but how to implement?
- competition/entry barriers
- extrinsic ⟨ econ. conditions laws/regul.

3. DECIDE ON A TENTATIVE POSITION, THEN ORGANIZE YOUR IDEAS

Using your notes from step 2, develop a tentative perspective or position on the Issue. Try to articulate it right on your scratch paper, then earmark it. Think of it as your working "thesis." You'll need to refer to it time and again throughout your writing task. Here's my tentative position (perspective) on each Issue:

Issue 1

Gov't regulation is problematic, but only gov't can enforce and ensure (qualified agreement).

Issue 2

There are contributing means, but teamwork is pivotal (agree on balance).

Using your tentative position and your notes as a starting point, organize your ideas in outline form. You might wish to indicate PRO or CON next to each one of the reasons and examples you jotted down during step 2. Arrange your ideas into 2–4 body paragraphs, then decide on a logical and persuasive order in which to present them. Number the points in your outline accordingly.

You can either construct a separate outline (as in the first outline) or use your notes as your outline, numbering the points in the order you intend to discuss them (as in the second outline).

Outline (Issue 1)

PRO

① • self-interest rules ind. & bus.
  • e.g. auto emissions
  • but nations too
④ • environ problems too widespread for ind. & bus.
  • but nations must cooperate

CON

② • lawmakers pander
  • but accountable to voters
  • enforcement problems
  • e.g. bus. relocate
③ • bureaucratic problems
  • e.g. delays
  • e.g. compromises
  • e.g. admin. expense
  • but must put up with problems to save environ.

Outline (Issue 2)

PRO ① *no worker is an island* < *programmers*
R & D
sales force

PRO ② *peer conflict → low prod. (e.g., my job)*

CON ③ ✓ *CEO—Apple (how to implement)*
✓ *entry barriers (not in info. age)*
✓ *ad gimmick (how to implement)*
✓ *extrinsic (uncontrollable, so not key)*

4. COMPOSE A BRIEF INTRODUCTORY PARAGRAPH

Now that you've spent about 5 minutes planning your essay, its time to compose it. You'll begin with a brief introductory paragraph in which you should accomplish each of the following tasks:

1. Demonstrate that you understand the complexities or implications of the issue.

2. Let the reader know that you have a clear perspective on the issue.

3. Anticipate the ideas you intend to present in your essay's body paragraphs.

You can probably accomplish all three tasks in 2–3 sentences. Keep in mind the following two caveats for your introductory paragraph:

- Don't go into detail about your reasoning, and don't provide specific examples. This is what your essay's body paragraphs are for.

- Don't begin your introductory paragraph by repeating the statement verbatim. This amounts to wasted time, since the reader is already familiar with the topic. Instead, show the reader from the very first sentence that you're thinking for yourself.

NOTE: Unless you are submitting a handwritten GRE essay, you may wish to wait until you've completed the rest of your essay before writing your introduction. Why? If your position on the issue evolves as you compose the body of your essay (it could happen), you won't have to rewrite your introduction.

Here's an introductory paragraph for each of the two simulated Issues—based on my outlines from step 3. For both Issues, I've decided to adopt a position in which I agree on balance with the statement (I've underlined words and phrases that you could use in nearly any introductory paragraph, regardless of the specific Issue):

Introductory Paragraph (Issue 1)

<u>In asserting that</u> government regulation is the "best" way to ensure environmental protection, <u>the speaker fails to acknowledge</u> certain problems inherent with government regulation. <u>Nevertheless, I agree with the statement to the extent that</u> exclusive reliance on individual or business volunteerism would be naive and imprudent, especially considering the stakes involved.

Introductory Paragraph (Issue 2)

<u>Whether</u> a particular business ultimately succeeds or fails <u>depends, of course, on</u> a variety of factors. <u>Nevertheless,</u> <u>since</u> teamwork is an essential ingredient for any large business to succeed, <u>I conclude that in most cases,</u> it is probably the pivotal factor.

5. COMPOSE THE BODY OF YOUR RESPONSE

During step 5, your chief ambition is to peck away at your keyboard (or write) like mad, in order to get your main points—and supporting reasons and examples—onto the screen! Here's what you need to keep in mind as you compose your body paragraphs:

- Be sure the first sentence of each paragraph begins a distinct train of thought and clearly conveys to the reader the essence of the paragraph.

- Arrange your paragraphs so your essay flows logically and persuasively from one point to the next. Try to stick to your outline, but be flexible.

- Try to devote no more than 3 or 4 sentences to any one point in your outline.

- Don't worry if you don't have time to include every single point from your outline. The readers understand that time constraints prevent most test takers from covering every point they want to make.

- Don't stray from the Issue at hand or even from the points you seek to make. Be sure to stay well focused on both.

If you're not sure where to begin, try starting with whichever point is easiest for you to articulate and seems most insightful or persuasive to you. Later, in step 7, if you determine that this point should appear elsewhere in your essay, you can rearrange your paragraphs for logical sense and continuity.

> **NOTE:** If you're a GRE test taker who opts to submit a handwritten essay, you won't have the luxury of rearranging sentences and paragraphs. You'll need to take greater care to get it right the first time.

Now, here are the body paragraphs of my response to each of the two simulated Issues. As you read these body paragraphs, note the following:

- I tried to stick to my outline while at the same time remaining flexible as new ideas for content or organization occurred to me. (Notice, for instance, that I repositioned certain points from my outlines.)

- I haven't included every single point from my outline. That's because you probably won't have time to cover every point you want to make.

- You might personally either agree or disagree with my positions or with my reasons for them. That's fine; when it comes to the Issue essay, it's all a matter of opinion—and not even your honest opinion at that!

- Again, I've underlined words and phrases that you might use in almost any Issue essay to help you see how the ideas flow naturally and persuasively from one to the next.

Four-Paragraph Body (Issue 1)

Experience tells us that individuals and private corporations tend to act in their own short-term economic and political interest, not on behalf of the environment or the public at large. For example, current technology makes possible the complete elimination of polluting emissions from automobiles. Nevertheless, neither automobile manufacturers nor consumers are willing or able to voluntarily make the short-term sacrifices necessary to accomplish this goal. Only the government holds the regulatory and enforcement power to impose the necessary standards and to ensure that we achieve these goals.

Admittedly, government penalties do not guarantee compliance with environmental regulations. Businesses often attempt to avoid compliance by concealing their activities, lobbying legislators to modify regulations, or moving operations to jurisdictions that allow their environmentally harmful activities. Others calculate the cost of polluting, in terms of punishment, then budget in advance for anticipated penalties and openly violate the law. However, this behavior only serves to underscore the need for government intervention, because left unfettered, this type of behavior would only exacerbate environmental problems.

One must admit as well that government regulation, environmental or otherwise, is fraught with bureaucratic and enforcement problems. Regulatory systems inherently call for legislative committees, investigations, and enforcement agencies, all of which add to the tax burden on the citizens whom these regulations are designed to protect. <u>Also</u>, delays typically associated with bureaucratic regulation can thwart the purpose of the regulations, because environmental problems can quickly become grave indeed. <u>However</u>, given that unjustifiable reliance on volunteerism is the only alternative, government regulation seems necessary. <u>Moreover</u>, such delays seem trivial when we consider that many environmental problems carry not only a real threat to public health but also a potential threat to the very survival of the human species.

<u>Finally</u>, environmental issues inherently involve public health and are far too pandemic in nature for individuals or even businesses to solve on their own. Many of the most egregious environmental violations traverse state and sometimes national borders. Individuals and businesses have neither the power nor the resources to address these widespread hazards.

Three-Paragraph Body (Issue 2)

<u>First</u>, cooperative interaction is an integral part of nearly all company jobs—including jobs performed in relative isolation and those in which technical knowledge or ability, not the ability to work with others, would seem to be most important. <u>For example</u>, scientists, researchers, and even computer programmers must collaborate to establish common goals and coordinate efforts. <u>Even</u> in businesses where individual tenacity and ambition of salespeople would seem to be the key for a firm's success, sales personnel must coordinate efforts with support staff and managers.

<u>Secondly</u>, in my experience, the kinds of problems that ultimately undermine an organization are those such as low employee morale, attrition, and diminishing productivity. These problems, in turn, almost invariably result from ill-will among coworkers and their unwillingness to communicate, cooperate, and compromise. Thus, problems in working together as a team pose the greatest threat to an organization's success.

<u>Some might argue</u> that the leadership and vision of a company's key executives is of paramount importance, citing specific cases such as Apple Computer's near demise and subsequent revival due to the departure and later return of its founding visionary, Steve Jobs. <u>Yet</u> chief executives of our most successful corporations would no doubt admit, as Jobs did, that without the cooperative efforts of their subordinates, their personal vision would never become reality. <u>Others might cite</u> the heavy manufacturing and natural-resource industries, where the value of tangible assets—raw materials and capital equipment—are often the most significant determinant of business success. <u>However</u>, such industries are diminishing in significance as we move from an industrial society to an information age.

6. COMPOSE A BRIEF CONCLUDING OR SUMMARY PARAGRAPH

Unless your essay has a clear end, the reader might think you didn't finish in time. That's not the impression you want to make; so be sure to make time to wrap up your discussion. Convey the main thrust of your essay in two or three sentences. If an especially insightful concluding point occurs to you, the final sentence of your essay is the place for it.

For each of the two simulated Issues, here's a brief summary that assures the reader I've organized my time well and finished my essay. Notice that this brief summary does not introduce any new reasons or examples; it's just a quick recapitulation. (Again, I've underlined words and phrases that you could use in any final paragraph.)

Final Paragraph (Issue 1)

In the final analysis, only the authority and scope of power that a government possesses can ensure the attainment of agreed-upon environmental goals. Since individuals are unable and businesses are by nature unwilling to assume this responsibility, government must do so.

Final Paragraph (Issue 2)

In sum, although leadership, individual ambition, and even the value of tangible assets play crucial roles in the success of many large business organizations, teamwork is the single ingredient common to all such organizations. It is, therefore, the key one.

7. REVIEW AND REVISE FOR COHERENCE AND BALANCE

Be sure to reserve time to revise and rework your essay as needed for a balanced, coherent discussion. Here's what you should try to accomplish during step 7:

1. Be sure you've presented varying perspectives on the issue. There's nothing wrong with adopting a strong position, but you should always acknowledge the merits and drawbacks of other viewpoints as well. If your essay appears too one-sided, now's the time to add a paragraph that remedies this problem.

2. Check your paragraphs to see if they are balanced in length. If they aren't, perhaps you dwelled too long on one area of discussion, while in another, you neglected to provide adequate support (reasons and/or examples). During step 7 is the time to trim back and fill out as needed to achieve a balanced presentation.

3. Check your introductory and concluding paragraphs to make sure they're consistent with each other.

8. Proofread for Significant Mechanical Problems

For a top score of 6, your essay need not be flawless. The readers won't decrease your mark for the occasional awkward sentence and minor errors in punctuation, spelling, grammar, or diction (word choice and usage). Don't get hung up on whether or not each sentence is something your English composition professor would be proud of. Instead, use whatever time remains to fix the most glaring mechanical problems. Here are three tasks you might attend to in step 8:

1. Find your one or two most awkward sentences, and rework them so they flow more naturally.

2. Correct your most glaring errors in diction (word choice and usage) and grammar.

3. Correct spelling errors *only* when they might prevent the reader from understanding the point at hand.

Don't spend *any* of your valuable time correcting punctuation, removing extra character spaces between words, or correcting minor spelling errors.

DEVELOPING A POSITION ON THE ISSUE

In analyzing an Issue statement, don't waste your time second-guessing what the reader might want to read or trying to guess what the "correct" response (politically or otherwise) to a topic might be. There is no "correct" answer, which the test itself emphasizes in its instructions:

"You are free to either *accept*, *reject*, or *qualify* the statement."

In this section, you'll learn some tips and caveats for your three options: accepting, rejecting, or qualifying the statement.

Qualifying an Issue Statement

You will not find a single irrefutable statement among the official Issues, nor will you find a statement that is utter nonsense, wholly without rational justification or supporting evidence. Typically, an Issue statement invites you to *qualify* it in one respect or another. By "hedging your position" on the Issue, you won't appear wishy-washy, but rather thoughtful and scholarly! Just be sure to persuade the reader (with sound reasons and relevant examples) that your lukewarm position is justifiable. Look especially for the following patterns among your list of official Issues:

- A statement whose accuracy depends on various factors
- A statement that overlooks legitimate competing interests (look for the key word *should*)

- A statement that raises two distinct but related issues (one might be a threshold issue, which you should address before analyzing the main issue)

- A statement that lists, or otherwise embraces, two or more distinct categories (different categories often lend differing degrees of support to the statement)

- A statement that might be true (or untrue) generally but fails to account for significant exceptional cases (look for all-inclusive words such as *only*, *all*, and *must*)

- A statement that is unclear or vague in some way (in other words, the statement's accuracy depends on the meaning of key terms or how you interpret the statement as a whole)

Keep these patterns in mind as you read any GRE or GMAT Issue statement. If you recognize a certain pattern behind the statement, try to develop a perspective, or thesis, that *qualifies* the statement accordingly.

STRONG AGREEMENT (ACCEPTANCE) OR DISAGREEMENT (REJECTION)

You don't need to qualify a statement to attain a top score. It's perfectly acceptable to strongly agree or disagree with the stated opinion. However, you must provide sound reasons and supporting examples to justify such strong agreement (or disagreement), and you must at least acknowledge a contrary view.

Adopting a Controversial Position

It's okay to take a controversial stance on an issue, but avoid coming across as fanatical or extreme. Many of the Issue topics are highly "charged" in the sense that they involve issues about which people tend to have strong opinions one way or the other. Don't worry that the reader may have a personal viewpoint that differs strongly from yours or that your position may appear somewhat "right-wing" or "left-wing." GRE and GMAT readers are trained to be objective! Moreover, graduate schools welcome students who are independent thinkers with distinct points of view.

Appealing to Morality, Spirituality, or Jingoism

Avoid inflammatory statements, and don't preach or proselytize. Approach the Issue writing task as an intellectual exercise in which you dispassionately examine various viewpoints. Do not use it as a forum for sharing your personal belief system. It is perfectly appropriate to criticize particular behavior, policies, or viewpoints as operating against the best interest of a business or of a society. But refrain from either condemning or extolling based on personal moral grounds. Also avoid demagoguery (appeals to prejudice or emotion) or jingoism (excessive patriotism).

SUPPORTING YOUR POSITION AND REFUTING OTHERS

Okay, so you've developed a position that recognizes the Issue's complexity and implications. So far, so good. Now you need to persuade the reader of your position with sound reasons and relevant examples—both in support of your viewpoint and in opposition to others. In this section, you'll learn a variety of tips and techniques for accomplishing both.

USING RHETORICAL TECHNIQUES TO PERSUADE THE READER

The word "rhetoric" refers to the art of persuasive argumentation. By now, you know that in your Issue essay, you should always acknowledge more than one position or perspective on the issue at hand. But to be rhetorically effective, your essay must:

- Never leave unchallenged any position that differs from yours

- Never leave unchallenged a reason or example that undermines your position

Otherwise, you've conceded the contrary point, and your essay will be unpersuasive. *Always* respond to contrary positions, reasons, and examples—with counter-reasons and/or counterexamples.

Hopefully, as you take notes, ideas for responding to other viewpoints and to possible problems with your own viewpoint will occur to you naturally, without you consciously considering particular rhetorical techniques. But if you do get stuck for ideas, draw upon the following five techniques to get your rhetorical juices flowing. For examples of these techniques, I'll cite excerpts from the two essays I composed earlier for Issue 1 (about the environment) and Issue 2 (about teamwork).

1. Turn It Around (Look for the "Silver Lining")

Argue that an apparent weakness (or strength) is actually not a weakness, if you view it from a different perspective. The essay for Issue 1 provides an example of this. First, the essay offers an example that lends *apparent* support to the opposing position:

> Admittedly, . . . [b]usinesses often attempt to avoid compliance by concealing their activities, . . . or calculate the cost of polluting, in terms of punishment, then budget in advance for anticipated penalties and openly violate the law.

Then, the essay indicates how this point *actually* undermines that position:

> . . . However, this behavior only serves to underscore the need for government intervention, because left unfettered, this type of behavior would only exacerbate environmental problems.

2. Trivialize It ("Explain It Away")

Argue that an apparent weakness of your position (or strength of a different position) is trivial, minor, or insignificant. The essay for Issue 2 provides an example. First the essay offers two examples that lend *apparent* support to the opposing position:

> Others might cite the heavy manufacturing and natural-resource industries, where the value of tangible assets—raw materials and capital equipment—are often the most significant determinant of business success.

Then, the essay *explains away* these examples:

> . . . However, such industries are diminishing in significance as we move from an industrial society to an information age.

3. Appeal to Broader Considerations

Argue that any minor problems with your position seem trivial in light of the broad, and serious, implications that the Issue raises. The essay for Issue 1 provides an example. First, the essay acknowledges a certain problem with its position:

> . . . [D]elays typically associated with bureaucratic regulation can thwart the purpose of the regulations, because environmental problems can quickly become grave indeed.

Then, the essay points out the broad societal consideration that puts this minor drawback in its proper perspective:

> . . . [S]uch delays seem trivial when we consider that many environmental problems carry not only a real threat to public health but also a potential threat to the very survival of the human species.

4. The "Lesser of Two Evils" Method

Argue that an opposing position is no stronger, or perhaps even weaker, in a certain respect. The essay for Issue 1 provides an example. First the essay acknowledges a certain weakness in its position:

> . . . [D]elays typically associated with bureaucratic regulation can thwart the purpose of the regulations, because environmental problems can quickly become grave indeed.

Then, the essay points out an even greater weakness in the opposing position:

> . . . However, given that unjustifiable reliance on volunteerism is the only alternative, government regulation seems necessary.

5. The "Greater of Two Virtues" Method

Argue that a certain merit of the opposing position is overshadowed by one or more virtues of your position. The essay for Issue 2 provides an example. First, the essay admits that the opposing position is not without merit:

> Some might argue that the leadership and vision of a company's key executives is of paramount importance, citing specific cases.

Then, the essay asserts that the contrary position has even greater merit:

> . . . Yet chief executives of our most successful corporations would no doubt admit . . . that without the cooperative efforts of their subordinates, their personal vision would never become reality.

YOUR SUPPORTING EXAMPLES

As noted earlier in Part 2, on both the GRE and GMAT, the official directions indicate that you should support your perspective with *reasons* and/or *examples* from your academic or other reading, your experience, or your observations. But should you try to include all of the listed example types? And what specific kinds of examples will leave the most positive impression on the reader? To answer these questions for yourself, keep in mind the following points of advice.

Spare the Reader the Technical Details

Don't try to impress the reader with your technical knowledge of any particular subject. Resist the temptation to use the Issue essay as a forum to recapitulate your senior-year thesis. This is not the place to convince the reader of your firm grasp of the finest points of foreign policy, macroeconomic theory, or nuclear physics. That's what your GPA and undergraduate transcripts are for.

Don't Be a "Know-It-All"

The Issue essay is not like a game of *Jeopardy!* or *Trivial Pursuit*. You will not score points by recounting statistics or by conjuring up the names of little-known historical figures. By all means, draw on both current and historical events to bolster your position. But try to use examples with which the reader is likely to be somewhat familiar. (Consider this point of advice, however, in light of the next one.)

Avoid the Trite and Hackneyed

Try to avoid using hackneyed, overused examples to make your point. Keep in mind: Many GRE and GMAT test takers will rely heavily on today's headlines and on history's most illustrious and notorious figures. Here are some names and events that currently (in the year 2002) come to mind:

- Osama bin Laden or the attack on the World Trade Center

- The Enron and Arthur Anderson accounting scandals

- Recent American presidential scandals

- Adolph Hitler and the Jewish Holocaust

- Bill Gates and Microsoft's business practices

Examples such as these are the all-too-obvious ones. Try to dig a bit deeper, showing the reader a broader, more literate perspective.

> **NOTE:** Most GRE and GMAT readers reside in the U.S. If your reside elsewhere, cite examples from your own region of the world. You're more likely to pique the reader's interest, which can only operate in your favor.

Draw Sparingly on Your Personal Experiences

Unless the specific directive accompanying the statement instructs otherwise, it's perfectly acceptable to draw on your own experiences at work, college, or elsewhere. However, avoid relying too heavily on personal experience. Strive to demonstrate through your essay a breadth of both real-world experience and academic knowledge.

Strive to Be a Generalist, Not a Specialist

Unless the specific directive accompanying the statement instructs otherwise, avoid harping on one particular reason that you believe is the most convincing one or on one example that you think is most illustrative. Try to round out your discussion as fully as you reasonably have time for. To guard against going off on a tangent with a single reason or example, try to adhere to one of the structural templates you'll learn about a bit later in Part 2.

BRAINSTORMING FOR ESSAY IDEAS

Many Issues in the official pool share common themes. Read again the lists of those themes on pages 13–15 in Part 1. You can be ready for several related Issues with an arsenal of your favorite examples. If you have time before your exam, try to develop an arsenal of your pet examples:

■❙❙ • For the GRE, develop an arsenal of supporting examples from science, philosophy, politics, and the arts. You can use many of the same historical figures, events, theories, and schools of thought for multiple Issue topics. Take notes, then review them shortly before exam day.

■❙❙❙ • For the GMAT, develop your general position on the broad business issues listed in Part 1 along with an inventory of examples. Take notes, then review them shortly before exam day.

> **NOTE:** At the end of Part 2 (see "If You Have More Time"), you'll find additional suggestions for brainstorming.

ORGANIZING YOUR IDEAS (YOUR ESSAY'S STRUCTURE)

Regardless of your brilliant and incisive ideas, the reader might not appreciate or even understand those ideas if you present them in a rambling, disorganized fashion. A clear organizational framework is a necessary ingredient for a high score. Although the testing service makes clear that there is no "correct" or "best" structure for the Issue essay, you should nevertheless adhere to certain guidelines, or risk losing your train of thought on the reader, thereby leaving a distinctively negative impression.

YOUR ESSAY'S LENGTH

There is no prescribed or "correct" length for an Issue essay. The only limitation on length that the testing system imposes is the practical limitation associated with the time limit. So do the readers prefer brief or longer Issue essays? Well, it all depends on the essay's quality. An essay that is concise and to the point can be more effective than a long-winded, rambling one. On the other hand, a longer essay that is nevertheless articulate and that includes many insightful ideas that are well supported by examples will score higher than a brief essay that lacks substance.

Number of Words

Don't worry about the word length of your essay. As long as you incorporate into your essay all the elements that I suggest here in Part 2, your essay's word length will be appropriate.

> **NOTE:** The sample GRE essays in Part 5 of this book range from 475 to 675 words in length, and the GMAT Issue essays in Part 7 range from 325 to 500 words in length. But for a top score of 6, your Issue essay need not be as lengthy as my samples, especially the longer ones. (GRE test takers have 50 percent more time for the Issue writing task, time enough for about 50 percent more words.)

Number of Paragraphs

There is no "correct" or "best" number of paragraphs *per se* for an Issue essay. Nevertheless, any GRE or GMAT Issue essay should include separate introductory and summary (or concluding) paragraphs. In addition, any GMAT Issue essay should contain *at least two* body paragraphs, and any GRE Issue essay should contain *at least three* body paragraphs.

> **NOTE:** GRE test takers have 50 percent more time for the Issue writing task, time enough for a more fully developed discussion with at least one additional paragraph.

RHETORICAL EMPHASIS AND YOUR ESSAY'S STRUCTURE

The principles of effective rhetoric you learned earlier should also apply to the manner in which you arrange your ideas (and opposing ideas) into paragraphs. While there are no hard-and-fast rules, here are a handful of ideas for you to put into practice:

- If you begin your body paragraphs with your position, start with the strongest ("chief," "main," or "primary") reason for that position. Then in subsequent paragraphs (or sentences), turn to your secondary reasons.

- If you begin your body paragraphs by discussing a position contrary to yours, start with the strongest ("chief," "main," or "primary") reason for that position—the one that most people would think of first. By turning right around to counter that reason, you disarm your detractors early in your essay.

- Among various opposing points, admit the strongest one first.

- Respond *immediately* to each contrary point, in turn. Don't pile them on, then risk running out of time to respond to them all.

TEMPLATES FOR YOUR ESSAY'S STRUCTURE

With the foregoing guidelines for paragraph number and rhetorical sequence in mind, your essay should build upon one of the following structural templates. Which template you should select depends on a variety of factors:

- The nature of the statement (e.g., whether it can be broken down into components, aspects, or applications, as discussed earlier in Part 2)

- The extent to which you agree (or disagree) with the statement

- The number of reasons and examples you intend to cite in support of your position (as well as other positions)

- Whether you're a GRE or GMAT test taker (GRE test takers have more time for a more fully developed analysis)

Be flexible; you might start out with a particular structure in mind, then, midway through your essay, discover that the pieces are not falling into place. Assuming you have enough time, switch to a structure that works better and rearrange your paragraphs accordingly. (Of course, this option is not available to GRE test takers who submit handwritten essays.) Also, you need not adhere strictly to one of these templates in order to write an effective Issue essay. You might discover some other, idiosyncratic format that works best for you personally, at least in most cases.

> **NOTE:** In the templates, brackets indicate optional elements. Also, the term "counterpoint" refers to a reason or example supporting a contrary position, and "rebuttal" refers to a response (reason or example) to a counterpoint (and in further support of the other position).

Template A

Try this template if your agreement or disagreement with the statement is nearly *unqualified*:

1st Paragraph: Main reason for your position → counterpoint → rebuttal

2nd Paragraph: Second reason for your position → counterpoint → rebuttal

3rd Paragraph: Third reason for your position → counterpoint → rebuttal

The following Issue essays in Part 5 and Part 7 are based essentially on this template:

■■I GRE Essay Nos. 16, 81, 87

■■■I GMAT Essay Nos. 22, 46, 53, 79, 90, 125

You can use the same template to discuss two or more examples (or distinct areas) that lend support to your position:

1st Paragraph: One example (or area) that supports your position → counterpoint → rebuttal

2nd Paragraph: Another example (or area) that supports your position → counterpoint → rebuttal

3rd Paragraph: Another example (or area) that supports your position → counterpoint → rebuttal

The following Issue essays in Part 5 and Part 7 are based essentially on this variation:

■▮▮ GRE Essay Nos. 66, 85
■■▮▮ GMAT Essay No. 74

Template B

Try this template to acknowledge *one* strong argument *against* your position but where you have more reasons or examples *in support of* your position:

1st Paragraph: One reason (and/or example) in support of your position

2nd Paragraph: Another reason (and/or example) in support of your position

3rd Paragraph: Another reason (and/or example) in support of your position

Final Paragraph: Chief counterargument → rebuttal

The following Issue essays in Part 5 and Part 7 are based essentially on this template:

■▮▮ GRE Essay Nos. 43, 48, 73
■■▮▮ GMAT Essay Nos. 11, 65, 84

Template C

Try this template to acknowledge *one or more* strong arguments *against* your position but where you have better reasons and/or examples in support of your position:

1st Paragraph: Chief counterargument

[*Next Paragraph:* Another counterargument]

Next Paragraph: One reason and/or example in support of your position

[*Next Paragraph:* Another reason and/or example in support of your position]

The following Issue essays in Part 5 and Part 7 are based essentially on this template:

■■I GRE Essay Nos. 25, 103, 115

■■■I GMAT Essay No. 43

Template D

If the arguments for and against the statement's position are equally strong (e.g., if it all depends on the area under consideration), try this template for a balanced essay:

1st Paragraph (or 1st and 2nd Paragraphs): Area(s) or examples supporting one position

2nd Paragraph (or 3rd and 4th Paragraphs): Area(s) or examples supporting a contrary position

The following Issue essays in Part 5 and Part 7 are based essentially on this template:

■■I GRE Essay No. 114

■■■I GMAT Essay Nos. 26, 60

Template E

Try this template to address two or more reasons in support of an opposing position, each one in turn:

1st Paragraph (or 1st and 2nd paragraphs): Counterargument → rebuttal

2nd Paragraph (or 3rd and 4th paragraphs): Counterargument → rebuttal

[*Next Paragraph:* Counterargument → rebuttal]

The following Issue essays in Part 5 and Part 7 are based essentially on this template:

■■I GRE Essay No. 46

■■■I GMAT Essay No. 54

DO'S AND DON'TS FOR YOUR ISSUE ESSAY

Now, review some of the key points from Part 2. Here's a list of DO's and DON'Ts to keep you on the right track when you organize and compose your Issue essay. To reinforce the ideas in this list, earmark it and refer to it from time to time as you practice the Issue writing task and as you read my sample essays in Part 5 and Part 7.

ADOPTING A PERSPECTIVE OR POSITION

Do try to break apart the statement into components or discrete areas of consideration. In fact, many GRE and GMAT Issue statements are intentionally designed for you to do so.

Don't waste time second-guessing what the reader might agree (or disagree) with. GRE and GMAT readers are trained to be objective. So don't try to anticipate what a reader would consider a "correct" position (politically or otherwise) on an Issue.

Do "hedge" your position by qualifying your viewpoint and acknowledging others. In doing so, you won't appear wishy-washy, but rather thoughtful and scholarly!

Don't be reluctant to take a strong stance on an Issue, but avoid coming across as fanatical or extreme. Approach the Issue essay is an intellectual exercise, not as a forum for sharing your personal belief system.

SUPPORTING YOUR POSITION AND COUNTERING OTHERS

Do admit and respond to the chief weakness of your position as well as to the chief merits of an opposing position. In doing so, use varied rhetorical techniques.

Don't overdo it when it comes to drawing on personal experiences to support your position. Try instead to demonstrate a breadth of both real-world and academic experience.

Do explain how each example you mention illustrates your point. Anyone can simply list a long string of examples and claim that they illustrate a point. But the readers are looking for incisive analysis, not fast typing (or writing).

Don't try to impress the reader with either your vast knowledge of trivia or your technical knowledge of the topic at hand.

ORGANIZATION

Do order your body paragraphs in a logical and persuasive manner.

DON'T dwell too long on details. Try to cover as many points in your outline as you have time for, devoting no more than one paragraph to each one.

Do save time for bookends: an introductory paragraph and a concluding or summary paragraph.

DON'T try to cover everything. The readers understand your time constraints. So don't worry if you're forced to leave the secondary and more tangential points on your scratch paper.

IF YOU HAVE MORE TIME

If you have ample time before your exam, consider supplementing the Issue materials in this book with additional resources. Here are some suggestions.

TAKE NOTES ON THE ISSUE STATEMENTS IN YOUR OFFICIAL POOL

Generate a printout of the complete pool of Issue questions. (See this book's introduction for how to obtain the questions via the testing service's GRE and GMAT Web sites.) Select ten or fifteen Issue statements covering diverse themes. For each one, perform the planning steps (1–3) you learned about here in Part 2. Keep your mind as well as your pencil moving!

CONSULT MY OTHER TWO ANALYTICAL WRITING BOOKS

Chances are, you'll have an easier time conjuring up supporting examples for some types of Issues than for others. Identify the thematic areas (from the lists on pages 13–15 in Part 1) in which you're deficient, then get up to speed for these areas by reading the relevant essays in one of my other two books:

GRE—Answer to the Real Essay Questions (Published by Peterson's). The book contains my essays for 125 Issues in the official pool.

GMAT CAT—Answer to the Real Essay Questions (Published by Peterson's). The book's 2nd edition contains my essays for 115 Issues in the official pool.

As you read the book's Issue essays, in addition to noting my supporting examples:

- Jot down *reasons* you find clearest, most convincing, or most useful.

- Pick up *thesis* ideas; even reading just the first and last paragraphs of each essay will afford you many useful insights.

- Highlight *transition* and *rhetorical* phrases, then try composing several essays yourself, making a special effort to incorporate your favorites into your essays so that they become part of your natural writing style.

> **NOTE:** For book information, see the books' Web supplements (www.west.net/~stewart).

DIG EVEN FURTHER FOR IDEAS AND EXAMPLES

Referring to the lists of common themes on pages 13–15 in Part 1, roll up your sleeves and hit the proverbial stacks for Issue ideas. All forms of media are fair game.

Magazines

The periodicals listed below feature articles that cover common Issue themes (the first two are especially relevant to the GMAT):

- *Inc.:* business ethics, management, leadership, entrepreneurship
- *Forbes:* same themes as those in *Inc.*
- *U.S. News & World Report:* notable current events
- *The Economist:* political and economic ideology
- *Reason:* ideology and culture (loads of "cross-discipline" articles)
- *The New Yorker:* arts, humanities, sociology, popular culture
- *The Futurist:* cultural and technological trends

With this list in hand, head to your local library or the magazine's Web site and rifle through some back issues or archived articles. You'll come away brimming over with ideas for Issue essays.

Books

Check out books that survey key people, events, and developments in various areas of human endeavor. Here are two useful ones to start with:

A History of Knowledge: Past, Present, and Future, by Charles van Doren (Birch Lane Press, 1991)

The World's Greatest Ideas: An Encyclopedia of Social Inventions, ed. by Nicholas Alberly, *et. al.* (New Society Publications, 2001)

Your Notes from College Course Work

Try dusting off your notes from college survey courses in art, science, history, politics, and sociology. You might surprise yourself with what you'll find that you can recycle into a GRE or GMAT Issue essay.

The Web

Take advantage of the World Wide Web to brush up on common Issue themes. At the Analytical Writing areas of my GRE Web site (www.west.net/~stewart/grewa) and GMAT Web site (www.west.net/~stewart/awa), I've provided links to some Web sites that are useful for this purpose.

Television and Video

If you're a couch potato, tune in to the History Channel or to your local PBS station for Issue-essay ideas. Also consider purchasing (or renting from a library) "History of the Millennium," a 3-hour A&E (Arts & Entertainment) channel production, which surveys the 100 most influential people of the most recent millennium (1000–1999). Zero in on a few of the featured artists, scientists, political leaders, and philosophers, and you'll be ready with good Issue examples, especially for the GRE.

KEEP YOUR PERSPECTIVE

The strategies listed above can be time-consuming. If you have ample time before exam day, then go the extra mile (or kilometer). But what if you don't have time for additional reading and brainstorming? Take heart: The specific reasons and supporting examples you cite are only one of several scoring criteria and by no means the most important. Your should primary be concerned with:

- Developing a position that accounts for the statement's complexity and implications and that acknowledges other viewpoints

- Expressing that position clearly, in a balanced, well-organized essay

REINFORCEMENT EXERCISES

Now, let's reinforce what you've learned in Part 2. The following series of exercises is designed to engage you more actively in planning, outlining, and composing effective Issue essays. Here are the five types of exercises you'll find here, along with the number of exercises per type:

- Outlining (3 exercises)

- Writing introductory paragraphs (5 exercises)

- Recognizing an essay's structure (8 exercises)

- Analytical writing (5 exercises)

- Composing a full-length Issue essay (1 essay)

For each group of exercises, directions for that group immediately precede the exercises. *My responses and comments begin on page 59.*

OUTLINING (3 EXERCISES)

On scratch paper, create an outline for each of the following three Issues. Your outline should contain notes for:

- At least one example and/or reason in support of each main point

- A basic position or thesis (for your introduction and concluding paragraphs)

Limit your time to 5 minutes per Issue.

1. For the following Issue, provide an outline for *two* body paragraphs—the first one in support of the statement's position, the second opposed to it:

   "In any field of endeavor, an individual's best critics are the individual's own peers in that field."

2. For the following Issue, provide an outline for *three* body paragraphs. You'll probably need at least three paragraphs to compare different types of professions or vocations and to define the statement's key terms.

   "Professional success usually depends on a person's ability to respond and adapt to unexpected problems and changing circumstances."

3. For the following Issue, provide an outline for *three* body paragraphs. You'll probably need at least three paragraphs to examine both areas listed and to consider other possible critiques of the statement.

   "How we react to public scandals—whether in business or politics—reflects our values and priorities as a society."

WRITING INTRODUCTORY PARAGRAPHS (5 EXERCISES)

For each of the following Issues, compose a two- or three-sentence introductory paragraph that:

- Reveals the complexity of the issue

- Suggests a general position on the issue

- Anticipates the structure of the essay

Limit your time to 5 minutes per Issue.

1. "Ads portraying attractive or successful people are effective only if consumers can actually become more attractive or successful by using the advertised product or service."

2. "Researchers at universities should concentrate on areas of research in which new ideas and discoveries are most likely to be of significant benefit to society."

3. "It is neither the proper nor necessary function of government to encourage the creation of art or to ensure its preservation."

4. "To truly succeed in life, an individual must assert his or her individuality, rather than conforming to the expectations of others."

5. "The only responsibility of a leader—whether in politics, business, or the military—is to serve the interests of his or her followers."

Recognizing an Essay's Structure (8 Exercises)

Not every essay in Parts 5 and 7 of this book conforms strictly to one of the structural templates you examined earlier in Part 2. For each of the following idiosyncratic essays, outline the essay's structure—paragraph by paragraph (except for the introductory and concluding paragraphs). In your outline, you may wish to use the following terms:

- *point*—to identify a reason in support of a position

- *counterpoint*—to describe a contrary position

- *rebuttal*—to identify a response to a counterpoint

Observe that for some of these essays, the structure is a variation on one of the five templates, while for others, the structure is more idiosyncratic.

■■I **Part 5**
1. GRE Essay No. 4
2. GRE Essay No. 21
3. GRE Essay No. 39
4. GRE Essay No. 55

■■■I **Part 7**
5. GMAT Essay No. 20
6. GMAT Essay No. 63
7. GMAT Essay No. 80
8. GMAT Essay No. 110

ANALYTICAL WRITING (5 EXERCISES)

Each of the following statements is one that most test takers would tend to agree with. Your task is to play devil's advocate. For each statement, compose a one-paragraph response in which you:

- Provide one reason and/or example in support of the statement's position

- Argue against the statement's position, by providing at least one reason and/or example

In your response, try to use rhetorical devices to convince the reader that your contrary position is the stronger one. Limit your time to 8 minutes per Issue.

1. "As adults, we prefer to define ourselves more by our occupation than by our affiliation with social groups."

2. "A democratic society is always better off when many people question authority."

3. "Parents should be free to make all important decisions regarding the formal education of their children."

4. "The proper focus of a college education should be on career preparation and not on the development of a personal value system."

5. "Most great achievements are the result of careful planning and a long, sustained effort rather than to sudden bursts of creativity or insight."

COMPOSING A FULL-LENGTH ISSUE ESSAY (1 ESSAY)

Early in Part 2, I constructed, step by step, a sample essay for each of these two simulated Issues:

Issue Statement 1
"The best way to ensure protection and preservation of our natural environment is through government regulatory measures. We cannot rely on the voluntary efforts of individuals and private businesses to achieve these objectives."

Issue Statement 2
"Large businesses should focus on teamwork as the primary means of achieving success."

My sample responses expressed overall *agreement* with both statements. Select either statement, and compose an essay in which you express overall *disagreement* with the statement, regardless of your personal opinions about the issue. Try to apply what you've learned in Part 2 about:

- Developing a perspective that recognizes the issue's complexities and implications

- Writing effective introductory and concluding paragraphs

- Adopting a structure that is rhetorically effective

- Using various rhetorical techniques to argue for your position and against others

Try to use your own reasons and examples. Limit your time to 45 minutes (GRE) or 30 minutes (GMAT). Unless you plan to submit a handwritten GRE essay, use a word processor to compose your response, limiting your use of word-processing functions to the ones built into the testing system.

REINFORCEMENT EXERCISES—SAMPLES AND COMMENTS

OUTLINING (3 EXERCISES)

1. Analysis

Here's an outline for a response with two body paragraphs—one in support of the statement and the other in opposition to it. The outline suggests that the test taker plans to rely chiefly on the art of film direction for examples. The outline's thesis notes indicate that weighing the issue's two sides requires agreement as to what makes for the "best" kind of criticism in the first place.

Paragraph 1 (Agree)
- Peers have best knowledge of field

  - technical and theoretical (e.g., cinematography: non-experts have no clue)

  - complex tasks can look simple to non-experts (e.g., good film editing goes unnoticed)

- People are more receptive to criticism from peers

  - expert opinions more worthy of respect

  - peers can speak the same language (communicate criticisms)

Paragraph 2 (Disagree)
- Peers might be dishonest (jealousy or competition)
- Outsiders are more objective
- Non-experts bring fresh insights (e.g., literary critic's focus differs from film director's)

Thesis
- Issue rests on definition of "best" (best informed vs. most objective)
- Key: Criticism must help you improve your craft or advance knowledge

2. Analysis

Here's an outline for a response with three body paragraphs. The first paragraph would provide two main reasons why the test taker fundamentally agrees with the statement. The second paragraph would consider possible exceptions, then explain them away. The third paragraph would recognize that the issue rests ultimately on the definition of "professional success." The outline suggests that the test taker plans to rely on examples from a variety of professions.

Paragraph 1 (Agree—2 Reasons)
- Many jobs inherently unpredictable (e.g., journalism, media, business)
- Multiple careers are common today (no job security)

Paragraph 2 (Exceptions)
- Exception: Jobs ensconced in convention/tradition (e.g., law, banking)
  - but evolving laws, regulations, and technology require adaptation
  - careers in these areas not secure
- A few theoretical fields might be insulated (e.g., history, math, or music theory)
  - but job circumstances often uncertain, so adapt or perish!
  - new developments still possible (e.g., historical evidence, math theories, new musical forms)

Paragraph 3 (Definition)
- Define success (Is the statement a tautology?)
- Maybe success depends on balancing career and personal life

Thesis
- Assuming a narrow definition of success, statement is true for all fields

3. Analysis

Here's an outline for a response with three body paragraphs. The first paragraph would provide examples of business scandals, while the second would examine two types of political scandals. For each type, the essay would basically agree with the statement. The third paragraph would distinguish this essay from less insightful ones by raising more fundamental questions about what our media's obsession with scandals reveals about us to begin with (i.e., the paragraph would critique the statement on another level).

Paragraph 1 (Business)
- E.g., Enron/Anderson
  - reaction was for reform and accountability
  - shows we value fairness, equity, proper functioning of markets
- E.g., Tobacco litigation
  - mixed reaction shows we tolerate unethical business behavior as part of free enterprise
  - court settlements show we are pragmatic
- Conclusion: We are a complex society with competing values (accurate)

Paragraph 2 (Politics)
- E.g., Fundraising scandals
  - response was campaign finance reform
  - shows concern for democratic ideals
- E.g., Clinton sex scandals
  - response was prurient interest
  - shows we are voyeurs and media puppets
- Conclusion: Same as in paragraph 1 (accurate)

Paragraph 3 (Queries)

- If we pay attention at all, what does this reflect about society?
- Is the fact that scandals are publicized more reflective of the media than of society?

Thesis

- In either area, scandals show we have many sides.
- Intuition tells me this is an accurate reflection.
- Musing: Issue raises questions about how media influences our values and priorities

WRITING INTRODUCTORY PARAGRAPHS (5 EXERCISES)

1. Analysis

The operative word in this statement is "only." This key word opens the door for you to discuss other reasons these ads are often effective and to provide supporting examples. Here's an introductory paragraph that leads appropriately into this discussion. Notice that the introduction anticipates *three* body paragraphs (one for the area of agreement and one for each of the two points of disagreement):

> Assuming that an "effective" ad is one that helps sell the advertised product or service, I agree with the statement to the extent that this advertising technique can be effective. However, the statement is problematic in two respects: (1) it overlooks other reasons that these types of ads are often effective, and (2) it wrongly assumes that consumers can accurately predict the benefits of a product before using it.

2. Analysis

Any statement with the word "should" invites the test taker to challenge certain normative assumptions underlying the statement. The following introductory paragraph tells the reader that the test taker recognizes those assumptions and will proceed to challenge them. Notice that the introduction anticipates *three* body paragraphs (one for the area of agreement and one for each of two challenges):

> I do not dispute the legitimacy of research aimed at improving the health and well-being of society and its members. However, the speaker misunderstands why we humans, by way of our very nature, are driven to advance our knowledge in the first place. The speaker fails to appreciate that in seeking knowledge for knowledge's own sake, researchers sometimes make the most profoundly beneficial discoveries.

62

3. Analysis

The following introduction lets the reader know that the test taker recognizes differing perspectives on this issue. The rhetorical phrase "[I]t might be tempting to agree . . ." suggests that in the final analysis, the test taker will, on balance, disagree with the statement. The introduction anticipates a separate paragraph for each of two reasons for agreement, followed by a separate paragraph for each of two sorts of benefits: "economic" and "other societal" (four body paragraphs altogether):

> The speaker's essential claim is that using public resources to support the arts is unjustifiable. It might be tempting to agree with the speaker on the basis that art is not a fundamental human need and that government is not entirely trustworthy when it comes to its motives and methods. However, the speaker overlooks certain economic and other societal benefits that accrue when government assumes an active role in supporting the arts.

4. Analysis

Like many GRE and GMAT Issue statements, this one overstates the speaker's case. (Notice the key word "must.") The statement invites the test taker to qualify the statement by carving out areas of exception and providing counterexamples. The first two sentences below inform the reader that the test taker is about to accomplish precisely that. The remainder of the introduction anticipates *three* body paragraphs.

> This statement amounts to an unfair generalization. The key to individual success in any activity is to strike the optimal balance between individuality and conformity—a balance that varies depending on the particular activity and goal involved. With respect to activities that are inherently creative, I am in full agreement with the statement. When it comes to certain other activities, however, conformity is the most important ingredient for success, while in still other activities, success depends equally on both.

5. Analysis

Notice that this statement lists three types of leaders. This list serves as an invitation to discuss each one in turn, in a separate paragraph. One way to approach this type of statement is to either agree or disagree with it, then provide supporting examples from each category. Another approach is to show (by reasons and examples) that the statement's accuracy depends on the category. The following introduction anticipates a four-paragraph analysis that follows the latter approach:

> Although this statement has merit, it is problematic in two respects. First, serving the interests of followers is not the only responsibility of a leader. Secondly, whether this responsibility is the "greatest" one

depends on the type of leadership involved. While legitimate political leadership must, by my definition, serve the citizenry, the same cannot be said for either business or military leadership.

RECOGNIZING AN ESSAY'S STRUCTURE (8 EXERCISES)

1. GRE Essay No. 4

The first three paragraphs concern one point of view, while the final two paragraphs turn to the opposing view. (The essay favors the latter view, on balance.)

P 1: Point
P 2: Example
P 3: Example
P 4: Counterpoint (one example)
P 5: Counterpoint (a second example)

2. GRE Essay No. 21

The first two paragraphs discuss the essay's main point (reason in support of the essay's position), while the third and fourth paragraphs each discuss another, distinct point.

P 1: Point 1
P 2: Point 1 (continued)
P 3: Point 2
P 4: Point 3

3. GRE Essay No. 39

The first paragraph acknowledge a contrary position, then rebuts it, while the remaining paragraphs provide examples in support of the rebuttal.

P 1: Point → counterpoint
P 2: Example (in support of counterpoint)
P 3: Example (in support of counterpoint)

4. GRE Essay No. 55

The first three paragraphs concern one point of view, while the final two paragraphs turn to the opposing view. (The essay favors the latter view, on balance.)

P 1: Point (one view)
P 2: Counterpoint
P 3: Rebuttal
P 4: Point (opposing view)
P 5: Counterpoint → Rebuttal

5. GMAT Essay No. 20

In the first paragraph, the test taker agrees with the statement in one respect; in the other two paragraphs, the test taker disagrees with the statement in another respect:

> P 1: Point
> P 2: Counterpoint
> P 3: Counterpoint (continued)

6. GMAT Essay No. 63

The first paragraph indicates the chief reason for the position taken in the essay; the second paragraph acknowledges a contrary argument, then responds to it:

> P 1: Point
> P 2: Counterpoint → Rebuttal

7. GMAT Essay No. 80

The first paragraph presents one side of the issue, while the second paragraph provides another side. (The essay favors the latter position.)

> P 1: Point
> P 2: Counterpoint

8. GMAT Essay No. 110

The first paragraph indicates one extreme position on the issue, while the second paragraph indicates the contrary extreme position. The final paragraph suggests a middle, more balanced position:

> P 1: Point
> P 2: Counterpoint
> P 3: Position (balances point and counterpoint)

ANALYTICAL WRITING (5 EXERCISES)

1. Analysis

The following response first pays lip service to the statement (with a reason and an example), then refutes it (again, with a reason and an example):

As adults take on the responsibilities of work, they <u>might appear</u> to define themselves less by their social affiliations and more by their occupation. <u>For example</u>, when two adults meet for the first time, beyond initial pleasantries, the initial question almost invariably is "What do you do for a living?" <u>Yet in my opinion,</u> this focus on occupation belies our true preferences as to how we would define ourselves. Rather, it is born of economic necessity; we don't have the leisure time or financial independence to concern ourselves with purely social activities. <u>After all</u>, when older people retire from the world of work, their true preference—for identifying with social groups (bridge clubs, investment clubs, or country clubs)—seems to emerge.

2. Analysis

The following response first acknowledges that the statement is generally correct. Then, rather than refuting the irrefutable, the response points out an important exception (and an illustrative example):

> <u>Admittedly</u>, in a democracy, citizens must question the fairness and relevance of current laws. It is not enough for a handful of legislators to challenge the status quo; ultimately, it is up to the electorate at large to call for changes in the law when they are needed to reflect evolving social values. <u>However</u>, when mass resistance to governmental authority escalates to violent protest, the end result is often more harm than good to the society, despite the worthiness of the social or political cause. <u>For instance</u>, although the violent challenge to authority during the 1992 Los Angeles riots was sparked by legitimate outrage against race-related police brutality, the protest ultimately resulted in a financially crippled community and, more broadly, a turning back of the clock with respect to racial tensions across America. Was the community and the society better off in the end? Perhaps not.

3. Analysis

The following response cites two reasons in support of the statement, then dispels them both (the first one with a reason, the second one by example):

> <u>Those who agree</u> with the statement, especially parents, <u>would argue</u> that only parents can truly know the unique needs of their children, including what educational choices are best suited for them, and that parents are more motivated than anyone else to ensure their children the best possible education. <u>In my view, both arguments are specious.</u> <u>As for the first one</u>, since parents lack both the objectivity and specialized training of professional educators, leaving crucial decisions about curriculum and pedagogy to parents might in many cases result in an incomplete education. <u>As for the second one</u>, although in a perfect world parents would always make their children's education one of their highest priorities, in fact many parents do not.

4. Analysis

The following response first acknowledges a narrow point of agreement, then provides two reasons for disagreeing with the statement generally (the second reason is supported by an example):

> I agree with the statement only with respect to certain aspects of a student's personal value system. For example, public colleges should not advocate the teachings of any particular religion or spiritual belief, or they would risk undermining our basic freedom of religion. Otherwise, I disagree with the statement for two reasons. First, rote technical knowledge and skill do not help a student determine which goals in life are worthwhile and whether or not the means of attaining those goals are ethically or morally acceptable. Secondly, by nurturing the development of thoughtful personal value systems, educators actually help prepare students for their careers. After all, for most people, jobs and even careers come and go throughout life, and a principled value system provides both the ballast and compass needed to navigate life's rough seas.

5. Analysis

The following response employs a certain rhetorical device that can be particularly effective. Notice that after providing counterexamples, the response "doubles back" to the attack the statement's supporting examples:

> I concede that careful planning and a sustained effort are essential ingredients for some forms of achievement. For example, none of the world's greatest democratic states or so-called "wonders" of architecture were built overnight—or by accident. However, I take issue with the statement with respect to artistic achievements. Query how many of the world's great artistic creations—visual, musical, or literary— would have come to fruition though mere planning and plodding. It seems to me that great creative accomplishment necessarily depends on moments of rare insight or brilliance. And even for works of architecture or for political states, greatness might not be the result of sustained effort as much as the product of an individual designer's extraordinary ingenuity and insight.

COMPOSING A FULL-LENGTH ISSUE ESSAY

Here are two sample responses, each of which express overall disagreement with the Issue at hand. Each one is brief enough to easily compose in 30 or 45 minutes. I've underlined transition and rhetorical phrases to help you see the structure and "flow" of the argument.

1. Sample Response for Issue 1 (370 words)

Imposing regulatory measures on those who would harm the natural environment is one way to preserve it. I disagree, however, that it is necessarily the best way. Laws might elicit grudging compliance; but other approaches—those that instill a sense of genuine commitment—are likely to be more effective in the long term.

Admittedly, motivating environmental protection by way of government regulation will serve environmental goals up to a point. However, many individuals and businesses will attempt to avoid compliance by concealing their activities. As for large businesses in particular, some will lobby legislators to modify regulations or move operations to jurisdictions that allow their environmentally harmful activities. Others might calculate the trade-off between accepting punishment and polluting, then budget in advance for anticipated penalties and openly violate the law. My intuition is that this practice is a standard operating mode among some of our largest manufacturers.

A better way to ensure environmental protection is to inculcate a sense of genuine commitment in our society and especially in our corporate culture—through education and shareholder involvement. When many individuals, including key corporate executives, are committed to values, the regulations associated with those values become a codification of conscience rather than obstacles to circumvent. Moreover, commitment-driven actions are likely to benefit the environment over and above what the law requires. For example, while a particular regulation might permit a certain amount of toxic effluents, individuals and businesses committed to environmental protection might avoid harmful emissions altogether.

Instilling a genuine sense of commitment through education and shareholder action is not just a better approach in theory, it is also less costly overall than a compliance-driven approach. Regulatory systems inherently call for legislative committees, investigations, and enforcement agencies, all of which add to the tax burden of the citizens whom these regulations are designed to protect. Also, delays typically associated with bureaucratic regulation can thwart the purpose of the regulations, because environmental problems can quickly become grave indeed.

In sum, environmental regulations are essentially expensive Band-Aids. A commitment-based approach, involving education at the individual level and shareholder activism at the corporate level, can instill in the society at large a sense of environmental conscience, resulting in far more effective environmental protection.

2. Sample Response for Issue 2 (325 words)

Whether a particular business ultimately succeeds or fails depends on a variety of factors. In my view, while teamwork is almost always important, in most instances, other factors are more pivotal to a firm's success.

The main reason for my view is simply that it accords with observation and common sense. For example, in many instances, it is clearly the policy decisions of key executives that determine whether or not a firm ultimately succeeds. Notable cases include the turnaround success of Coca-Cola after Roberto Goizueta assumed the position of CEO and, in contrast, the Apple Computer debacle years ago following the departure of its founding visionary Steve Jobs. Also, consider industries such as financial services, where product differentiation is difficult. It seems to me that a creative marketing ploy or the tenacity of a sales force would be the key factor here. Finally, in manufacturing and mining, the value of raw materials or capital equipment is surely more significant than the cooperative efforts of employees or, for that matter, any other asset.

Another reason for my view is that technical knowledge and competence would seem to be more fundamental to most jobs. Specifically, without adequate knowledge of the systems, procedures, and vocabulary used in one's department or division, an employee cannot communicate effectively with peers or contribute meaningfully to organizational goals. Admittedly, nearly all jobs in an organization require some cooperative interaction with coworkers, even jobs performed in relative isolation and those calling for a high level of technical knowledge or ability. For instance, researchers, scientists, and computer programmers must agree on specifications and coordinate efforts to meet timelines. However, some substantive knowledge is necessary to perform virtually any job, whereas the ability to work effectively with others is merely helpful.

In sum, I agree that teamwork is an important ingredient for organizational success. However, it is generally not the most important one. On balance, some other factor—such as leadership, ambition, tangible assets, or especially technical knowledge—usually plays a more pivotal role.

Part 3

HOW TO WRITE A HIGH-SCORING ARGUMENT ESSAY

Here in Part 3, you'll learn all you need to score your best on your GRE or GMAT Argument essay. At the end of Part 3, you'll put into practice what you've learned through a series of skill-building exercises.

For a high-scoring Argument essay, you need to accomplish these three basic tasks:

1. Determine the argument's key elements

2. Organize, develop, and express your critique manner

3. Support your ideas with sound reasons and supporting examples

> **NOTE:** You'll also need to demonstrate adequate control of the elements of standard written English (grammar, syntax, and usage). You'll focus on that task later, in Part 4.

To make sure you accomplish all three tasks within your 30-minute time limit, follow this 8-step approach (suggested times are parenthesized):

8 STEPS TO THE ARGUMENT WRITING TASK

Plan Your Essay (5 min.)

1. Read the Argument, and identify its conclusions. (2 min.)

2. Identify and examine the Argument's evidence to determine how strongly it supports the Argument's conclusion(s). (2 min.)

3. Organize and prioritize your points of critique. (1 min.)

Compose Your Essay (20 min.)

4. Compose a brief introductory paragraph. (2 min.)

5. Compose the body of your response. (16 min.)

6. Compose a concluding paragraph. (2 min.)

Refine Your Essay (5 min.)

7. Review and revise for coherence and balance. (3 min.)

8. Proofread for significant mechanical problems. (2 min.)

> **NOTE:** The suggested time limits for each step are merely guidelines, not hard-and-fast rules. As you practice composing your own Argument essays under timed conditions, start with my guidelines, then develop a pace that works best for you personally.

In the following pages, I'll walk you through each step in turn, applying the following simulated Argument:

Argument

The following appeared in a memo from the manager of UpperCuts hair salon:

> "According to a nationwide demographic study, more and more people today are moving from suburbs to downtown areas. In order to boost sagging profits at UpperCuts, we should take advantage of this trend by relocating the salon from its current location in Apton's suburban mall to downtown Apton, while retaining the salon's decidedly upscale ambiance. Besides, Hair-Dooz, our chief competitor at the mall, has just relocated downtown and is thriving at its new location, and the most prosperous hair salon in nearby Brainard is located in that city's downtown area. By emulating the locations of these two successful salons, UpperCuts is certain to attract more customers."

1. READ THE ARGUMENT, AND IDENTIFY ITS CONCLUSION(S)

Every GRE and GMAT Argument consists of the following basic elements:

1. **Evidence** (stated premises that the Argument does not dispute)

2. **Assumptions** (unstated premises needed to justify a conclusion)

3. **Conclusions** (inferences drawn from evidence and assumptions)

As you read an Argument for the first time, identify its *final* conclusion as well as its *intermediate* conclusion (if any). Why is this first step so important? Unless you are clear about the Argument's conclusions, it's impossible to evaluate the author's reasoning or the strength of the evidence offered in support of them. And that's what the Argument writing task is all about!

You'll probably find the *final* conclusion in the Argument's first or last sentence. The Argument might refer to it as a "claim," a "recommendation," or a "prediction." An intermediate conclusion, upon which the final conclusion depends, might appear anywhere in the Argument. Not every Argument contains an intermediate conclusion.

Did you identify and distinguish between the intermediate and final conclusions in the Argument involving UpperCuts? Here they are:

Intermediate Conclusion

"By emulating the locations of these two successful salons, UpperCuts is certain to attract more customers."

Final Conclusion

"In order to boost sagging profits at UpperCuts, we should . . . relocat[e] the salon from its current location in Apton's suburban mall to downtown Apton, while retaining the salon's decidedly upscale ambiance."

Notice that the Argument's final conclusion relies on its intermediate conclusions. Here's the essential line of reasoning:

UpperCuts will gain customers if it moves downtown. *(Intermediate conclusion)*

Therefore, UpperCuts will boost its profits *simply* by moving downtown. *(Final conclusion)*

Always jot down an Argument's intermediate conclusion (if any) and its final conclusion—in shorthand form like I've provided above. You'll need to refer to them time and again as you develop your points of critique and compose your essay.

2. IDENTIFY AND EXAMINE THE ARGUMENT'S EVIDENCE TO DETERMINE HOW STRONGLY IT SUPPORTS THE ARGUMENT'S CONCLUSION(S)

Most Arguments contain at least two or three items of information, or evidence, that it uses in support of its conclusion(s). Identify them, label them, and jot them down in shorthand form on your scratch paper. The Argument involving UpperCuts contains three distinct items of evidence:

Evidence (Item 1)

"According to a nationwide demographic study, more and more people today are moving from suburbs to downtown areas."

Evidence (Item 2)

"Hair-Dooz, our chief competitor at the mall, has just relocated downtown and is thriving at its new location."

Evidence (Item 3)

". . . the most prosperous hair salon in nearby Brainard is located in that city's downtown area."

Then, analyze each item as to how much support it lends to the Argument's intermediate and final conclusions. Be on special lookout for any unsubstantiated or unreasonable *assumptions* upon which the Argument's conclusions depend. For each major piece of evidence, you should also note any *additional information* you would need to determine how strongly the evidence supports whatever conclusion (intermediate or final) is based on that evidence.

During step 2 you should also:

1. Look for problems with the Argument's *internal logic* (e.g., self-contradictions or circular reasoning).

2. Determine whether the Argument relies on any *vague* or *undefined* key terms.

As in the Issue essay, don't filter your ideas during this crucial brainstorming step! Let them all flow onto your scratch paper. (You'll sort them out in step 3.)

> **NOTE:** Without exception, each Argument in the official GRE and GMAT pools contains at least three or four discrete reasoning flaws. Later, in Part 3, you'll examine in greater detail the most common such flaws in GRE and GMAT Arguments.

Here's what your notes for the Argument involving UpperCuts might look like after a few minutes of brainstorming:

inter. concl.—UC will gain customers downtown
final concl.—UC will improve profits downtown

● demog. study—is Apton typical?   no trend
                                        reverse trend

● success of HD—is location key?   marketing
                                        key stylist

● success of B salon—downtown location key?
            —is Apton like Brainard?
            (demog.)

● other problems
      —relocation expenses offset revenues
      —UC must establish new clientele
      —competition from HD
         (suff. demand for <u>both</u> salons?)
      —demand for "upscale" salon downtown?

3. ORGANIZE AND PRIORITIZE YOUR POINTS OF CRITIQUE

Using your notes from step 2 as a guide, arrange your ideas into paragraphs (probably three or four, depending on the number of problems built into the Argument). Take a minute to consider whether any of the flaws you identified overlap and whether any can be separated into two distinct problems. In many cases, the best sequence in which to organize your points of critique is the same order in which they appear in the Argument.

For the Argument writing task, there's no need to create a separate outline. You can probably use your notes as your outline, numbering them according to the most logical sequence to discuss them. Here's what my notes for the Argument involving UpperCuts look like after organizing them (arrows indicate where I intend to discuss a point; [FC] denotes "final conclusion"):

NOTE: Later in Part 3, you'll learn specific guidelines for organizing the points of your critique.

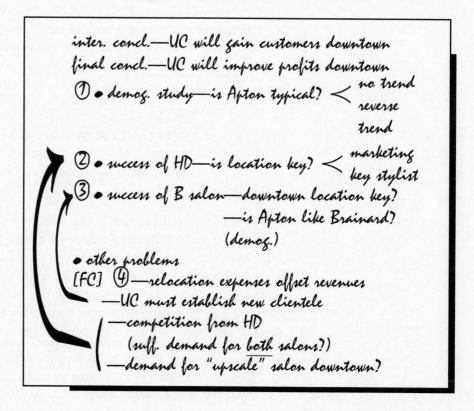

4. COMPOSE A BRIEF INTRODUCTORY PARAGRAPH

Now that you've spent about five minutes planning your essay, it's time to compose it. Don't waste time repeating the Argument at hand; the reader, whom you can assume is already well familiar with the Argument, is interested in your critique—not in your transcription skills. Here's what you should try to accomplish in your initial paragraph:

1. **Identify** the Argument's final conclusion.

2. **Describe** briefly the Argument's line of reasoning and evidence in support of its conclusion.

3. **Allude** generally to the problems with the Argument's line of reasoning and use of evidence.

You can probably accomplish all three tasks in 2–3 sentences. Here's a concise introductory paragraph for the Argument involving UpperCuts (I've underlined words and phrases that you could use in the introductory paragraph of any Argument essay):

Citing a general demographic trend and certain evidence about two other hair salons, the manager of UpperCuts (UC) concludes here that UC should relocate from suburban to downtown Apton in order to attract more customers and, in turn, improve its profitability. However, the manager's argument relies on a series of unproven assumptions and is therefore unconvincing as it stands.

> **NOTE:** The essays in Parts 6 and 8 include longer introductory paragraphs that paraphrase the entire Argument—for your reference. There's no need for you to include as much detail in your initial paragraph.

Your introductory paragraph is the least important component of your essay. Thus, you might consider waiting until you've completed your critique of the Argument before composing your introduction (unless you are a GRE test taker who will submit handwritten essays). If you're running out of time for your introduction, begin your essay with a sentence like one of the following two, then delve right into your first point of critique—without a paragraph break:

This argument suffers from numerous flaws that, considered together, render untenable the conclusion that UpperCuts should relocate to downtown Apton. One such flaw involves . . .

I find the argument for moving UpperCuts salon downtown specious at best, because it relies on a series of unproven, and doubtful, assumptions. One such assumption is that . . .

5. COMPOSE THE BODY OF YOUR RESPONSE

After spending no more than 5 minutes planning your response, it's time to compose it. As in the Issue essay, during this step, your chief aim is to peck madly at your keyboard in order to get your ideas onto the screen! Here's what you need to keep in mind as you compose your body paragraphs:

- Try to devote a separate paragraph to each point of your critique.

- Be sure the first sentence of each paragraph conveys to the reader the essence of the problem that you intend to discuss in that paragraph.

- Try to provide at least one example (scenario) that would undermine each major assumption.

- Try to devote no more than three or four sentences to any one point in your outline. Otherwise, you risk running out of time without discussing all of the Argument's major problems.

- Arrange your paragraphs so your essay flows logically from one point of critique to the next.

- Don't worry if you don't have time to include every possible point of critique. The readers understand your time constraint. Just be sure to hit the most critical problems.

Try to stick to your outline, but be flexible. Start with whichever points of critique strike you as the most important, are clearest in your mind, and are easiest to articulate. (You can always rearrange your points later, during step 7, assuming you're using the testing system's word processor.)

NOTE: If you're a GRE test taker who opts to submit a handwritten essay, you won't be able to easily rearrange sentences and paragraphs. You'll need to take greater care to get the sequence right the first time.

Here's the body of my response to the Argument involving UpperCuts. As you read these four paragraphs, note the following:

- Each paragraph addresses a distinct, critical assumption—a certain condition that must be true to justify the Argument's conclusions.

- Each paragraph describes at least one scenario that, if true, would serve to undermine an assumption.

- I've underlined certain transitional words and phrases—just to help you see how the ideas flow from one to the next.

    To begin with, the argument assumes that Apton's demographic trend reflects the national trend. Yet, the mere fact that one hair salon has moved downtown hardly suffices to infer any such trend in Apton; Hair-Dooz might owe its success at its new location to factors unrelated to Apton's demographics. Without better evidence of a demographic shift toward downtown Apton, it is just as likely that there is no such trend in Apton. For that matter, the trend might be in the opposite direction, in which event the manager's recommendation would amount to especially poor advice.

Even if Apton's demographics do reflect the national trend, it is unfair to assume that UC will attract more customers simply by relocating downtown. It is entirely possible that the types of people who prefer living in downtown areas tend not to patronize upscale salons. It is also possible that Hair-Dooz will continue to impede upon UC's business, just as it might have at the mall. Without ruling out these and other reasons why UC might not benefit from the demographic trend, the manager cannot convince me that UC would attract more customers, let alone increase its profits, by moving downtown.

Nor can the manager justify the recommended course of action on the basis of the Brainard salon's success. Perhaps hair salons generally fare better in downtown Brainard than downtown Apton, due to demographic differences between the two areas. Or perhaps the salon thrives only because it is long-established in downtown Brainard—an advantage that UC clearly would not have in its new location. In short, the manager cannot defend the recommended course of action on the basis of what might be a false analogy between two hair salons.

Finally, even assuming that the proposed relocation would attract more customers, an increase in the number of patrons would not necessarily result in improved profits. After all, profit is a function of expenses as well as revenue. Thus, an increase in UC's expenses—due perhaps to higher rents downtown than at the mall—might very well offset increasing revenues, thereby frustrating UC's efforts to improve its profitability.

6. COMPOSE A CONCLUDING PARAGRAPH

Unless your essay has a clear end, the reader might think you didn't finish on time; so be sure to make time for a final paragraph that clearly "wraps up" your essay. Your final paragraph is *not* the place to introduce any new points of critique. Instead, try to accomplish the following two tasks:

1. **Recapitulate** the Argument's problems—e.g., a series of unproven assumptions (1–2 sentences)

2. **Indicate** how the Argument can be strengthened *and/or* indicate what additional information would be helpful in evaluating the Argument. (2–3 sentences)

> **NOTE:** You can perform the second task as you compose your body paragraphs, incorporating this additional information into those paragraphs. You'll explore this alternative a bit later in Part 3.

Now, here's my final paragraph for the Argument involving UpperCuts. Notice that this paragraph does not introduce any new points of critique (I've underlined words and phrases that you could use in the final paragraph of nearly any Argument essay):

> In sum, the argument is a dubious one that relies on a series of unproven assumptions—about Apton's and Brainard's demographics, the reasons for the success of the two other salons, and UC's future expenses. To strengthen the argument, the manager should provide better evidence of a demographic shift in Apton toward the downtown area and clear evidence that those demographics portend success there for an upscale hair salon. Even with this additional evidence, in order to properly evaluate the argument, I would need to know why Hair-Dooz relocated, what factors have contributed to the Brainard salon's success, what factors other than location might have contributed to UC's sagging profits at the mall, and what additional, offsetting expenses UC might incur at the new location.

7. REVIEW AND REVISE YOUR ESSAY TO ENSURE COHERENCE AND BALANCE

Be sure to reserve time to revise and rework your essay. Check the flow of your essay, paying particular attention to the first sentence of each paragraph. If you have time, rearrange paragraphs so they appear in their most logical sequence.

8. PROOFREAD FOR SIGNIFICANT MECHANICAL PROBLEMS

Your Argument essay, like your Issue essay, need not be flawless in order to earn a top score. The readers won't decrease your score for the occasional awkward sentence and minor error in punctuation, spelling, grammar, or diction (word choice and usage). Use whatever time remains to fix the most glaring mechanical problems. Correct spelling errors only when they're likely to interfere with the reader's understanding of the point at hand. Don't spend any time correcting punctuation or minor spelling errors.

ORGANIZING YOUR IDEAS (YOUR ESSAY'S STRUCTURE)

Just as for the Issue essay, the testing service makes clear that there is no correct structure *per se* for an Argument essay. Nevertheless, you should adhere to certain guidelines or risk losing your train of thought on the reader.

NUMBER OF WORDS

Don't worry about the word length of your essay. As long as you incorporate into your essay all the elements that I suggest here in Part 3, your essay's word length will be appropriate.

> **NOTE:** The sample Argument essays in Parts 6 and 8 of this book range from 425 to 625 words in length. But for a top score of 6, your Issue essay need not be as lengthy as my samples, especially my longer ones.

NUMBER OF PARAGRAPHS

There is no "correct" or "best" number of paragraphs for an Argument essay. However, any GRE or GMAT Argument essay should contain at least *three* body paragraphs, because every official Argument contains at least three significant, and distinct, reasoning problems. In addition, your essay should include a final "recap" paragraph and, if you have time, an introductory paragraph.

AN ARGUMENT'S LINE OF REASONING AND YOUR ESSAY'S STRUCTURE

The structure of your essay should reflect the Argument's line of reasoning as much as possible. Your points of critique should lead the reader, item by item, from the Argument's evidence and assumptions to the Argument's intermediate conclusion (if any), then to its final conclusion. Here's an example of a typical Argument, stripped down to its structure, revealing its flawed line of reasoning and use of evidence:

Example 1—Three Distinct Points of Critique, One per Paragraph

1. A *first* major assumption (about an item of evidence) is needed to justify the intermediate conclusion.

2. A *second* major assumption (about an item of evidence) is also needed to justify the intermediate conclusion.

3. If the intermediate conclusion is true, a *third* major assumption is still needed to justify the *final* conclusion.

Some Arguments rely on threshold assumptions—for example, a certain definition of a key term. Here's an example of this type of Argument—again, stripped down to its structure, revealing its flawed line of reasoning and use of evidence (this one does not contain an intermediate conclusion):

Example 2—Four Distinct Points of Critique, One per Paragraph

1. The *threshold assumption* is needed before addressing the Argument's main line of reasoning.

2. If the threshold assumption is true, a *first* major assumption (about an item of evidence) is still needed to justify the Argument's conclusion.

3. If the threshold assumption is true, a *second* major assumption (about an item of evidence) is still needed to justify the Argument's conclusion.

4. Even if all of the foregoing assumptions are true, a *third* (and final) major assumption is still needed to justify the Argument's conclusion.

Of course, most GRE and GMAT Arguments do not fit *precisely* into one of these two patterns. But your essential approach for any Argument should be the same: to trace the Argument's line of reasoning from its evidence and assumptions to its intermediate conclusion (if any) through to its final conclusion. Here are some rules of thumb to keep in mind as you put into practice this principle:

- Many Arguments rely on some sort of "threshold" assumption (e.g., about the meaning of a vague, ambiguous, or undefined term). The most logical place to address this type of assumption is in your *first* body paragraph—because clearing up the threshold problem might very well be needed before you need to address the overall Argument to begin with.

- Many Arguments rely on the assumption that the recommended course of action is either *necessary* or *sufficient* (or both) to achieve a stated objective or outcome. Usually, the most logical place to discuss these assumptions is in your *final* body paragraph—during which you grant all other assumptions (for the sake of argument).

- Some (but not many) Arguments suffer from problems with their *internal logic* (e.g., contradictory recommendations or objectives, or circular reasoning). Usually, the most logical place to address these problems is in your *final* body paragraph—during which you grant all other assumptions (for the sake of argument).

OPTIONAL ELEMENTS AND YOUR ESSAY'S STRUCTURE

The foregoing guidelines for paragraph number and logical sequence should dictate your Argument essay's structure, for the most part. However, you do have a few personal choices when it comes to either of the following optional elements:

- Suggestions as to how the Argument can be strengthened

- Additional information needed to evaluate the Argument

If you have time to add either element to your critique, you have two realistic choices:

1. List the suggestions (or additional information needed) in your *final* paragraph.

2. Incorporate the list of suggestions (or additional information needed) into your *body paragraphs* as you compose each one in turn. For example, indicate additional evidence needed to substantiate a particular assumption (i.e., to show that the assumption is true) as you point out that assumption.

> **NOTE:** The sample Argument essays in Part 6 and Part 8 employ the first method.

Regardless of which structure you use, consider adding these optional elements only *after* you've completed your critique of the Argument. Otherwise, you risk running out of time for addressing all of the Argument's major problems.

APPLYING STRUCTURAL PRINCIPLES TO A SAMPLE ARGUMENT

Earlier in Part 3, I walked you through each step in composing a response to the Argument involving UpperCuts. The final essay contained a full introductory paragraph, and it incorporated both optional elements into its final paragraph. The end result was a 540-word essay—an ambitious response for any test taker with a 30-minute time limit.

Now, here's a briefer response (360 words), which incorporates only *one* of the two optional elements—directly into the essay's body paragraphs rather than into the final paragraph. This response does not include a separate introductory paragraph, and its analysis is a bit more concise. Nevertheless, it would score a 6 with any GRE or GMAT reader (again I've underlined words and phrases that you could use in almost any Argument essay):

This argument relies on a series of unproven assumptions, which together undermine its conclusion that UpperCuts (UC) should relocate to downtown Apton. One such assumption is that Apton reflects the cited demographic trend. The mere fact that one hair salon has moved downtown hardly suffices to show that the national trend applies to Apton specifically. For all we know, in Apton there is no such trend, or perhaps the trend is in the opposite direction. Thus, I would need to know whether more people are in fact moving to downtown Apton before I could either accept or reject the manager's proposal.

Even assuming that downtown Apton is attracting more residents, relocating downtown might not result in more customers for UC, especially if downtown residents are not interested in UC's upscale style and prices. Besides, Hair-Dooz might draw potential customers away from UC, just as it might have at the mall. Before I can accept that UC would attract more customers downtown, the manager would need to supply clear proof of a sufficient demand downtown for UC's service.

Even if there would be a high demand for UC's service in downtown Apton, an increase in the number of patrons would not necessarily improve UC's profitability. UC's expenses might be higher downtown, in which case it might be no more, or perhaps even less, profitable downtown than at the mall. Therefore, before I could agree with the proposal, I would need to examine a comparative cost-benefit analysis for the two locations.

As for the Brainard salon, its success might be due to particular factors that don't apply to UC. For example, perhaps the Brainard salon thrives only because it is long-established in downtown Brainard. Accordingly, in order to determine whether the success of the

Brainard salon portends success for UC in downtown Apton, <u>I would need to know</u> why the former salon is successful in the first place.

<u>In sum, the argument relies on</u> what might amount to two poor analogies between UC and two other salons, as well as a sweeping generalization about demographic trends, which may or may not apply to Apton. <u>As a result, without the additional information indicated above</u>, I find the argument unconvincing at best.

RECOGNIZING AND HANDLING FLAWS IN GRE AND GMAT ARGUMENTS

The test maker intentionally incorporates into each Argument numerous reasoning flaws that render the Argument vulnerable to criticism. In a typical Argument, you can find three or four distinct areas for critique. (Glance through the essays in Parts 6 and 8, and you'll notice that most of them contain three or four body paragraphs—one for each distinct reasoning flaw built into the Argument.)

In this section, you'll explore the reasoning flaws that are most common in GRE and GMAT Arguments. I've presented them here in order—from more frequent to less frequent. For each type of flaw, you'll find at least one simulated Argument that illustrates the problem, along with at least one effective response. The simulated Arguments and responses in this section are each designed to focus on one particular reasoning flaw. They are not intended as complete Arguments or essays.

> **NOTE:** I've intentionally avoided the use of the technical terminology of formal logic to identify types of logical fallacies here. You don't need to know these terms, and you don't need any formal course work in logic, in order to recognize and handle reasoning problems in GRE and GMAT Arguments.

CONFUSING A CAUSE-AND-EFFECT RELATIONSHIP WITH A MERE CORRELATION OR TEMPORAL SEQUENCE

Many GRE and GMAT Arguments rely on the claim that certain events cause other certain events. A cause-and-effect claim might be based on

1. A significant *correlation* between the occurrence of two phenomena (both phenomena generally occur together), or

2. A *temporal relationship* between the two (one event occurred after another).

A significant correlation or a temporal relationship between two phenomena is one indication of a cause-and-effect relationship between them. However, neither in itself suffices to prove such a relationship. Unless the Argument also considers and eliminates all other plausible causes of the presumed "result" (by the way, it won't), the Argument is vulnerable to criticism.

To show the reader you understand a false-cause problem, you need to accomplish all three of the following tasks:

1. **Identify** the false-cause problem (e.g., as one of the Argument's crucial assumptions).

2. **Elucidate** by providing at least one or two examples of other possible causes.

3. **Explain** how the false-cause problem undermines the Argument.

You'll probably need at least three sentences to accomplish all three steps (one sentence for each step). If the Argument involves an intermediate "link" in the cause-and-effect chain (as both of the following Arguments do), you'll probably need additional sentences—and perhaps an additional paragraph—to discuss that link.

Once you've accomplished all three tasks, if you have extra time to discuss a false-cause problem:

- Indicate what type of additional information (e.g., statistical data) would help prove a cause-and-effect relationship, and/or

- List additional types of information (e.g., statistical data, cost-benefit analyses, projections for the future) needed to determine whether the assumed cause-and-effect relationship actually exists.

> **NOTE:** An Argument might also confuse *sole* cause with mere *contributing* cause. In other words, a certain condition contributes to an outcome ("effect") but is insufficient by itself for the outcome. You'll examine this type of flaw (the *sufficient-condition* assumption) a bit later.

Example (Cause-and-Effect Confused with Mere Correlation)

Here's an Argument that might confuse causation with mere correlation. (The Argument might suffer from other reasoning problems as well, but here I'm focusing on false cause.) Response A provides a brief but adequate one-paragraph analysis that contains each of the three elements needed to address this false-cause problem. Response B goes further, to identify and discuss an intermediate link in the chain of reasoning, as well as to list additional information needed to properly evaluate the Argument.

Argument

The following appeared in a memo from a television network's programming director:

> "Parents of young children are becoming increasingly concerned about how depictions of violence on television might influence a child's behavior and attitudes. During the past year, the ratings for *Real Crime*, one of our network's most popular prime-time shows, have steadily declined. Therefore, in order to boost our prime-time ratings, we should replace *Real Crime* with a situation comedy show."

Response A

The argument relies on an unproven cause-and-effect relationship between certain parental concerns and the show's ratings problem. The director has not ruled out other possible causes for the show's ratings decline—for example, a change in the show's specific time slot. If it turns out that the show's ratings problem has nothing to do with it's depictions of violence, then simply replacing the show with one that contains no violence will probably not solve the problem.

Response B

To begin with, the memo indicates neither that young children are interested in watching *Real Crime* nor that the show actually depicts violence. Yet both conditions are necessary in order for the show to carry the kind of deleterious influence on young children with which parents seem concerned. Thus, unless both conditions are met, the director cannot convince me that any change involving the show will address these parental concerns, let alone boost the show's ratings.

Even if *Real Crime* does portray violence and does have a potentially undesirable impact on young children as a result, the director has not shown that the show's waning popularity is attributable to this impact. Perhaps the show owed its popularity to some other feature, such as a certain celebrity narrator, that the show now lacks. Or perhaps a new competing show, one that is at least as violent as *Real Crime*, has drawn viewers away from *Real Crime*. In short, until the director rules out all other possible reasons for the rating's decline, I will remain unconvinced that the show's violent portrayals, if any, are responsible for the trend and therefore that any change would serve to reverse it.

In order to evaluate the argument properly, at the very least, I would need to know whether the content of *Real Crime* is cause for parental concern and what percentage of the show's viewers are young children. It would also be useful to know the reasons for the show's relative popularity in the past and why former *Real Crime* viewers, especially those with young children, no longer watch the show.

Example (Cause-and-Effect Confused with Temporal Sequence)

Here's an Argument that might confuse causation with mere temporal sequence. (The Argument might suffer from other reasoning problems as well, but here I'm focusing on false cause.) Response A provides a brief but adequate one-paragraph analysis that contains each of the three elements needed to address this false-cause problem. Response B goes further, to identify and discusses an intermediate link in the chain of reasoning, as well as to suggest how to strengthen the Argument.

Argument

The following appeared in the editorial section of a newspaper:

> "Two years ago, State X enacted a law prohibiting environmental emissions of certain nitrocarbon byproducts, on the basis that these byproducts have been shown to cause Urkin's Disease in humans. Last year, fewer State X residents reported symptoms of Urkin's Disease than in any prior year. Since the law is clearly effective in preventing the disease, in the interest of public health, this state should adopt a similar law."

Response A

The editorial infers that State X's new law is responsible for the apparent decline in the incidence of Urkin's Disease (UD) symptoms. However, the editorial's author ignores other possible causes of the decline—for example, a new UD cure or new treatment for UD symptoms. Without eliminating alternative explanations such as these, the author cannot justify either the inference or the additional assertion that a similar law would be similarly effective in the author's state.

Response B

Based on State X's reported decline in the incidence of Urkin's Disease (UD) symptoms since the passage of the law, the speaker infers that the law's enactment is responsible for the decline. However, the sequence of these events, in itself, does not suffice to prove that the earlier development caused the later one. A decline could have resulted from some other event instead: a cure for UD or new treatment for its symptoms, a demographic shift away from contaminated areas, or an increasing mortality rate among State X's UD sufferers—to list just a few possibilities. Without ruling out scenarios such as these, the editorial's author cannot establish a cause-and-effect relationship (between the new law and the decline in reports) upon which the editorial's recommendation depends.

Moreover, the argument overlooks the fact that it is the level of compliance with a law, not its enactment, that determines its effectiveness. The editorial's author has not accounted for the possibility that despite the new law, the emissions have continued unabated. If this is the case, then the claim that the law has been effective in preventing Urkin's Disease in State X would lack any merit whatsoever—as would the ultimate claim that a similar law would be effective in this state.

To strengthen the argument, the editorial's author must supply evidence that since the law was enacted two years ago (1) State X residents are just as likely to report UD symptoms as before, (2) emissions that violate the law have abated, and (3) all other factors in the incidence of UD symptoms have remain essentially unchanged.

False-Cause Problems in the Official Arguments (Parts 6 and 8)

As you study my essays in Part 6 ("Essays for 20 Official GRE Arguments"), look for my analysis of false-cause problems in the following paragraphs:

■■| GRE Argument No. 1 (fourth essay paragraph)
GRE Argument No. 20 (second and third essay paragraphs)
GRE Argument No. 42 (third essay paragraph)
GRE Argument No. 46 (fourth essay paragraph)
GRE Argument No. 59 (third essay paragraph)
GRE Argument No. 68 (second essay paragraph)
GRE Argument No. 88 (third essay paragraph)
GRE Argument No. 91 (third essay paragraph)
GRE Argument No. 96 (fifth essay paragraph)
GRE Argument No. 105 (second and third essay paragraphs)
GRE Argument No. 122 (second essay paragraph)

As you study my essays in Part 8 ("Essays for 20 Official GMAT Arguments"), look for my analysis of false-cause problems in the following paragraphs:

■■■| GMAT Argument No. 23 (third essay paragraph)
GMAT Argument No. 28 (second and fifth essay paragraphs)
GMAT Argument No. 37 (second essay paragraph)
GMAT Argument No. 42 (fourth essay paragraph)
GMAT Argument No. 48 (third essay paragraph)
GMAT Argument No. 74 (third essay paragraph)
GMAT Argument No. 84 (second essay paragraph)
GMAT Argument No. 89 (third and fourth essay paragraphs)
GMAT Argument No. 93 (second essay paragraph)
GMAT Argument No. 105 (second and third essay paragraphs)
GMAT Argument No. 124 (fourth essay paragraph)

DRAWING A WEAK ANALOGY BETWEEN TWO THINGS

A GRE or GMAT Argument might draw a conclusion about one thing (perhaps a city, school, or company) on the basis of an observation about a similar thing. However, in doing so, the Argument might assume that because the two things are similar in certain respects, they are similar in all respects, at least as far as the Argument is concerned. Unless the Argument provides sufficient evidence to substantiate this assumption (by the way, it won't), the Argument is vulnerable to criticism.

To show the reader you understand the weak-analogy problem, you need to accomplish all three of the following tasks:

1. **Identify** the analogy (e.g., as one of the Argument's crucial assumptions).

2. **Elucidate** by providing at least one or two significant ways in which the two things might differ.

3. **Explain** how those differences, which render the analogy weak, undermine the Argument's conclusion.

You'll probably need at least three sentences to accomplish all three steps (one sentence for each step). Once you've accomplished all three tasks, if you have extra time to discuss the problem, add one of these two optional elements:

- Indicate what sort of additional evidence the argument's author could supply to either strengthen the analogy or, if the analogy is especially poor, to make a convincing argument without the analogy.

- Indicate what else you would need to know to determine whether the analogy is a fair one—that warrants the argument's conclusion.

> **NOTE:** An Argument that relies on a weak analogy between two things (A and B) typically assumes that emulating just one certain feature of B will *suffice* for A to see a similar result as B. You'll examine this *sufficient-condition* assumption separately, just a bit later.

Example

Here's an Argument that contains a questionable analogy. (The Argument might suffer from other reasoning problems as well, but here I'm focusing on the analogy.) Response A provides a brief but adequate one-paragraph analysis that contains each of the three elements needed to address this problem. Response B provides a more detailed analysis, as well as indicating how the argument can be strengthened.

Argument

The following was part of a speech made by the principal of Valley High School:

> "Every year, Dunston High School wins the school district's student Math SuperBowl competition. The average salary of teachers at Dunston is greater than at any other school in the district. Hence in order for Valley High students to improve their scores on the state's standardized achievement exams, Valley should begin awarding bonuses to Valley teachers whenever Valley defeats Dunston in the Math SuperBowl."

Response A

The principal's recommendation relies on what might be a poor analogy between Dunston and Valley. Valley teachers might be less responsive than Dunston teachers when it comes to monetary incentives, or Valley students might be less gifted than Dunston students when it comes to math. In short, what might have helped Dunston perform well at the Math SuperBowl would not necessarily help Valley perform better either at the SuperBowl or on the state exams.

Response B

Even assuming Dunston's stellar performance at the SuperBowl is attributable to its high teacher salaries, a different monetary incentive (bonuses) for a different group of teachers and students (Valley's) will not necessarily carry a similar result. The mere prospect of a bonus might not provide as great an incentive as a salary raise. For that matter, any form of monetary reward might provide far less motivation for Valley's teachers than for Dunston's. As for the students, Dunston's might be exceptionally gifted in math and would win the SuperBowl every year, regardless of efforts at other schools. In short, without accounting for important possible differences between Valley and Dunston, the principal cannot reasonably rely on Dunston's salaries to prove that the proposed bonuses will help Valley defeat Dunston, let alone score high on the state's exams.

To strengthen the argument, instead of relying on a dubious analogy between Dunston and Valley, the principal should supply evidence, perhaps by way of a teacher survey or pilot program at Valley, that the proposed bonuses would provide sufficient incentive for Valley's teachers to help their students perform better in math competitions and on math tests. The evidence should also show that Valley's teachers are capable of improving their effectiveness as math teachers and that their students are capable of improving their performance.

Analogies in the Official Arguments (Parts 6 and 8)

As you study my essays in Part 6 ("Essays for 20 Official GRE Arguments"), look for my analysis of analogies in the following paragraphs:

■■I GRE Argument No. 1 (third essay paragraph)
GRE Argument No. 46 (second essay paragraph)
GRE Argument No. 52 (fifth essay paragraph)
GRE Argument No. 59 (second essay paragraph)
GRE Argument No. 88 (fifth essay paragraph)
GRE Argument No. 91 (third essay paragraph)
GRE Argument No. 105 (fourth essay paragraph)

As you study my essays in Part 8 ("Essays for 20 Official GMAT Arguments"), look for my analysis of analogies in the following paragraphs:

■■■I GMAT Argument No. 37 (second essay paragraph)
GMAT Argument No. 71 (second essay paragraph)
GMAT Argument No. 79 (third essay paragraph)
GMAT Argument No. 84 (fourth essay paragraph)
GMAT Argument No. 93 (third essay paragraph)
GMAT Argument No. 95 (third essay paragraph)
GMAT Argument No. 105 (fourth essay paragraph)
GMAT Argument No. 117 (third essay paragraph)
GMAT Argument No. 122 (fourth essay paragraph)
GMAT Argument No. 124 (third essay paragraph)

RELYING ON A POTENTIALLY UNREPRESENTATIVE STATISTICAL SAMPLES

A GRE or GMAT Argument might cite statistical evidence from a study, survey, or poll involving a "sample" group, then draw a conclusion about a larger group or population that the sample supposedly represents. But in order for a statistical sample to accurately reflect a larger population, the sample must meet two requirements:

1. The sample must be *significant in size* (number) as a portion of the overall population.

2. The sample must be *representative* of the overall population in terms of relevant characteristics.

Arguments that cite statistics from studies, surveys, and polls often fail to establish either of these two requirements. Of course, this failure is by design of the test maker, who is inviting you to call into question the reliability of the evidence.

To show the reader you understand this statistical problem, you need to accomplish all three of the following tasks:

1. **Identify** the problem (e.g., as one of the Argument's crucial assumptions).

2. **Elucidate** by providing at least one or two respects in which key characteristics of sample group might differ from those of the larger population.

3. **Explain** how those differences would undermine the Argument's conclusion.

You'll probably need at least three sentences to accomplish all three steps (one sentence for each step). Once you've accomplished all three tasks, if you have extra time to discuss the problem, add one of these two optional elements:

- Indicate how the Argument's author can prove that the sample group is representative, or in the alternative, make a convincing argument without the statistic.

- Indicate what else you would need to know to determine whether the sample group is representative of the larger population.

Example

Here's an Argument that relies on *two* potentially unrepresentative sample groups: (1) new graduates from a certain state's undergraduate programs and (2) new graduates from the state's graduate-level programs. (The Argument might suffer from other reasoning problems as well, but here I'm focusing on this statistical problem.) Response A provides a brief but adequate one-paragraph analysis that contains each of the three elements needed to address this problem. Response B provides a more detailed analysis with more examples, as well as indicating (in a final paragraph) what additional information is needed to fully evaluate the Argument.

Argument
The following was part of an article appearing in a national magazine:

> "Our nation's new college graduates will have better success obtaining jobs if they do not pursue advanced degrees after graduation. After all, more than 90 percent of State X's undergraduate students are employed full-time within one year after they graduate, while less than half of State X's graduate-level students find employment within one year after receiving their graduate degrees."

Response A
The argument fails to consider that State X's new graduates might not be representative of the nation's as a whole, especially if the former group constitutes only a small percentage of the latter group. If it turns out, for example, that State X's undergraduate students are less motivated than the nation's average college student to pursue graduate-level study, then the argument's recommendation for all undergraduate students would be unwarranted.

Response B

One problem with the argument involves the cited statistics about State X's new graduates. It is unreasonable to draw any conclusions about new graduates of all colleges in the nation based on statistics from only one state. Depending on the total number of colleges and college students in the nation, it is entirely possible that State X's students are not representative of our nation's students as a whole. Perhaps in State X, undergraduate students as a group are particularly outstanding academically due to comparatively high admission standards among State X's largest universities and colleges. Or perhaps in State X, graduate-level programs are relatively few in number and focus on disciplines for which job prospects are unusually poor. In either event, the editorial's recommendation might amount to poor advice for new college graduates in other states.

To better assess the argument, I would need to determine the extent to which State X's students are representative of the nation's college students generally, in terms of the ease with which its undergraduate and graduate students find immediate employment. At a minimum, I would need to know the total number of undergraduate and graduate students in State X and compare these totals to the numbers for the entire nation. I would also need to know the comparative caliber of State X's students, as well as more information about other features of State X's colleges and universities that might affect the ability of their graduates to find jobs.

Statistical-Sample Problems in the Official Arguments (Parts 6 and 8)

As you study my essays in Part 6 ("Essays for 20 Official GRE Arguments"), look for my analysis of statistical-sample problems in the following paragraphs:

■ ■ I GRE Argument No. 1 (second essay paragraph)
GRE Argument No. 9 (fourth essay paragraph)
GRE Argument No. 22 (second essay paragraph)
GRE Argument No. 42 (second essay paragraph)
GRE Argument No. 80 (sixth essay paragraph)
GRE Argument No. 91 (second essay paragraph)
GRE Argument No. 96 (second essay paragraph)

As you study my essays in Part 8 ("Essays for 20 Official GMAT Arguments"), look for my analysis of statistical-sample problems in the following paragraphs:

■ ■ ■ I GMAT Argument No. 8 (third essay paragraph)
GMAT Argument No. 74 (second essay paragraph)
GMAT Argument No. 98 (fourth essay paragraph)

RELYING ON TAINTED RESULTS FROM A SURVEY OR POLL

As you just learned, a GRE or GMAT Argument might draw some conclusion involving a group based on statistical data about an *insufficient* or *unrepresentative* sample. However, this is not the only potential problem with statistical data. The process of collecting the data (i.e., the methodology) might be flawed in a way that calls into question the *quality* of the data, rendering the data "tainted" and therefore unreliable for the purpose of drawing any conclusions. In order for survey or poll results to be reliable in quality:

- The survey or poll responses must be *credible* (truthful and accurate). If respondents have reason to provide incomplete or false responses, the results are tainted and unreliable.

- The method of collecting the data must be *unbiased*. If responses are not mandatory or if the survey's form predisposes subjects to respond in certain ways, then the results are tainted and unreliable.

To show the reader that you recognize and understand this statistical problem, you need to accomplish all three of the following tasks:

1. **Identify** the problem (e.g., as one of the Argument's crucial assumptions).

2. **Elucidate** by providing at least one or two reasons, based on the Argument's information, why the statistical data might be tainted and unreliable.

3. **Explain** how the potentially tainted data might undermine the Argument's conclusion.

You'll probably need at least three sentences to accomplish all three steps (one sentence for each step). Once you've accomplished all three tasks, if you have extra time to discuss the problem, add one of these two optional elements:

- Indicate how the argument's proponent can establish that the statistical evidence is reliable (not tainted).

- Indicate what else you would need to know to determine whether the statistical evidence is reliable (not tainted).

Example

The following Argument relies on survey that poses a potential *bias* as well as a *credibility* problem. (The Argument might suffer from other reasoning problems as well, but here I'm focusing on tainted-data problems.) The response contains all three elements required to address each problem, in a single paragraph.

Argument

The following appeared in a memo from the Director of Human Resources at Webco:

> "Among Webco employees participating in our department's most recent survey, about half indicated that they are happy with our current four-day work week. These survey results show that the most effective way to improve overall productivity at Webco is to allow each employee to choose for himself or herself either a four-day or five-day work week."

Response

The survey methodology might be problematic in two respects. First, we are not informed whether the survey required that respondents choose their work-week preference between alternatives. If it did, then the results might distort the preferences of the respondents, who might very well prefer a work-schedule choice not provided for in the survey. Secondly, we are not informed whether survey responses were anonymous or even confidential. If they were not, then respondents might have provided responses that they believed their superiors would approve of, regardless of whether the responses were truthful. In either event, the survey results would be unreliable for the purpose of drawing any conclusions about Webco employee preferences, let alone about how to improve overall productivity at Webco.

Tainted Data Problems in the Official Arguments (Parts 6 and 8)

As you study my essays in Part 6 ("Essays for 20 Official GRE Arguments"), look for my analysis of potentially tainted statistical data in the following paragraphs:

■ I I GRE Argument No. 9 (second and fifth essay paragraphs)
   GRE Argument No. 22 (second essay paragraph)
   GRE Argument No. 80 (third and fourth essay paragraphs)
   GRE Argument No. 96 (second essay paragraph)

As you study my essays in Part 8 ("Essays for 20 Official GMAT Arguments"), look for my analysis of potentially tainted statistical data in the following paragraphs:

■ ■ I I GMAT Argument No. 8 (fourth essay paragraph)
   GMAT Argument No. 98 (second and third essay paragraphs)
   GMAT Argument No. 122 (second essay paragraph)

Assuming That a Certain Condition Is Necessary and/or Sufficient for a Certain Outcome

A GRE or GMAT Argument might recommend a certain course of action, based on one or both of the following claims:

1. The course of action is *necessary* to achieve a desired result.

2. The course of action is *sufficient* to achieve the desired result.

Both claims often occur in the same Argument, and both are potentially vulnerable to criticism. With respect to claim 1, the Argument must provide evidence that no other means of achieving the same result are available (by the way, it won't). With respect to claim 2, the Argument must provide strong evidence that the proposed course of action by itself would be sufficient to bring about the desired result (by the way, it won't). Lacking this sort of evidence, the Argument cannot rely on these claims to support its recommendation.

An Argument that relies on one of these two assumptions does not necessarily rely on the other as well. Read the Argument very carefully—because a few words can make all the difference. For instance, consider the following alternative recommendations for reversing a profit decline at XYZ Company (the italicized words are the key):

Unless XYZ Company hires the former marketing director of ABC Company, XYZ *will not* reverse its current profit decline.

[This conclusion relies on the necessary-condition assumption only.]

By hiring the former marketing director of ABC Company, XYZ Company *will* boost its profits.

[This conclusion relies on the sufficient-condition assumption only.]

In order to boost its profits, XYZ Company *should* hire the former marketing director of ABC Company.

[This conclusion relies on both assumptions. The language implies that the recommended course of action is needed to, and in fact will, bring about the stated objective.]

To show the reader you understand necessary-condition and sufficient-condition problems, you need to accomplish all three of the following tasks:

1. **Identify** the problem (e.g., as one of the Argument's crucial assumptions).

2. **Elucidate** by providing at least one or two examples.

   - For a necessary-condition problem, suggest other possible means of achieving the stated objective.

   - For a sufficient-condition problem, suggest other conditions that might also be necessary for the outcome.

3. **Explain** how the problem undermines the Argument's conclusion.

You'll probably need at least three sentences to accomplish all three steps (one sentence for each step). Once you've accomplished all three tasks, if you have extra time to discuss the problem, add one of these two optional elements:

- Indicate what sort of additional information the argument's author could provide to strengthen the inference that the condition is necessary and/or sufficient for the outcome.

- Indicate what else you would need to know to determine whether the condition is necessary/sufficient for the outcome.

Example—Both Assumptions

Here's an Argument that relies on both assumptions. (The Argument might suffer from other reasoning problems as well, but here I'm focusing on these two problems.) Although you might be able to address both assumptions in a single paragraph, if you have time, you should devote a separate paragraph to each one, as in my response to the Argument:

Argument

The following appeared in a memo from the superintendent of the Harper County school district:

"In order to raise the level of reading skills among our district's elementary-school students to a level that at least represents the national average, we should adopt the "Back to Basics" reading program. After all, this reading program has a superior record for improving reading skills among youngsters nationwide. By adopting Back to Basics, the parents of our young students would be assured that their children will develop the reading skills they will need throughout their lives."

Response

The superintendent fails to account for other possible means of improving the students' reading skills to the desired extent. Admittedly, the superior record of Back to Basics (BTB) amounts to some evidence that no other "program" is as likely to achieve the stated objective. However, the superintendent must at least examine and rule out other programs. She must also consider and eliminate other alternatives—for example, encouraging parents to read with their children or simply devoting more time during school to reading. Otherwise, it seems hasty at best to conclude that the district must adopt the BTB program, or for that matter any reading program, in order to achieve its objective.

The superintendent also neglects to substantiate her assumption that adopting BTB would suffice by itself to improve students' reading skills to the desired extent. Common sense tells me that BTB will be largely ineffective unless other conditions are met as well. Most notably, students must be sufficiently attentive and motivated. In short, until the superintendent shows that the program will be effectively implemented and received, I simply cannot accept the recommendation.

Necessary- and Sufficient-Condition Assumptions in the Official Arguments (Parts 6 and 8)

As you study my essays in Part 6 ("Essays for 20 Official GRE Arguments"), look for my analysis of necessary- and sufficient-condition assumptions in the following paragraphs:

Necessary Conditions

■ ❙ ❙ GRE Argument No. 20 (second essay paragraph)
GRE Argument No. 59 (fifth essay paragraph)
GRE Argument No. 109 (second essay paragraph)
GRE Argument No. 122 (fifth essay paragraph)

Sufficient Conditions

■ ❙ ❙ GRE Argument No. 20 (fourth essay paragraph)
GRE Argument No. 46 (third and fifth essay paragraphs)
GRE Argument No. 68 (third essay paragraph)
GRE Argument No. 76 (second essay paragraph)
GRE Argument No. 96 (fourth essay paragraph)
GRE Argument No. 122 (third essay paragraph)

As you study my essays in Part 8 ("Essays for 20 Official GMAT Arguments"), look for my analysis of necessary- and sufficient-condition problems in the following paragraphs:

Necessary Conditions

■ ■ ❙ GMAT Argument No. 28 (third essay paragraph)
GMAT Argument No. 53 (fourth essay paragraph)
GMAT Argument No. 59 (third essay paragraph)
GMAT Argument No. 79 (fifth essay paragraph)
GMAT Argument No. 89 (fifth essay paragraph)
GMAT Argument No. 93 (fourth essay paragraph)
GMAT Argument No. 117 (fourth essay paragraph)
GMAT Argument No. 124 (fifth essay paragraph)

Sufficient Conditions

■ ■ I I GMAT Argument No. 42 (third and fifth essay paragraphs)

GMAT Argument No. 74 (fourth essay paragraph)

GMAT Argument No. 79 (fifth essay paragraph)

GMAT Argument No. 93 (fifth essay paragraph)

GMAT Argument No. 122 (third essay paragraph)

ASSUMING THAT CHARACTERISTICS OF A GROUP APPLY TO EACH GROUP MEMBER (OR VICE VERSA)

A GRE or GMAT Argument might point out some fact about a general group—such as students, employees, or cities—to support a claim about one particular member of that group. Or conversely, the Argument might point out some fact about a particular group member to support a claim about the entire group. In either scenario, unless the Argument supplies clear evidence that the member is representative of the group as a whole (by the way, it won't), the Argument is vulnerable to criticism.

To show the reader you understand a group-member problem, you need to accomplish all three of the following tasks:

1. **Identify** the problem (e.g., as one of the Argument's crucial assumptions).

2. **Elucidate** by providing at least one or two significant ways in which the member might differ from the general group.

3. **Explain** how those key differences, which serve to refute the assumption, would undermine the Argument's conclusion.

You'll probably need at least three sentences to accomplish all three steps (one sentence for each step). Once you've accomplished all three tasks, if you have extra time to discuss the problem, add one of these two optional elements:

- Indicate what sort of additional evidence the Argument's author could supply to show that the member's relevant characteristics are similar to those of the group as a whole.

- Indicate what additional information would help you determine the extent to which the member is representative of the group.

Example—What's True for a Group Is also True for Any Member

The following Argument assumes that characteristics of a group apply to every member of the group. (The Argument might suffer from other reasoning problems as well, but here I'm focusing on this group-member problem.) The response provides a brief but adequate one-paragraph analysis that contains each of the three elements needed to address this problem. The response also indicates how the Argument can be strengthened.

Argument

The following appeared in a local newspaper editorial:

> "According to a recent nationwide survey, a greater percentage of our nation's teenagers complain of depression today than ever before. Here in the town of Seaside, we need to do more to ensure that our teenagers fill their days with meaningful, productive activities, so that they grow up to be happy, well-adjusted adults."

Response

Although the editorial assumes that Seaside's teenagers are typical of the nation's teenagers in general, it supplies no evidence whatsoever to substantiate this assumption. For all we know, the incidence of depression among Seaside's teens is far lower than the national average—low enough that teen depression does not pose a community-wide problem for Seaside. If so, the editorial cannot justify its recommendation to the community, at least not based on the nationwide survey.

To bolster the recommendation, instead of relying on a sweeping generalization, the editorial's author should provide specific evidence that among Seaside teenagers, depression is a widespread problem that is likely to continue unless the community takes specific measures to reverse the trend.

Example—What's True for a Member Is also True for the Group

The following Argument assumes that characteristics of a particular member of a group apply to the group as a whole. (The Argument might suffer from other reasoning problems as well, but here I'm focusing on this group-member problem.) Response A provides a brief but adequate one-paragraph analysis that contains each of the three elements needed to address the problem. Response B provides a more detailed analysis with more examples, as well as listing additional information needed to properly evaluate the Argument.

Argument

The following is part of an article appearing in the entertainment section of a local newspaper:

> "At the local Viewer Choice video store, the number of available movies in VHS-tape format remains about the same as three years ago, even though the number of available movies on digital video disk, or DVD, has increased tenfold over the past three years. People who predict the impending obsolescence of the VHS format are mistaken, since demand for VHS movie rentals today clearly remains just as strong as ever."

Response A

This argument assumes that Video Choice (VC) is typical of all video stores, as a group. However, this isn't necessarily the case; VC might carry far more VHS tapes, as a percentage of its total inventory, than the average store. Is so, then the argument has failed to discredit the prediction for the industry as a whole.

Response B

The article's position unfairly assumes that Viewer Choice (VC) is typical of the video rental and sales industry generally. Perhaps VC is attempting to serve a niche market by specializing in older movies that are not yet available on DVD. Or perhaps the percentage of households in VC's neighborhood that have DVD players is lower than the national average, for whatever reason. For that matter, perhaps much of VC's current VHS inventory is for sale but not for rent, because VC is trying to clear its shelves of VHS tapes in order to further expand its selection of DVDs. Since the article fails to consider and eliminate these and other possible reasons why VC continues to stock as many VHS tapes as three years ago, the article has not succeeded in dispelling the predicted demise of VHS.

In order to fully evaluate the article's position, I would need more information about worldwide trends in VHS sales and rentals vis-a-vis trends in DVD sales and rentals. Lacking this information, it would be helpful to learn why VC carries as many VHS tapes today as three years ago.

Group-Member Problems in the Official Arguments (Parts 6 and 8)

As you study my essays in Part 6 ("Essays for 20 Official GRE Arguments"), look for my analysis of group-member problems in the following paragraphs:

■■I GRE Argument No. 9 (fourth essay paragraph)
GRE Argument No. 14 (fifth essay paragraph)
GRE Argument No. 20 (fifth essay paragraph)
GRE Argument No. 109 (fifth essay paragraph)

As you study my essays in Part 8 ("Essays for 20 Official GMAT Arguments"), look for my analysis of group-member problems in the following paragraphs:

■■■I GMAT Argument No. 48 (fourth essay paragraph)
GMAT Argument No. 89 (second essay paragraph)

ASSUMING THAT ALL THINGS REMAIN UNCHANGED OVER TIME

A GRE or GMAT Argument might rely on evidence collected in the *past* in order to formulate some conclusion or recommendation concerning the *present* or the *future*. Similarly, an Argument might rely on evidence about *present* conditions to make a prediction or recommendation for the *future*. But unless the Argument provides clear evidence that key circumstances have remained, or will remain, unchanged over the relevant time period (by the way, it won't), the Argument is vulnerable to criticism.

To address a time-shift problem, you should accomplish each of the following three tasks:

1. **Identify** the problem (i.e., the poor assumption that all key circumstances remain fixed over time).

2. **Elucidate** by providing examples of conditions that might change from one time frame to the other.

3. **Evaluate** the argument in light of the problem.

You'll probably need three sentences to accomplish all three tasks. If you have more time, you can perform either of the following optional tasks as well:

- Indicate that to strengthen the argument, the author must convince that other relevant conditions remain unchanged from one time frame to the next.

- List additional information about past and present (or present and future) circumstances that you need in order to evaluate the recommendation, prediction, or other conclusion.

Example—Past Conditions Remain Unchanged in the Present *and* Future

Here's an Argument that provides evidence about the past to draw a conclusion about the present as well as the future. (The Argument might suffer from other reasoning problems as well, but here I'm focusing on this time-shift problem.) The response accomplishes all three required tasks, as well as suggesting how to strengthen the argument, all in a single, concise paragraph.

Argument

The following appeared in a political campaign advertisement:

> "Residents of this state should vote to elect Kravitz as state governor in the upcoming election. During Kravitz's final term as a state senator, she was a member of a special legislative committee that explored ways the state can reduce its escalating rate of violent crime. Elect Kravitz for governor, and our cities' streets will be safer than ever."

Response

Assuming that at one time Kravitz was genuinely committed to fighting violent crime, the ad unfairly infers a similar commitment on Kravitz's part today and in the future while Kravitz serves as governor. Kravitz might hold entirely different views today, especially if her participation as a member of the committee occurred some time ago. Lacking better evidence that as governor Kravitz would continue to make crime-fighting a high priority, the ad cannot persuade me to vote for Kravitz based on her committee membership.

Example—Present Conditions Will Remain Unchanged into the Future

Here's an Argument that makes a prediction based on present conditions, ignoring possible future developments. (The Argument might suffer from other reasoning problems as well, but here I'm focusing on this time-shift problem.) Response A provides a brief but adequate analysis of the time-shift problem. Response B goes further, to provide more examples as well as suggestions for strengthening the argument.

Argument

The following appeared in a regional business magazine:

> "Yoga Essentials, a small retail store located in Mountcrest, has been in business for about a decade, even though the store's owner has never advertised in Mountcrest's local newspaper. Now Yoga Essentials is offering franchise opportunities in other areas. In the nearby town of Lakeview, there are more yoga studios and health clubs than in Mountcrest. Thus, a Yoga Essentials franchise in Lakeview would surely be a profitable investment."

Response A

The argument assumes that the apparent interest in yoga (and yoga-related products) among Lakeview residents will remain strong. However, it fails to consider that this interest might wane or that Lakeview will lose many of its residents, for whatever reason. Since the argument fails to account for possibilities such as these, I am unconvinced that a Lakeview franchise would be profitable.

Response B

The argument's claim that a Yoga Essentials store in Lakeview would succeed relies on the assumption that the apparent interest in yoga (and yoga-related products) among Lakeview residents will continue to remain strong enough to support the store. However, in Lakeview, yoga might turn out to be a passing fad or a luxury that the town's residents will no longer be able to afford in the future, for whatever reason. For that matter, a newer competing store might run Yoga Essentials out of business in Lakeview. Thus, the argument's proponent must supply better evidence—perhaps by way of a Lakeview survey and a Lakeview economic forecast—of a sufficient demand in Lakeview for the kinds of products Yoga Essentials sells, at least for the foreseeable future. Otherwise, the author cannot persuade me that a Lakeview franchise would be profitable.

Time-Shift Problems in the Official Arguments (Parts 6 and 8)

As you study my essays in Part 6 ("Essays for 20 Official GRE Arguments"), look for my analysis of time-shift problems in the following paragraphs:

■■I GRE Argument No. 9 (third essay paragraph)
GRE Argument No. 31 (fourth essay paragraph)
GRE Argument No. 96 (sixth essay paragraph)
GRE Argument No. 109 (third essay paragraph)
GRE Argument No. 113 (fourth essay paragraph)

As you study my essays in Part 8 ("Essays for 20 Official GMAT Arguments"), look for my analysis of time-shift problems in the following paragraphs:

■■■I GMAT Argument No. 23 (fourth essay paragraph)
GMAT Argument No. 28 (fourth essay paragraph)
GMAT Argument No. 53 (second and third essay paragraphs)
GMAT Argument No. 79 (fourth essay paragraph)
GMAT Argument No. 131 (second essay paragraph)

OTHER REASONING PROBLEMS WITH GRE AND GMAT ARGUMENTS

Now that you've examined the most common GRE and GMAT reasoning problems, briefly survey some other reasoning problems you might find with an Argument. Although each of these problems is less common than any of the ones I've already covered, you should be ready for them anyway—just in case.

Failing to Define Important Terms

An Argument might rely on a certain term without providing an adequate definition of it. Look especially for references to a particular class, category, or group, without a clear explanation of what it includes or excludes. For examples of this problem, see

■■I GRE Argument No. 59 (fourth essay paragraph)

■■■I GMAT Argument No. 23 (fifth essay paragraph)
GMAT Argument No. 71 (fourth essay paragraph)
GMAT Argument No. 89 (first essay paragraph)
GMAT Argument No. 122 (fourth essay paragraph)

Relying on Vague or Ambiguous Evidence

An Argument might contain a statement (or word or phrase) that carries more than one possible meaning or is simply too vague to reasonably rely upon when it comes to drawing conclusions. Look especially for references to "some," "many," and "several" in lieu of providing precise percentages or numbers. For examples of this problem, see

■■I GRE Argument No. 52 (third and fourth essay paragraphs)
GRE Argument No. 80 (fifth essay paragraph)
GRE Argument No. 88 (third essay paragraph)

■■■I GMAT Argument No. 48 (first and second essay paragraphs)
GMAT Argument No. 84 (third essay paragraph)

Drawing a Conclusion that Is Too Broad in Degree or Scope

An Argument's conclusion might be well supported but only to a certain *extent* or only with respect to a certain *subclass*. An Argument that fails to limit the degree or scope of its conclusion in accordance with the evidence is vulnerable to criticism. For examples of this problem, see

■■I GRE Argument No. 42 (fourth essay paragraph)
GRE Argument No. 91 (second essay paragraph)

■■■I GMAT Argument No. 48 (fifth essay paragraph)
GMAT Argument No. 59 (second essay paragraph)

Assuming that Two Courses of Action Are Mutually Exclusive

A GRE or GMAT Argument might recommend one course of action over another in order to achieve the stated objective, without considering that it is possible to pursue both courses (that is, they are not mutually exclusive alternatives), thereby increasing the likelihood of achieving the objective. For examples of this problem, see

■■■I GMAT Argument No. 71 (third essay paragraph)
GMAT Argument No. 79 (fifth essay paragraph)

> **NOTE:** An Argument that suffers from this "either-or" reasoning problem will probably also overlook other courses of action that might achieve the stated objective. (In other words, neither course of action is a *necessary* condition.) If both problems arise, you should discuss both.

Arguing Simultaneously for Two Competing Objectives

A GRE or GMAT Argument might seek to achieve two distinct objectives, which appear to compete with each other; in other words, accomplishing one objective decreases the likelihood of achieving the other. For an example of this problem, see

■■■I GMAT Argument No. 59 (fifth essay paragraph)

Engaging in Circular Reasoning

A GRE or GMAT Argument might rely, at least partly, on its own line of reasoning to support that very reasoning. This general problem is known by the terms "circular reasoning" and "tautology" as well as by the idiom "begging the question." For an example of this problem, see

■■I GRE Argument No. 42 (fifth essay paragraph)

DO'S AND DON'TS FOR YOUR ARGUMENT ESSAY

Now, review some of the key points from Part 3. Here are two lists of DO's and DON'Ts—for content and organization—to keep you on the right track in organizing and composing your Argument essay. To reinforce the ideas in this list, earmark the list and refer to it from time to time as you practice the Argument writing task and as you read my sample essays in Part 6 and Part 8.

CONTENT—YOUR CRITIQUE OF THE ARGUMENT

Do identify and keep in mind the Argument's final and intermediate conclusions so that you can analyze the Argument's use of evidence and line of reasoning in support of those conclusions.

Don't merely restate or rehash the stated Argument. The only way to score points is to tell the reader what's wrong with the Argument.

Do analyze the Argument with an eye for uncovering three or four flaws—in the author's line of reasoning and use of evidence.

Do commit to memory the types of reasoning flaws you learned in Part 3, and look for at least three of them in your Argument.

Don't rely on the technical terminology of formal logic to identify reasoning problems; plain English will suffice.

DO identify unsubstantiated or unreasonable assumptions upon which the Argument's conclusion depends.

Do support each challenge to an assumption with at least one example (scenario).

Do discuss what is required to make the Argument more convincing and/or what would help you better evaluate it—if you have sufficient time.

Don't stray from the Argument at hand. Your personal opinions about any issue discussed in the Argument are irrelevant to the Argument writing task.

ORGANIZATION

Do organize your points of critique in a logical order, one per paragraph. The sequence should mirror the Argument's line of reasoning.

Don't introduce any new points of critique in the concluding paragraph. Your job here is simply to reiterate the Argument's main problems and possibly to indicate what is required to strengthen or fully evaluate the Argument.

Do use transition words and phrases that connect the various points of your critique in a way that helps your ideas flow naturally and logically from one to the next.

Don't worry about the word length of your Argument essay. Focus instead on identifying at least three problems and providing an adequate and coherent critique of each one.

IF YOU HAVE MORE TIME

If you have ample time before your exam, consider supplementing the Argument materials in this book with other resources. Here are some suggestions:

TAKE NOTES ON THE ARGUMENTS IN YOUR OFFICIAL POOL

Generate a printout of the complete pool of Arguments. (See this book's introduction for how to obtain the questions via the testing service's GRE and GMAT Web sites.) Randomly select up to fifteen Arguments from the pool. Pause for a minute to ponder the Argument, referring to my list of common reasoning problems. At least three or four points of critique should pop into your mind; jot them down. Then move on to the next Argument. With a little practice, the common reasoning flaws you learned about in this workshop will fly off the page at you!

CONSULT MY OTHER TWO ANALYTICAL WRITING BOOKS

If you have trouble ferreting out reasoning problems in a particular Argument, consult the corresponding essay in one of my other two Analytical Writing books:

GRE—Answer to the Real Essay Questions (Published by Peterson's). The book contains my essays for 125 Arguments in the official pool.

GMAT CAT—Answer to the Real Essay Questions (Published by Peterson's). The book's 2nd edition contains my essays for 115 Arguments in the official pool.

As you read the book's Argument essays, jot down points of critique you find clearest or most convincing. Also, highlight transitional phrases, which connect the essay's points of critique. Review the phrases, then try composing several essays yourself, making a special effort to incorporate similar phrases into your essays.

NOTE: For book information, see the books' Web supplements (www.west.net/~stewart).

Practice, Practice, Practice!

Compose as many practice essays as you reasonably have time for, responding to the official questions. Be sure to practice under timed conditions with a word processor, restricting your use of editing functions to the ones provided on the real exam. Evaluate your practice essays, referring to the official scoring criteria; reflect on your weaknesses, and concentrate on improving in those areas next time.

REINFORCEMENT EXERCISES

Now let's reinforce what you've learned in Part 3. Each of the following exercises contains an Argument designed to highlight a particular reasoning problem. For each Argument:

1. Compose a brief (one- or two-paragraph) essay response that focuses *only on that problem*.

2. Try to incorporate all the required elements for an adequate analysis of the problem.

3. You may also discuss how to remedy the problem (strengthen the argument) and/or what additional information is needed to fully evaluate the Argument, in terms of the specific problem.

4. On scratch paper, outline additional reasoning problems with the Argument that you would anticipate discussing were this a full-length (30-minute) writing task.

Limit your time to 10 minutes per exercise.

For each group of exercises, directions for that group immediately precede the exercises. *My responses and comments begin on page 111.*

EXERCISES 1–2

In each of these first two exercises, identify and discuss the *false-cause problem*. Also note other possible problems you would anticipate discussing in a full-length Argument essay.

1. In order to revitalize this city's economy, we should increase the number of police officers that patrol the city's downtown business district during daytime business hours. Three years ago, the city reduced the total size of its police force by nearly 30 percent. Since then, retail businesses in the district have experienced a steady decline in revenue.

2. At Xenon Company, workers who bring their own lunches from home are generally more productive than workers who purchase lunch at the company's cafeteria. Therefore, in order for Xenon to enhance overall worker productivity, and in turn profits, the company's cafeteria should offer the same types of lunch foods that workers bring from home.

EXERCISES 3–4

In each of the next two exercises, identify and discuss the *potentially weak analogy*. Also note other possible problems you would anticipate discussing in a full-length Argument essay.

3. In order to prevent a decline of Oak City's property values and in rents that Oak City property owners can command, the residents of Oak City must speak out against the approval of a new four-year private college in their town. After all, in the nearby town of Mapleton, the average rent for apartments has decreased by 10 percent since its new community college opened last year, while the average value of Mapleton's single-family homes has declined by an even greater percentage over the same time period.

4. Trashco provides refuse pickup and disposal as well as recycling services for the town of Plattsburg, all at about two thirds the total cost of Hillsville's total cost for Ridco's refuse and recycling services. In order to save enough money to construct a refuse transfer station within its city limits, Hillsville should discontinue using Ridco's services and use Trashco's services instead.

EXERCISES 5–6

In Exercise 5, identify and discuss the *potentially unrepresentative statistical results*. In Exercise 6, identify and discuss the potential *tainted-data problem*. For each Argument, also note other possible problems you would anticipate discussing in a full-length essay.

5. Workforce Systems, a consulting firm specializing in workplace productivity and efficiency, reports that nearly 70 percent of Max-tech's employees who enrolled in Workforce Systems' one-week seminar last year claim to be more content with their current jobs than prior to enrolling in the seminar. By requiring managers at all large corporations to enroll in the kinds of seminars that Workforce System offers, productivity in our economy's private sector is certain to improve.

6. A significant percentage of this county's residents who receive unemployment benefits from the state report that they would prefer to work but have difficulty finding work for which they are qualified. In order to reduce the strain on our county's State Employment Development office, which is currently understaffed, the county should establish an adult job-training program.

EXERCISES 7–8

In each of the next two exercises, identify and discuss the *necessary-condition* or *sufficient-condition* assumption. Also note other possible problems you would anticipate discussing in a full-length Argument essay.

7. The juvenile justice department of one of the nation's largest cities recently reported that children who engage in any of the city's organized sports programs are less likely than other children to be convicted of a felony crime later in life. Therefore, the federal government can reduce the national crime rate by mandating daily physical-education classes at every high school in the nation.

8. Rivertown's historic Hill district used to be one of the city's main tourist attractions. Since the construction of a new shopping center in the district, the district's quaint older shops and restaurants have had difficulty attracting patrons. In order to preserve the historic value of the Hill district's older buildings and to prevent further loss of revenue from tourists, the city must impose a moratorium on the construction of any new structures in the Hill district.

EXERCISES 9–10

In each of the next two exercises, identify and discuss the potential *group-member problem*. Also note other possible problems you would anticipate discussing in a full-length Argument essay.

9. At Giant Industries, our state's largest private business, the average production worker is now 42 years old. Recently, Giant's revenue from the sale of textiles and paper, which together account for the majority of Giant's manufacturing business, has declined significantly. Since an increasing percentage of new graduates from our state's

colleges and universities are finding jobs in other states, our state will soon face a crisis in which the size of our workforce will be insufficient to replace our current workers as they retire, in turn resulting in widespread business failure and a reduced quality of life in our state.

10. A recent issue of the *Journal of Education* observes that last year's decline in the total number of applicants to our nation's law schools was accompanied by an increase in the total number of applications to our nation's medical schools. In order to be take advantage of these current trends, Claybrook Community College should replace its associate-degree program in legal assistantship with a nursing program.

EXERCISES 11–12

In each of the next two exercises, identify and discuss potential *time-shift problems*. Also note other possible problems you would anticipate discussing in a full-length Argument essay.

11. According to a recent report by the federal government, last year, the total declared value of goods exported from this country to other countries was less than the annual total ten years ago, adjusted for inflation. Since our federal government seems unwilling to impose tariffs on imported goods, our country is destined to continue its dependency on foreign goods and services.

12. During the last five years, the volume of recyclable materials produced in Blackburn County has increased steadily, while the volume of nonrecyclable refuse has been declining. Since our current resources for accommodating refuse are ample, the county should reduce spending in this area and apply the savings to subsidies for businesses willing to collect, recycle, and resell recyclable materials.

REINFORCEMENT EXERCISES—SAMPLES AND COMMENTS

1. ANALYSIS

This Argument might confuse cause and effect with mere temporal sequence. Here's a response that handles the problem:

Just because the police-force reduction occurred before the decline in retail revenue, it is unfair to assume that the former is responsible for the latter. The business slowdown might be due instead to factors such as a general economic downturn or increasing competition in outlying suburbs, to list just a few possibilities. Besides, for all we know, the number of police officers patrolling the business district itself has remained the same, or even increased, during the last three years, and the city's other areas are the ones that have seen a reduction in police presence. Since the argument fails to prove that the police-force reduction is the actual cause of the retail business slump, or even contributed to it, the argument's proponent cannot justifiably infer that a police-force increase would serve to reverse that slump, let alone that it would revitalize the city's economy in general.

In a full-length (30-minute) essay, you might also address the following questions about the Argument's reasoning:

- A *threshold* problem: Does the city have an economic problem to begin with? (Is it fair to assume that the city's economy is suffering merely because retail revenues in one particular district have declined?)

- Would the proposed course of action *suffice* to attain the stated objective? (Perhaps additional measures, such as renovating the district or patrolling it at night, would also be needed.)

- Is the proposed course of action *necessary* to attain the stated objective? (A city might revitalize its economy through other means instead.)

2. ANALYSIS

This Argument might confuse cause and effect with mere correlation. Here's a response that handles the problem:

The argument unfairly assumes that Xenon's worker productivity is simply a function of what a worker eats for lunch. Although this might be the case, a mere correlation between lunch diet and productivity does not suffice to establish a cause-and-effect relationship. The argument's author must also consider and eliminate all other reasonable explanations for the difference in productivity levels between the two groups of workers. Perhaps the most plausible alternative explanation is that workers who bring their own lunch are more productive because they spend less time eating lunch and more time working. In short, lacking better evidence that at Xenon productivity depends primarily on lunch diet, asserting that changing the cafeteria's lunch menu will improve worker productivity amounts to little more than conjecture.

In a full-length (30-minute) essay, you might also address the following questions about the Argument's reasoning:

- A *threshold* problem: Are cafeteria lunches actually much different from lunches that workers bring from home? (If not, then the entire argument is pointless.)

- Would the proposed course of action *suffice* to attain the stated objective? (e.g., workers who prefer cafeteria dining might choose menu items that are different from lunch foods that other workers bring from home.)

- Is the proposed course of action *necessary* to attain the stated objective? (Perhaps Xenon can enhance worker productivity through other means instead.)

- Does the argument draw an *unfair analogy* between the two groups of workers? (Perhaps people who pay for meals are generally lazier than people who prepare their own meals.)

3. ANALYSIS

This Argument relies on a questionable analogy between two towns and between two types of colleges. Here's a response that handles both analogies together in one paragraph:

> The argument draws what might be a poor analogy between Oak City's circumstances and Mapleton's. The argument ignores possible differences that are relevant to the influence a new college exerts on property values and rents. For instance, perhaps the percentage of college students needing off-campus rental housing is less in Mapleton than it would be in Oak City with its new college, in which case the forces of supply and demand suggest less upward pressure on rents in the former than in the latter. Also, perhaps a four-year college brings to a town greater prestige or high culture than a community college, in turn exerting more upward pressure on overall property values. In short, without accounting for possible key differences between the two towns and the two types of colleges, the argument cannot justifiably rely on the cited trend in Mapleton to show that Oak City's property values and rents would face a similar fate were the new college approved.

In a full-length (30-minute) essay, you might also address the following questions about the Argument's reasoning:

- Is the presence of Mapleton's new community college the *true cause* of the decline in property values and rents in that town? (Perhaps some other recent development is responsible instead.)

- Is it *necessary* to refuse the new college in order to prevent a decline in property values and rents? (Perhaps Oak City can counteract downward pressure on property values and rents through some means.)

4. ANALYSIS

This Argument relies on a questionable analogy between two towns as well as between two trash companies. Here's a concise response that handles both analogies together in one paragraph:

> The argument's inference that Trashco's service is more costly than Ridco's depends on the unproven assumption that the two refuse companies provide the same degree and amount of service to both towns. Perhaps Trashco's services to Plattsburg is provided less frequently or to fewer households than Ridco's services to Hillsville, for whatever reason. Either scenario would explain Plattsburg's lower total cost, which in turn would undermine the argument's contention that Hillsville would save money by switching from Ridco to Trashco. Thus, to better evaluate the argument, I would need to know how much Trashco would charge Hillsville, not Plattsburg, for the same service that Ridco now charges.

In a full-length (30-minute) essay, you might also address the following questions about the Argument's reasoning:

- What does the argument assume about *future conditions* in Hillsville? (If the town's residents increase the volume of refuse or recyclables or begin insisting on more frequent pickups, Hillsville might regret its decision to switch to Trashco.)

- Is the proposed switch to Trashco *necessary* for the city to achieve its stated objective? (Perhaps the city has other means to reduce its costs, or means to enhance its revenue, for the purpose of affording the new station.)

- Might Hillsville incur *countervailing expenses* by constructing the new transfer station? (Perhaps refuse would need to be taken from the center to a more remote location, at additional expense.)

5. ANALYSIS

This Argument relies on a potentially unrepresentative statistical sample to draw a general inference. Here's a response that handles the problem:

> The argument assumes that Maxtech employees who reported these results are typical of private-sector workers in general, in terms of how they are likely to respond to this type of seminar. However, this isn't necessarily the case. It is entirely possible, for example, that Maxtech employees were unusually receptive or responsive to Workforce's particular methods, for whatever reason. In any event, Maxtech's seminar participants might constitute an insufficiently small sample for the purpose of making recommendations for the private-sector workforce in general. Since the argument fails to show that Maxtech's experience is typical, I simply cannot accept the argument's sweeping conclusion.

In a full-length (30-minute) essay, you might also address the following questions about the Argument's reasoning:

- Is the report from Workforce Systems *credible*? (Perhaps the company overstates the benefits of its seminars in order to attract clients.)

- Was the seminar the *true cause* of the improved level of content-ment among the participants from Maxtech? (The answer might depend on how much time has passed since the seminar, whether Maxtech's participants have the same jobs as before, and whether the seminar is designed to help workers become more content to begin with.)

- Are the claims by Maxtech's employees *credible*? (Perhaps they felt pressure to exaggerate the benefits of the seminar or falsely report improvement in order to take time off from work to enroll again in the seminar.)

- Might the argument assume that *all other conditions remain unchanged*? (Overall productivity of the economy's private sector depends also on many extrinsic factors having nothing to do with the benefits of these types of seminars.)

6. ANALYSIS

This Argument relies on reports that suffer from a potential credibility problem. Here's a response that handles the problem:

The recommendation relies on certain "reports" that may or may not be credible. The argument's proponent needs to consider the possibility that the unemployed people who report difficulty in finding work actually prefer unemployment because they can receive money while not working. Since the argument fails to rule out this possibility, I cannot be convinced that the proposed job-training program would succeed in reducing the ranks of the county's unemployed residents.

In a full-length (30-minute) essay, you might also address the following questions about the Argument's reasoning:

- Is the proposed program *necessary* for achieving the stated objective? (It might be possible to reduce the strain on the office by other means instead—e.g., by hiring additional staff, perhaps even from the pool of unemployed county residents.)

- Would the proposed program *suffice* to achieve the stated objec-tive? (A sufficient number of unemployed residents who might be able to find work through the program would actually need to participate in the program.)

- Would reducing the number of residents who receive unemployment benefits *suffice* to attain the stated objective? (Perhaps the office can easily accommodate the current number of residents applying for and receiving unemployment benefits, and the source of the strain lies elsewhere.)

- Does the argument suggest a course of action that would actually *undermine the stated objective*? (To staff the new job-training program, it might be necessary to reduce staff elsewhere in the office, which might exacerbate the strain.)

7. ANALYSIS

This Argument relies on a sufficient-condition assumption. Here's a response that handles the problem:

> The argument assumes that the proposed mandate in itself will suffice to lower the national crime rate yet fails to account for other conditions that might also be necessary for that outcome. Perhaps to be effective in this respect, physical-education classes must also be accompanied by after-school activity programs; or perhaps the classes must begin earlier in a youngster's academic life to have any appreciable impact on delinquent behavior. Without considering these and a myriad of other conditions that might be needed to ensure that a young person grows up to become law-abiding, the argument's author cannot justify the mandate.

In a full-length (30-minute) essay, you might also address the following questions about the Argument's reasoning:

- A *threshold* problem: Are "physical-education classes" sufficiently similar to "organized sports programs" that their impact on long-term behavior would be similar? (If not, then the entire argument can be dismissed out of hand.)

- Might the argument mistake *mere correlation*—between organized-sports participation and adult criminal behavior—for a *cause-and-effect* relationship? (We might need to know what percentage of youngsters participate to begin with and whether those youngsters are less inclined in any event toward delinquent behavior.)

- Is the sample group (children in one large city) *representative* of all children throughout the nation? (Perhaps participation in these programs is more effective in large cities than in smaller cities and rural areas.)

8. ANALYSIS

This Argument relies on two necessary-condition assumptions—one for each stated objective. Here's a response that handles both assumptions (one paragraph for each one):

> The argument assumes without justification that the proposed moratorium is the only available means of preserving the historic value of the district's older buildings. To begin with, the argument supplies absolutely no evidence that the new shopping center adversely impacts that value at all. Even if it does, the argument fails to account for alternative means of preserving that value. For instance, a focused effort on restoring the most historically significant buildings to their original condition might be just as effective as, or even more effective than, a moratorium.

> Nor is the moratorium necessarily the only means of stabilizing revenue from tourism. Rivertown might very well boast other features that hold the potential of attracting tourist dollars. For that matter, an intensive public-relations campaign might be just as effective, or more effective, in reversing the decline. Moreover, common sense tells me that means such as these would probably be more effective than a moratorium, which might come too late now that the shopping center is already built. In short, the argument's author must convince me that the moratorium is the only feasible means of achieving both goals; otherwise I cannot agree that the city should impose it.

In a full-length (30-minute) essay, you might also address the following questions about the Argument's reasoning:

- Is the shopping center the *true cause* of the slowdown in the district's restaurant and retail businesses? (Perhaps some other change in the district is responsible instead.)

- Is the slowdown referred to above the *true cause* of the decline in tourism revenue? (Perhaps it is local residents, not tourists, who have been patronizing the district's shops and restaurants less frequently.)

9. ANALYSIS

This Argument draws *two* inferences about a group (all employers in a certain state) based on characteristics of one member of the group (Giant Industries). Here's a response that handles both inferences in a single paragraph:

> This prediction relies on the assumption that Giant is typical of the state's employers, as a group, with respect to financial strength as well as average worker age. However, the argument provides no

information to substantiate either assumption. Perhaps non-manufacturing businesses that require a college-degreed workforce now account for an increasing majority of the state's jobs. (The argument's information suggests this might be the case.) If so, then the mere fact that one employer, albeit the state's largest business, is losing business while its workforce nears retirement age proves almost nothing about the prospects for the state's overall economy.

In a full-length (30-minute) essay, you might also address the following questions about the Argument's reasoning:

- Does the term "largest private business" necessarily mean that Giant employs more workers than any other business in the state? (The smaller the workforce at Giant, the less likely that Giant is representative of the state's employers as a group.)

- Doesn't the prediction's accuracy require that other *future conditions* remain unchanged? (E.g., the argument ignores a possible influx of workers from other states.)

- Would a reduced workforce necessarily result in business failure? (Perhaps businesses will be more profitable by trimming their workforce.)

- What is the *definition* of "quality of life"? (The argument's ultimate prediction depends on this missing definition.)

10. ANALYSIS

This Argument draws an inference about a single community (Claybrook) based on characteristics of a group (the nation's communities as a whole). Here's a response that handles the inference:

The argument depends partly on the assumption that future employment trends in Claybrook's job market will reflect nationwide trends. However, the argument fails to consider that Claybrook might be atypical. Perhaps Claybrook's job market will buck the trend (for one reason or another), and the demand for legal assistants from CCC's legal-assistant program will remain strong compared to demand for nurses from the school's nursing program. If so, then the cited statistics would portend nothing about the future employment prospect for graduates of either program at CCC or about whether the proposed course of action would be prudent.

In a full-length (30-minute) essay, you might also address the following questions about the Argument's reasoning:

- Do statistics from only one year constitute *sufficient data* for proving a clear trend? (Perhaps last year was an exception to a contrary trend, or perhaps there is no trend at all.)

- Does a continuation of the assumed trends depend on certain *other conditions* remaining *unchanged in the future*? (E.g., an unexpected national event might spark renewed interest in law among college students.)

- Even if the assumed trends continue, would they necessarily result in the predicted job trends for legal assistants or nurses? (E.g., perhaps new technologies will render obsolete many traditional nursing functions.)

11. ANALYSIS

This Argument assumes that current circumstances will remain unchanged into the future. Here's a succinct response that handles the problem:

> The argument relies on the assumption that all other factors (besides tariffs) determining the country's balance of trade will remain unchanged in the foreseeable future. However, common sense tells me that this assumption is dubious at best and that any one of a myriad of possible future developments—political, economic, and social—might render the proposed tariff unnecessary in order to reduce the country's dependency on foreign goods.

In a full-length (30-minute) essay, you might also address the following questions about the Argument's reasoning:

- Do totals from only two years constitute *sufficient data* to show a dependency on foreign goods? (Perhaps one or both of the two years were unusual in terms of the total value of exports.)

- Do export totals alone suffice to show a past or current dependency on foreign goods? (E.g., a recent increase in import totals or domestic sales would help refute the implication that the country has been dependent on foreign goods.)

- Is the argument's prediction *too broad*? (Statistics about the value of imported or exported *goods* don't prove anything about a country's dependency on foreign *services*.)

- Are tariffs *necessary* in order to reduce the country's dependency on foreign goods? (Other means, such as reducing sales taxes on domestic sales of goods, might be just as effective.)

12. ANALYSIS

This Argument assumes that current circumstances will remain unchanged into the future. Here's a response that handles the problem:

> The argument assumes that the current decline in refuse volume will continue, or at least not reverse itself, in the foreseeable future.

However, the argument fails to account for possible future developments that might prove this assumption erroneous. For example, the county might experience an influx of new residents, or its residents' willingness to recycle might wane. In either case, the volume of refuse is likely to increase, and the proposed course of action might result in a shortage of resources for handling refuse. To bolster the recommendation, the argument's proponent should provide better evidence, perhaps in the form of population projections and county-resident surveys, that the volume of refuse in Blackburn County will not increase in the foreseeable future.

In a full-length (30-minute) essay, you might also address the following questions about the Argument's reasoning:

- A *threshold* issue: Is there a recycling problem to begin with that the county needs to address? (The argument provides no evidence that current means are less than adequate for current as well as future needs.)

- Are the proposed subsidies *necessary* to ensure that the county can handle a continued increase in the volume of recyclables? (Perhaps businesses would not require subsidies to provide needed service, or perhaps the county itself could provide the service.)

Part 4

WRITING STYLE AND MECHANICS

ETS instructs its readers to place less weight on writing style and mechanics than on content and organization. This does not mean, however, that the first two factors won't influence the reader or affect your Analytical Writing score. Indeed, they might! If the way you write interferes with the reader's understanding of your ideas, you will not attain a score of 5 or 6. And, in any event, poor writing will predispose the reader to award a lower score, regardless of your ideas or how you organize them. To ensure yourself a score of 5 or 6 on your essays, strive for writing that is:

- Persuasive in style (using rhetorical devices effectively)

- Varied in sentence length and structure (to add interest and variety as well as to demonstrate maturity and sophistication in writing style)

- Clear and concise (easy to follow and direct rather than wordy or verbose)

- Correct in grammar, mechanics, and usage (conforming to the requirements of standard written English)

All of this is easier said than done, of course. Don't worry if you're not a natural when it comes to writing effective prose. You can improve your writing significantly for your exam even if your time is short. Just follow the suggestions and guidelines here in Part 4.

YOUR OVERALL TONE AND VOICE

In general, you should try to maintain a somewhat formal tone throughout both your essays. If your essay comes across as conversational, it's probably a bit too informal for the GRE or GMAT. Here's a brief list of additional guidelines:

1. The overall tone should be critical but not inflammatory or emotional. Don't try to overstate your position by using extreme or harsh language. Don't attempt to elicit a visceral or emotional response from the reader. Appeal instead to the reader's intellect.

2. When it comes to your main points, a very direct, even forceful voice is perfectly acceptable. But don't overdo it; when it comes to the details, use a more dispassionate approach.

3. Don't try to make your point with "cutesy" or humorous remarks. Avoid puns, double-meanings, plays on words, and other forms of humor. Not that GRE and GMAT readers don't have a sense of humor; it's just that they leave it at the door when they go to work for ETS. (That sentence exhibits just the sort of "humor" you should avoid in your essays.)

4. Sarcasm is entirely inappropriate for your GRE or GMAT essays. Besides, the reader might not realize that you're being sarcastic, in which case your remark will only serve to confuse the reader.

DEVELOPING A PERSUASIVE WRITING STYLE

In Parts 2 and 3, you learned how to develop persuasive ideas as well as a structure and sequence for your paragraphs that serve to enhance their persuasiveness. To ensure a high Analytical Writing score, you should also develop a persuasive style, using rhetorical devices effectively.

RHETORICAL WORDS AND PHRASES—BY FUNCTIONAL CATEGORY

Here's a reference list of rhetorical words and phrases, categorized by function. Some list items you encountered as underlined words and phrases in the examples throughout Parts 2 and 3. Others are new here. To learn how you might incorporate these and other rhetorical phrases into your sentences, read my essays in Parts 5–8, highlighting rhetorical phrases as you encounter them. Review them, then try to incorporate them into your practice essays to enhance your power of persuasion.

Use phrases such as these to subordinate an idea:

- although it might appear that, at first glance it would seem/appear that, admittedly

Use phrases such as these to argue for a position, thesis, or viewpoint:

- promotes, facilitates, provides a strong impetus, serves to, directly, furthers, accomplishes, achieves, demonstrates, suggests, indicates

Use phrases such as these to argue for a solution or direction based on public policy or some other normative basis:

- ultimate goal/objective/purpose, overriding, primary concern, subordinate, subsumed

Use phrases such as these to refute, rebut, or counter a proposition, theory, or viewpoint:

- however, closer scrutiny reveals, upon closer inspection/examination, a more thorough analysis, in reality, actually, when viewed more closely, when viewed from another perspective, further observation shows

Use phrases such as these to point out problems with a proposition, theory, or viewpoint:

- however, nevertheless, yet, still, despite, of course, serious drawbacks, problematic, countervailing factors

Use phrases such as these to argue against a position or viewpoint:

- works against, undermines, thwarts, defeats, runs contrary to, fails to achieve/promote/accomplish, is inconsistent with, impedes

Use phrases such as these to argue that the merits of one position outweigh those of another:

- on balance, on the whole, all things considered, in the final analysis

AVOID EMPTY RHETORIC

Many test takers try to mask weak ideas by relying on strong rhetoric. Be careful in using words and phrases such as these for emphasis:

clearly, absolutely, definitely, without a doubt, nobody could dispute that, extremely, positively, emphatically, unquestionably, certainly, undeniably, without reservation

It's okay to use these phrases. But keep in mind: By themselves, they add absolutely no substance to your ideas. So be sure that you have convincing reasons and/or examples to back up your rhetoric!

USING IRONY AS A RHETORICAL DEVICE

In your Issue essay, look for the opportunity to use words in their ironic sense or as misnomers for rhetorical emphasis—in other words, to help make your point. Read the Issue statement closely for key words. Here's one example of each:

Example (Irony)
The speaker fails to consider the long-term cultural impact of the kinds of technological "advancements" I've just described.

Example (Misnomer)
The "knowledge" to which the statement refers is, in actuality, only subjective perception.

Be sure to use quotation marks for the ironic term or misnomer, whether or not you're quoting the Issue statement.

Using Punctuation for Rhetorical Emphasis

Use punctuation for rhetorical emphasis *very* sparingly, heeding the following points of advice:

- Use em dashes (two hyphens or one hyphen preceded and followed by a space) in the middle of a sentence—instead of commas or parentheses—to set off particularly important parenthetical material (just like in this sentence). You can also use an em dash instead of a comma before a concluding phrase—to help set off and emphasize what follows (just like in this sentence). But don't overuse the dash—or it will lose its punch (as in this paragraph).

- Use exclamation points for emphasis very sparingly. As in this paragraph, one per essay is plenty!

- Use the question mark *very* sparingly (once or twice per essay is enough) and only for posing rhetorical questions. (You'll return to this topic a bit later.)

> **NOTE:** Avoid using UPPERCASE letters, *asterisks*, or similar devices to flag words you'd emphasize in rhetorical *speech*. To get your point across, rely instead on your choice of words and phrases as well as your sentence construction. Also, as noted in Part 1, the testing system's word processor does not permit the use of attributes such as bold, underlining, and italics—so those devices are not available for emphasis in any event.

CONNECTING YOUR IDEAS TOGETHER

Your essays will not earn top scores unless your ideas flow naturally from one to the next, so the reader can easily follow your train of thought. To connect your ideas together, develop your own arsenal of transition devices—words and phrases that serve as bridges between ideas and help to convey your line of reasoning to the reader.

Each transition device should help the reader make certain connections or assumptions about the two areas that you are connecting together. For example, some lead your reader forward and imply the building of an idea or thought, while others prompt the reader to compare ideas or draw conclusions from the preceding thoughts. In the examples throughout Parts 2 and 3, you encountered devices such as underlined words and phrases. Now here's a reference list that includes many of those underlined words and phrases, along with some additional ones—by functional category.

To Signal Addition
and, again, and then, besides, equally important, finally, further, furthermore, nor, too, next, lastly, what's more

To Connect Ideas Together
furthermore, additionally, in addition, also, [first, second, . . .], moreover, most important/significantly, consequently, simultaneously, concurrently, next, finally

To Signal Comparison or Contrast
but, although, conversely, in contrast, on the other hand, whereas, but, except, by comparison, where, compared to, weighed against, *vis-à-vis*, while, meanwhile

To Signal Proof
because, for, since, for the same reason, obviously, evidently, furthermore, moreover, besides, indeed, in fact, in addition, in any case, that is

To Signal Exception
yet, still, however, nevertheless, in spite of, despite, of course, occasionally, sometimes, in rare instances, infrequently

To Signal Sequence—Chronological, Logical, or Rhetorical
[first, second(ly), third(ly), . . .], next, then, now, at this point, then, after, in turn, subsequently, finally, consequently, previously, beforehand, simultaneously, concurrently

To Signal Examples
for example, for instance, perhaps, consider, take the case of ..., to demonstrate, to illustrate, as an illustration, one possible scenario, in this case, in another case, on this occasion, in this situation

To Signal Your Reasoning from Premise to Conclusion
therefore, thus, hence, accordingly, as a result, it follows that, hence, therefore, accordingly, thus, in turn

Use These Phrases for Your Concluding or Summary Paragraph
in sum, in the final analysis, in brief, summing up, in conclusion, to conclude, to recapitulate, in essence, in a nutshell

REFERENCES TO YOURSELF AND TO THE STATEMENT OR ARGUMENT

Occasionally in your essays, you'll need to refer to the Issue statement (or Argument) as well to its hypothetical source, whether a person or entity. You might also wish to refer to yourself from time to time. Here are some guidelines for handling these references.

SELF-REFERENCES

Self-references—singular as well as plural—are perfectly acceptable, though optional. Just be consistent:

> I disagree with . . .

> In my view, . . .

> Without additional evidence, we cannot assume that . . .

REFERENCES TO THE STATEMENT OR ARGUMENT

In your Issue essay, refer to a statement or statement as "this statement" or an alternative such as "this claim" or "this assertion." In your Argument essay, try using "argument" to refer to the passage's line of reasoning as a whole or "recommendation" or "claim" to refer to the specific conclusions.

REFERENCES TO THE SOURCE OF THE STATEMENT OR ARGUMENT

Be sure your references to a statement or Argument's source are appropriate. In your Issue essay, you can simply refer to the statement's source as the "speaker." In your Argument essay, the first time you refer to the source, be specific and correct—e.g., "this editorial," "the ad," "the vice president," or "ACME Shoes." If no specific source is provided, try using "author" or "argument."

PRONOUN REFERENCES TO AN ARGUMENT'S PROPONENT

In your Argument essay, it's okay to save keystrokes by using an occasional pronoun. Just be sure that your pronouns are appropriate and consistent (male, female, or neither):

> The speaker argues. . . . *Her* line of reasoning is . . . ; but *she* overlooks . . .

> The manager cites . . . in support of *his* argument. . . . *He* then recommends . . .

> To strengthen *its* conclusion, the board must . . . . *It* must also . . .

Also, be sure that your pronoun references are clear. If a pronoun is separated from its antecedent (the noun that it describes) by one or more sentences, don't use a pronoun.

> **NOTE:** Readers will disregard whether you use masculine, feminine, or gender-neutral terms in your essays. In other words, don't worry about your political correctness (or incorrectness) when it comes to gender. If you wish to use gender-neutral pronouns, that's fine. However, avoid alternating male and female examples and expressions; you might confuse the reader.

SHORTHAND REFERENCES TO AN ARGUMENT'S SOURCE AND EVIDENCE

It's perfectly acceptable to save keystrokes with shorthand names or acronyms in place of multiple-word proper nouns. If you use an acronym, be sure to identify it the first time you use it. For example:

> In this Argument, the marketing director for Specialty Manufacturing (SM) recommends that SM discontinue its line of . . .

QUOTING THE STATEMENT OR ARGUMENT

Occasionally, it may be appropriate to quote key words or phrases from the Issue statement or Argument at hand. For example, you might wish to point out to the reader a key phrase that is ambiguous or vague (e.g., "certain respondents") or a term that is overly inclusive or exclusive (e.g., "only" or "all"). Just keep the number of quoted words and phrases to a minimum. Also, there's never any justification for quoting entire sentences.

YOUR SENTENCES

This section provides a checklist of the most common pitfalls to avoid when constructing sentences. You'll find few hard-and-fast rules here, because we're not dealing with rules of grammar but rather rules of thumb for the art of effective writing.

SENTENCE LENGTH AND VARIETY

In order to ensure top scores on your essays, strive for sentences that are varied in length and structured in a manner that helps convey their intended meaning, rather than obscuring or distorting it. Here are some tips for both writing tasks:

1. Sentences that vary in length make for a more interesting and persuasive essay. For rhetorical emphasis, try using an abrupt short sentence for a crucial point, either before or after longer sentences that elucidate that point.

2. Sentences that use the same essential structure can help convey your line of reasoning to the reader. Try using the same structure for a list of reasons or examples.

3. Sentences that essentially repeat (verbatim) throughout your essay suggest an immature, unsophisticated writing style. Try to avoid using so-called "template" sentences over and over—especially for the first (or last) sentence of each body paragraph. There's nothing wrong with copying and pasting certain sentences to speed up the writing process; just be sure to "tweak" them so each one is distinct.

4. Sentences that pose questions can be a useful rhetorical device. Like short, abrupt sentences, rhetorical questions can help persuade the reader—or at least help to make your point. They can be quite effective, especially in Issue essays. They also add interest and variety. Yet how many test takers think to incorporate them into their essays? Not many. (By the way, I just posed a rhetorical question.) Just be sure to provide an answer to your question. And don't overdo it; one rhetorical question per essay is plenty.

5. For additional variety, use a semicolon to transform two sentences involving the same train of thought into one; and use the word "and" to connect your two independent clauses (just as in this sentence).

PART OF A SENTENCE OUT OF BALANCE WITH ANOTHER PART

An effective sentence gets its point across by placing appropriate emphasis on its different parts. Be sure that the main idea receives greater emphasis (as a main clause) than subordinate ideas.

Equal Emphasis (Confusing)
Treating bodily disorders by noninvasive methods is generally painless, and these methods are less likely than those of conventional Western medicine to result in permanent healing.

Emphasis on Second Clause (Better)
Although treating bodily disorders by noninvasive methods is generally painless, these methods are less likely than those of conventional Western medicine to result in permanent healing.

AWKWARD USE OF THE PASSIVE AND ACTIVE "VOICES"

In a sentence expressed using the active voice, the subject "acts upon" an object. Conversely, in a sentence expressed in the passive voice, the subject "is acted upon" by an object. You can generally use either voice in your GRE or GMAT essays. However, one may be clearer and less awkward than the other, depending on the particular sentence. In any event, never mix the two voices in the same sentence, and try not to shift voice from one sentence to the next. Here's a sentence where the active voice is better.

Passive (Acceptable)

While repetitive tasks are not generally performed reliably by humans for prolonged time periods, such tasks can be performed reliably by computers almost endlessly.

Active (Better)

While most humans cannot perform repetitive tasks reliably for a prolonged time period, computers can perform such tasks endlessly and reliably.

Mixed (Awkward)

While humans generally cannot perform repetitive tasks reliably for a prolonged time period, repetitive tasks can be performed endlessly by computers in a reliable manner.

In this next sentence, the passive voice is needed for emphasis and clarity.

Active (Acceptable)

It is actually a chemical in the brain that creates the sensation of having eaten enough, a chemical that consuming simple sugars depletes.

Passive (More Effective)

The sensation of having eaten enough is actually created by a chemical in the brain that is depleted by consuming simple sugars.

Mixed (Awkward)

The sensation of having eaten enough is actually created by a chemical in the brain that consuming simple sugars depletes.

CONFUSING OR VAGUE PRONOUN REFERENCES

A pronoun (e.g., she, him, their, its) is a shorthand way of referring to an identifiable noun (person, place, or thing). Nouns to which pronouns refer are called *antecedents*. Make sure every pronoun in a sentence has a clear antecedent. One way to correct a pronoun-reference error is to reposition the noun and pronoun as near as possible to each other.

Confusing

During *their* burgeoning independence from England, Madison and Hamilton, among others, recognized the need to foster allegiances between all the *states*.

Clear

Madison and Hamilton, among others, recognized the need to foster allegiances among all the *states* during *their* burgeoning independence from England.

Another way to correct a pronoun-reference error is to replace the pronoun with its antecedent.

> **Confusing**
> E-mail accounts administered by employers belong to *them*, and *they* can be seized and used as evidence against the employee.
>
> **Clear**
> E-mail accounts administered by an employer belong to *the employer*, *who* can seize and use the accounts as evidence against the employee.

IMPROPER PLACEMENT OF MODIFIERS

A *modifier* is a word or phrase that describes, restricts, or qualifies another word or phrase. Modifying phrases are typically set off with commas. Try to place modifiers as close as possible to the word(s) they modify; otherwise, you could end up with an ambiguous and confusing sentence.

> **Ambiguous**
> *Exercising frequently contributes* to not only a sense of well being but also to longevity.
>
> **Clear**
> *Frequent exercise contributes* not only to a sense of well being but also to longevity.
>
> **Ambiguous**
> Through careful examination, competent diagnosis, and successful treatment, *patients* grow to trust their physicians.
>
> **Clear**
> Through careful examination, competent diagnosis, and successful treatment, *physicians* help their patients grow to trust them.

IMPROPER SPLITTING OF A GRAMMATICAL UNIT

Splitting apart clauses or phrases (by inserting a word or clause between them) often results in an awkward and confusing sentence.

> **Split**
> The value of the dollar *is not*, relative to other currencies, *rising* universally.
>
> **Better**
> The value of the dollar *is not rising* universally relative to other currencies.

Split

Typographer Lucian Bernhard was *influenced*, perhaps more so than any of his contemporaries, *by* Toulouse-Lautrec's emphasis on large, unharmonious lettering.

Better

Perhaps more so than any of his contemporaries, typographer Lucian Bernhard was *influenced by* Toulouse-Lautrec's emphasis on large, unharmonious lettering.

DANGLING MODIFIER ERRORS

A *dangling modifier* is a modifier that fails to refer to any particular word(s) in the sentence. The best way to correct a dangling-modifier problem is to reconstruct the sentence.

Dangling

By imposing artificial restrictions in price on oil suppliers, these suppliers will be forced to lower production costs. (Who or what is imposing restrictions?)

Clear

Imposing artificial price restrictions on oil suppliers will force these suppliers to lower production costs.

Certain dangling modifiers are nevertheless acceptable:

Acceptable

Judging from the number of violent crimes committed every year by minors, our nation must overhaul its juvenile justice system. (The sentence makes no reference to whomever is judging; but it is acceptable anyway.)

STRINGING TOGETHER TOO MANY ADJECTIVES

Avoid juxtaposing more then two adjectives, especially if the string includes a possessive (a noun with an apostrophe to indicate possession). The following sentence also uses the gerund *confusing* in a "confusing" manner.

Awkward String

To avoid confusing oral medications, *different pills' coatings* should have different colors, and pills should be different in shape and size.

Clear and Less Awkward

To avoid confusion between different oral medications, pills should differ in color as well as in shape and size.

USING TOO FEW (OR TOO MANY) COMMAS

Although punctuation is the least important aspect of your GRE or GMAT essay, too few or too many commas might interfere with the reader's understanding of a sentence, at which point the punctuation becomes important. Too few commas might confuse the reader, while too many can unduly interrupt the sentence's flow. Here's the guideline: Use the minimum number of commas needed for a reader to understand the intended meaning of the sentence.

Too Few Commas

Enzyme catalysis takes place in living systems and as it is not a laboratory procedure is therefore subject to cellular controls.

Better

Enzyme catalysis takes place in living systems, and as it is not a laboratory procedure is therefore subject to cellular controls.

Also Acceptable

Enzyme catalysis takes place in living systems, and, as it is not a laboratory procedure, is therefore subject to cellular controls.

WORDY AND AWKWARD PHRASES

With an unlimited amount of words, anyone can make the point; but it requires skill and effort to make your point with *concise* phrases. If your sentences seem too long, check for wordy, awkward phrases that can be replaced with more clear and concise ones. Here are three examples (replace italicized phrases with the ones in parentheses):

Discipline is crucial to *the attainment of one's* objectives. (attain)

To indicate the fact that they are in opposition to a bill, legislators sometimes engage in filibusters. (To show their)

In Norse poetry, the stories rarely stand as substitutes or symbols for anything *other than the stories themselves*. (else)

Look for the opportunity to change prepositional phrases into one-word modifiers:

The employee *with ambition*...

The *ambitious* employee...

You can often rework clauses with relative pronouns (*that, who, which,* etc.), omitting the pronoun:

The system *that is* most efficient and accurate . . .

The most efficient and accurate system . . .

Using *it is*, *there is*, and *there are* at the beginning of sentences can result in a wordy and awkward sentence. You might need to restructure an entire sentence to remedy this problem.

Wordy and Awkward

There is a gene that causes hemophilia, which if paired with a healthy gene results in the individual's not developing the disease's symptoms.

Clear and Concise

If paired with a healthy gene, the gene that causes hemophilia will not result in the development of the disease's symptoms.

In your Argument essay, you can replace wordy phrases that signal a premise with a single word.

Wordier

the reason for, for the reason that, due to the fact that, in light of the fact that, on the grounds that

More Concise

because, since, considering that

REDUNDANT WORDS AND PHRASES

Check your essays for words and phrases that express the same essential idea twice.

Both unemployment levels *as well as* interest rates can affect stock prices. (Replace *as well as* with *and* or omit *both*.)

The reason science is being blamed for threats to the natural environment *is because* scientists fail to see that technology is only as useful, or as harmful, as those who decide how to use it. (Replace *because* with *that* or omit *the reason* and *is*.)

YOUR FACILITY WITH THE ENGLISH LANGUAGE

To ensure yourself top scores for your essays, strive to convince the readers that you possess a strong command of the English language—i.e., that you can use the language and its conventions clearly and persuasively in writing. To show the reader the requisite linguistic prowess, try to:

- Demonstrate a solid vocabulary

- Use proper idioms (especially prepositional phrases)

- Use proper diction (word usage and choice)

DEMONSTRATING A SOLID VOCABULARY

By all means, show the reader that you possess the vocabulary of a broadly educated individual and that you know how to use it. But keep the following caveats in mind:

1. Don't overuse SAT-style words just to make an impression. Doing so will only serve to warn the reader that you're trying to mask poor content with "window dressing."

2. Avoid obscure or archaic words that few readers are likely to know. The readers will not take time while reading essays to consult their unabridged dictionaries.

3. Avoid technical terminology that only specialists and scholars in a specific field understand. Most readers are English-language generalists from the academic fields of English and Communications, not biochemists or economic-policy analysts.

4. Use Latin and other non-English terms *very* sparingly. After all, one of the primary skills being tested through the GRE and GMAT essays is your facility with the *English* language. However, the occasional use of Latin terms and acronyms—for example, *per se*, *de facto*, *ad hoc*, and especially *i.e.*, and *e.g.*,—is perfectly acceptable. Non-English words used commonly in academic writing—such as *vis-à-vis*, *caveat*, and *laissez faire*—are acceptable as well. Again, however, don't overdo it. before a concluding phrase

> **NOTE:** The rules for standard written English require that Latin and other non-English terms be italicized (or underlined). However, the GRE and GMAT word processors do not allow you to incorporate these attributes or special diacritical marks (as in *vis-à-vis*). So leave words such as these as is, but be sure they are terms that most educated people are familiar with.

5. Avoid colloquialisms (slang and vernacular). Otherwise, instead of hitting a home run with your essay, your essay will turn out lousy, and you'll be out of luck and need to snake your way in to a bottom-barrel graduate program. (Did you catch the *five* colloquialisms in the preceding sentence?)

USING THE LANGUAGE OF CRITICAL REASONING

As noted above, you need not resort to the obscure terminology of formal logic—especially Latin terms such as "*ipso facto*" and "*Q.E.D.*" However, in all likelihood, you'll need to use the more commonly used ones, such as "argument," "assumption," "conclusion," and possibly "premise" and "inference"—especially in your Argument essay. Be sure you understand what these words mean and that your use of them is idiomatically proper. Here are definitions for these terms and usage guidelines.

Argument

The process of reasoning from premises to conclusion.

To describe a flawed argument, use adjectives such as *weak*, *poor*, *unsound*, *poorly reasoned*, *dubious*, *poorly supported*, and *problematic*.

To describe a good argument use adjectives such as *strong*, *convincing*, *well reasoned*, and *well supported*.

You don't "prove an argument"; rather, you "prove an argument (to be) true." (However, the word "prove" implies deduction and should be used sparingly, if at all, in your Argument essay.)

Premise

A proposition helping to support an argument's conclusion.

Use the words *premise* and *evidence* interchangeably to refer to stated information that is not in dispute.

Assumption

Something taken for granted to be true in the argument (Strictly speaking, assumptions are unstated, assumed premises.)

To describe an assumption, use adjectives such as *unsupported*, *unsubstantiated*, and *unproven*.

To describe a particularly bad assumption, use adjectives such as *unlikely*, *poor*, *questionable*, *doubtful*, *dubious*, and *improbable*.

To strengthen an argument, you *substantiate* an assumption or *prove* (or *show* or *demonstrate*) that the assumption is true. (However, be careful in using the word *prove*; it is a strong word that implies deduction.)

Strictly speaking, an assumption is neither "true" nor "false," neither "correct" nor "incorrect." Also, you don't "prove an assumption."

Conclusion

A proposition derived by deduction or inference from the premises of an argument

To describe a poor conclusion, use adjectives such as *indefensible*, *unjustified*, *unsupported*, *improbable*, and *weak*.

To describe a good conclusion, use adjectives such as *well-supported*, *proper*, *probable*, *well-justified*, and *strong*.

Although you can "prove a conclusion" or "provide proof for a conclusion," again the word *proof* implies deduction. You're better off "supporting a conclusion" or "showing that the conclusion is probable."

Inference
The process of deriving from assumed premises (assumptions) either a strict conclusion or a conclusion that is to some degree probable

You can describe an inference as *poor*, *unjustified*, *improbable*, or *unlikely*.

You can also describe an inference as *strong*, *justified*, *probable*, or *likely*.

You can "infer that . . ."; but the phrase "infer a conclusion" is awkward.

Deduction
The process of reasoning in which the conclusion follows necessarily from the premises (Deduction is a specific kind of inference.)

NOTE: GRE and GMAT Arguments do not involve deduction; all inferences and conclusions involve probabilities, not certainties. So there's no reason to use any form of the word "deduction" in your Argument essay.

YOUR DICTION AND USE OF IDIOMS

When evaluating your essays, GRE and GMAT readers take into account your *diction* and use of *idioms*—albeit to a far lesser degree than your essay's ideas and how you organize them. In the previous section, you learned some specific suggestions for diction and idiom. Here you'll learn tips for avoiding, or at least minimizing, diction and idiom errors in your essays.

Diction (Word Choice and Usage)

Diction chiefly refers to your choice of word as well as to the manner in which a word is used. When you commit an error in diction, you might be confusing one word with another because the two words look or sound similar. Or you might be using a word that isn't the best one to convey the idea you have in mind. Here's an example of each type of diction error:

One Type of Diction Error

The best way to *impede* employees to improve their productivity is to allow them to determine for themselves the most efficient way of performing their individual job tasks.

(The word *impede* means "to hinder or hamper"; in the context of this sentence, *impede* should be replaced with a word such as *impel*, which means "propel or drive." The test taker might have confused these two words.)

Another Type of Diction Error

Unless the department can supply a comparative cost-benefit analysis for the two alternative courses of action, I would remain *diffident* about following the department's recommendation.

(The word *diffident* means "reluctant, unwilling, or shy." A more appropriate word here would be *ambivalent*, which means "undecided or indecisive." Or perhaps the test taker meant to use the word *indifferent* (thereby committing the first type of diction error).

What appear to be diction errors might in many instances be mere clerical (typing) errors. Accordingly, problems with your word choice and usage will adversely affect your scores only if they are obvious and occur frequently.

Idiom

An *idiom* is a distinctive (*idio*syncratic) phrase that is either proper or improper simply based upon whether it has become acceptable over time—through repeated and common use. Here are two sentences, each of which contains an idiomatic prepositional phrase as well as another idiom:

Example—from a Typical Issue Essay

The speaker's contention *flies in the face of* the empirical evidence and, *in any event*, runs contrary to common sense.

Example—from a Typical Argument Essay

For all we know, last year was the only year in which the company earned a profit, in which case the vice president's advice might *turn out* especially poor in retrospect.

Tips for Avoiding Diction and Idiom Errors

Idioms don't rely on any particular rules of grammar; hence, they are learned over time by experience. As you might suspect, the English language contains more idiomatic expressions than you can shake a thesaurus at. Moreover, the number of possible diction errors isn't even limited only to the number of entries in a good unabridged English dictionary. Although it is impossible in these pages to provide an adequate diction or idiom review, here are some guidelines to keep you on the straight and narrow when it comes to these aspects of your writing:

- If you're the least bit unsure about the meaning of a word you intend to use in your essay, don't use it. Why risk committing a diction blunder just to impress the reader with an erudite vocabulary? (And if you're not sure what "erudite" means, either find out or don't use it in your essays!)

- If a phrase sounds wrong to your ear, change it until it sounds correct to you.

- The fewer words you use, the less likely you'll commit an error in diction or idiom. So when in doubt, go with a relatively brief phrase that you still think conveys your point.

- If English is your second language, take heart: In evaluating and scoring your essays, GRE and GMAT readers take into account diction or idiom problems only to the extent that those problems interfere with a reader's understanding of your sentence's intended meaning. As long as your writing is understandable to your EFL (English-as-first-language) friends, you need not worry.

- If you have ample time before your exam, and you think your diction and use of idioms could stand considerable improvement, check for errors in your practice essays by consulting a reputable guide to English usage—or a trusted professor, colleague, or acquaintance who has a firm grasp of the conventions of standard written English.

YOUR GRAMMAR

In this section, you'll learn the grammatical errors that test takers make most often in their GRE and GMAT essays. Of course, I can't cover the entire area of English grammar here. Consult a comprehensive grammar guide for more details about the various errors listed here.

ERROR IN CHOICE OF ADJECTIVE FOR COMPARISONS

Use adjectives ending in *-er* and *-ier* to compare *two* things; use adjectives ending in *-est* and *-iest* to compare three or more things.

Correct
The island of Hawaii is the *largest* of the Hawaiian islands.

Correct
The island of Hawaii is *larger* than *any* other Hawaiian island.

Another way to make a comparison is to precede the adjective by a word such as *more*, *less*, *most*, or *least*. As a rule of thumb, use this method when describing longer nouns, but use the *-er* or *-est* suffix for short nouns. Also, be sure to use *less/least* to compare amounts, but use *fewer/fewest* to compare numbers.

IMPROPER USE OF REFLEXIVE PRONOUNS

Reflexive pronouns include such words as *oneself*, *itself*, and *themselves*. In general, use reflexive pronouns only when the subject of the sentence is acting upon itself (in other words, when the subject is also the object).

Incorrect
Contrary to popular myth, war heroes rarely earn their status by acting *as if they themselves are invincible*.

Correct
Contrary to popular myth, war heroes rarely earn their status by acting *as if they were invincible*.

Correct
Contrary to popular myth, war heroes rarely *consider themselves invincible* and rarely act as if they were.

ERROR IN PRONOUN-ANTECEDENT AGREEMENT

An *antecedent* is simply the noun to which a pronoun refers. Be sure that pronouns agree in *number* (singular or plural) with their antecedents.

Singular (Correct)
Studying other artists actually helps a young *painter* develop *his* or *her* own style.

Plural (Correct)
Studying other artists actually helps young *painters* develop *their* own style.

Singular pronouns are generally used in referring to antecedents such as *each*, *either*, *neither*, and *one*.

Singular (Correct)
The Republican and Democratic parties *each* seem to prefer criticizing *the other's* policies over making constructive proposals *itself*.

Plural (Correct)
The Republican and Democratic parties *both* seem to prefer criticizing *each other's* policies over making constructive proposals *themselves*.

ERROR IN SUBJECT-VERB AGREEMENT

A verb should always agree in number—either singular or plural—with its subject. An intervening clause set off by commas masks a subject-verb agreement error. Both sentences below include a singular subject and therefore call for a singular verb (in parentheses).

Incorrect
Improved sonar *technology*, together with less stringent quotas, *account* for the recent increase in the amount of fish caught by commercial vessels. (accounts)

Incorrect
Grade school *instruction* in ethical and social values, particularly the values of respect and of tolerance, *are* required for any democracy to thrive. (is)

Compound subjects (multiple subjects joined by connectors such as the word *and* or the word *or*) can also mask agreement errors. Remember: If joined by *and*, a compound subject is usually plural (and takes a plural verb). But if joined by *or*, *either . . . or*, or *neither . . . nor*, compound subjects are usually singular.

Plural Subject (Correct)
Raising a child alone and holding down a full-time job *require* good organizational skills.

Singular Subject (Correct)
Neither his financial patron nor Copernicus himself *was* expecting the societal backlash resulting from his denouncing the Earth-centered Ptolemaic model of the universe.

IMPROPER MIXING OF GERUNDS, NOMINATIVES, AND INFINITIVES

A *gerund* is a verb turned into a noun by tacking on *-ing* (by the way, *tacking* is a gerund). A *nominative* is a noun phrase that substitutes for a gerund (*the use of* is a substitute for *using*). An *infinitive* is the plural form of an action verb, preceded by *to* (as in *to go*). Avoid mixing gerunds with either infinitives or nominatives. In the next sentence, use either the italicized pair or the parenthesized pair:

To Assert
(Asserting) that the nation's health-care crisis can be remedied only by political means would essentially be *to ignore* (ignoring) the role of technological innovation.

In some cases, however, it is acceptable to mix forms:

Mixed But Acceptable

Harnessing the power of nature has resulted in our *control over* it rather than our *submitting to* it.

Also Acceptable

Harnessing the power of nature has resulted in our *controlling* it rather than our *submitting to* it.

Use whichever form most clearly conveys the intended meaning of the sentence. In the next sentence, the gerund *using* obscures the identity of the user:

Unclear

Opposition to *using* prison labor by private manufacturing companies began to emerge alongside the burgeoning of the organized labor movement in the latter part of the nineteenth century. (Replace *using* with *the use of*.)

FAULTY PARALLELISM—LISTS

Sentence elements that are grammatically equal—such as a list of items—should be constructed similarly. Check all lists for inconsistent or mixed use of:

- Prepositions (such as *in*, *with*, or *on*)

- Gerunds (verbs with an *-ing* added to the end)

- Infinitives (plural verbs preceded by *to*)

- Articles (such as *a* and *the*)

Correct

Long before the abolition of slavery, many freed indentured servants were able *to* acquire property, *to* interact with people of other races, and *to* maintain their freedom.

Correct

Long before the abolition of slavery, many freed indentured servants were able *to* acquire property, interact with people of other races, and maintain their freedom.

FAULTY PARALLELISM—CORRELATIVES

Also check for faulty parallelism wherever you've used *correlatives*. Here are the most commonly used correlatives:

- Either . . . or . . .

- Neither . . . nor . . .

- Both . . . and . . .

- Not only . . . but also . . .

Make sure that the element immediately following the first correlative term is parallel in construction to the element following the second term. Here's an example that contains the correlative pair *not only . . . but also*:

Faulty Parallelism

According to behavioral psychology, physiological responses to external stimuli *are not only* observable and measurable *but also can* explain why humans behave as they do.

Parallel (One Construction)

According to behavioral psychology, physiological responses to external stimuli *not only are* observable and measurable *but also can* explain why humans behave as they do.

Parallel (Alternative Construction)

According to behavioral psychology, *not only are* physiological responses to external stimuli observable and measurable, *but they can also* explain why humans behave as they do.

ERROR IN VERB TENSE

Tense refers to how a verb's form indicates the *time frame* (past, present, or future) of the sentence's action. Do not *mix* tenses or *shift* tense from one time frame to another in a confusing manner.

Confusing

Due to the fact that fewer makers of personal computers *are* turning a profit *lately*, many such companies plan to hold prices at current levels. *(The word "lately" establishes the present perfect tense, requiring the verb form "have been" instead of "are.")*

Confusing

The underlying philosophy of our current juvenile justice system *was* the centuries-old "age of accountability" legal doctrine, which *exonerates* children under a particular age for their misdeeds. *(The verb "was" should be replaced with "is" because it shifts tense in a way that confuses the meaning of the sentence; the philosophy behind the current system is necessarily a current philosophy.)*

ERROR IN USING THE SUBJUNCTIVE MOOD

The *subjunctive mood* should be used to express a *wish* or a *contrary-to-fact* condition. These sentences should include words such as *if, had, were,* and *should*. In the following sentences, the words in parentheses should replace italicized words.

If empty space *was* (were) nothing real, then any two atoms located in this "nothingness" would contact each other since nothing would be between them.

The Environmental Protection Agency would be overburdened by its detection and enforcement duties *if it fully implemented* (were it to fully implement) all of its own regulations.

Had each nation had its own way during the course of the negotiations, international relations *could quickly degenerate* (could have quickly degenerated) into chaos, thereby threatening humanity's very existence.

DO'S AND DON'TS FOR WRITING STYLE AND MECHANICS

Finally, review some of the key points from Part 4. Here are two lists of DO's and DON'Ts—for writing style and mechanics. To reinforce the ideas in this list, earmark the list and refer to it from time to time as you practice both writing tasks and as you read my sample essays in Parts 5–8.

DO maintain a somewhat formal tone; avoid slang and colloquialisms.

DON'T try to make your point with humor or sarcasm.

DO use rhetorical and transitional phrases for persuasiveness and cohesiveness.

DO vary your sentence length.

DO use a consistent sentence structure for related ideas, examples, or reasons.

DO strive for concise writing that avoids undue wordiness, repetition, and redundancy.

DON'T try too hard to impress the readers with your vocabulary or use of distinctive idioms.

DON'T overuse Latin and other non-English terms.

DO refer to yourself, at your option.

DO be sure your references to the source of the statement or argument are appropriate.

DON'T be overly concerned about your grammar, spelling, or punctuation.

Part 5

SAMPLE ESSAYS FOR 20 OFFICIAL GRE ISSUES

Part 5 contains my responses to 20 of the Issues in the test maker's official pool. You can obtain the entire list of official Issues via my GRE Analytical Writing Web site (www.west.net/~stewart/grewa). As you study the responses here in Part 5, keep in mind the following:

- Each essay provides merely one of many possible viewpoints on the issue at hand. Keep in mind: there is no single "correct" perspective on any GRE Issue.

- I did not compose these essays under timed conditions. Also, I did quite a bit of fine-tuning to make them better models for you to study. So don't be concerned if your essays aren't as polished as mine. Be realistic about what *you* can produce in 45 minutes.

- These essays are intended to provide you with substantive, organizational, and style ideas for composing your GRE Issue essay; but they are not for copying word-for-word. Be forewarned: GRE readers will be on the lookout for plagiarism.

IMPORTANT! From time to time, ETS changes the sequence of Issues in its pool; so be sure to check my online updates (www.west.net/~stewart) for the current sequence. Preceding each essay here in Part 5 is a brief phrase that describes the Issue's topic; this description should help you match the essay to the corresponding Issue in the official pool.

ISSUE No. 4

Is Moderation in All Things Poor Advice?

Should we strive for moderation in all things, as the adage suggests? I tend to agree with the speaker that worthwhile endeavors sometimes require, or at least call for, intense focus at the expense of moderation.

The virtues of moderation are undeniable. Moderation in all things affords us the time and energy to sample more of what life and the world have to offer. In contrast, lack of moderation leads to a life out of balance. As a society, we are slowly coming to realize what many astute psychologists and medical practitioners have known all along: we are at our best as humans only when we strike a proper balance between the mind, body, and spirit. The call for a balanced life is essentially a call for moderation in all things.

For instance, while moderate exercise improves our health and sense of well-being, overexercise and intense exercise can cause injury or psychological burnout, either of which defeat our purpose by requiring us to discontinue exercise altogether. Lack of moderation in diet can cause obesity at one extreme or anorexia at the other, either of which endangers one's health—and even life. And when it comes to potentially addictive substances—alcohol, tobacco, and the like—the deleterious effects of overconsumption are clear enough.

The virtues of moderation apply to work as well. Stress associated with a high-pressure job increases one's vulnerability to heart disease and other physical disorders. And overwork can result in psychological burnout, thereby jeopardizing one's job and career. Overwork can even kill, as demonstrated by the alarmingly high death rate among young Japanese men, many of whom work 100 or more hours each week.

Having acknowledged the wisdom of the old adage, I nevertheless agree that under some circumstances, and for some people, abandoning moderation might be well justified. Consider how many of the world's great artistic creations—in the visual arts, music, and even literature—would have come to fruition without intense, focused efforts on the part of their creators. Creative work necessarily involves a large measure of intense focus—a single-minded, obsessive pursuit of aesthetic perfection.

Or, consider athletic performance. Admittedly, intensity can be counterproductive when it results in burnout or injury. Yet who could disagree that a great athletic performance necessarily requires great focus and intensity—both in preparation and in the performance itself? In short, when it comes to athletics, moderation breeds mediocrity, while intensity breeds excellence and victory. Finally, consider the increasingly competitive world of business. An intense, focused company-wide effort is sometimes needed to ensure a company's competitiveness and even survival. This is particularly true in today's technology-driven industries where keeping up with the frantic pace of change is essential for almost any high-tech firm's survival.

In sum, the old adage amounts to sound advice for most people under most circumstances. Nevertheless, when it comes to creative accomplishment and to competitive success in areas such as athletics and business, I agree with the speaker that abandoning or suspending moderation is often appropriate, and sometimes necessary, in the interest of achieving worthwhile goals.

ISSUE No. 6
Do People Prefer Constraints on Freedom?

Do people prefer constraints on absolute freedom of choice, regardless of what they might claim? I believe so, because in order for any democratic society to thrive, it must strike a balance between freedom and order.

History informs us that attempts to quell basic individual freedoms—of expression, of opinion and belief, and to come and go as we please—invariably fail. People ultimately rise up against unreasonable constraints on freedom of choice. The desire for freedom seems to spring from our fundamental nature as human beings. But does this mean that people would prefer absolute freedom of choice to any constraints whatsoever? No. Reasonable constraints on freedom are needed to protect freedom—and to prevent a society from devolving into a state of anarchy where life is short and brutish.

To appreciate our preference for constraining our own freedom of choice, one need look no further than the neighborhood playground. Even without any adult supervision, a group of youngsters at play invariably establish mutually agreed-upon rules for conduct—whether or not a sport or game is involved. Children learn at an early age that without any rules for behavior, the playground bully usually prevails. And short of beating up on others, bullies enjoy taking prisoners—i.e., restricting the freedom of choice of others. Thus our preference for constraining our freedom of choice stems from our desire to protect and preserve that freedom.

Our preference for constraining our own freedom of choice continues into our adult lives. We freely enter into exclusive pair-bonding relationships; during our teens, we agree to "go steady," then as adults, we voluntarily enter into marriage contracts. Most of us eagerly enter into exclusive employment relationships—preferring the security of steady income to the "freedom" of not knowing where our next paycheck will come from. Even people who prefer self-employment to job security quickly learn that the only way to preserve their "autonomy" is to constrain themselves in terms of their agreements with clients and customers and especially in terms of how they use their time. Admittedly, our self-inflicted job constraints are born largely of economic necessity. Yet even the wealthiest individuals usually choose to constrain their freedom by devoting most of their time and attention to a few pet projects.

Our preference for constraining our own freedom of choice is evident on a societal level as well. Just as children at a playground recognize the need for self-imposed rules and regulations, as a society, we recognize the same need. After all, in a democratic society, our system of laws is an invention of the people. For example, we insist on being bound by rules for operating motor vehicles, for buying and selling both real and personal property, and for making public statements about other people. Without these rules, we would live in continual fear for our physical safety, the security of our property, and our personal reputation and dignity.

In sum, I agree with the fundamental assertion that people prefer reasonable constraints on their freedom of choice. In fact, in a democratic society, we insist on imposing these constraints on ourselves in order to preserve that freedom.

ISSUE No. 16

Government's Duty to Preserve Cultural Tradition

The speaker's claim is actually threefold: (1) ensuring the survival of large cities and, in turn, that of cultural traditions, is a proper function of government; (2) government support is needed for our large cities and cultural traditions to survive and thrive; and (3) cultural traditions are preserved and generated primarily in our large cities. I strongly disagree with all three claims.

First of all, subsidizing cultural traditions is not a proper role of government. Admittedly, certain objectives, such as public health and safety, are so essential to the survival of large cities and of nations that government has a duty to ensure that they are met. However, these objectives should not extend tenuously to preserving cultural traditions. Moreover, government cannot possibly play an evenhanded role as cultural patron. Inadequate resources call for restrictions, priorities, and choices. It is unconscionable to relegate normative decisions as to which cities or cultural traditions are more deserving, valuable, or needy to a few legislators, whose notions about culture might be misguided or unrepresentative of those of the general populace. Also, legislators are all too likely to make choices in favor of the cultural agendas of their hometowns and states or of lobbyists with the most money and influence.

Secondly, subsidizing cultural traditions is not a necessary role of government. A lack of private funding might justify an exception. However, culture—by which I chiefly mean the fine arts—has always depended primarily on the patronage of private individuals and businesses and not on the government. The Medicis, a powerful banking family of Renaissance Italy, supported artists Michelangelo and Raphael. During the twentieth century, the primary source of cultural support were private foundations established by industrial magnates Carnegie, Mellon, Rockefeller, and Getty. And tomorrow, cultural support will come from our new technology and media moguls—including the likes of Ted Turner and Bill Gates. In short, philanthropy is alive and well today, and so government need not intervene to ensure that our cultural traditions are preserved and promoted.

Finally, and perhaps most importantly, the speaker unfairly suggests that large cities serve as the primary breeding ground and sanctuaries for a nation's cultural traditions. Today, a nation's distinct cultural traditions—its folk art, crafts, traditional songs, customs, and ceremonies—burgeon instead in small towns and rural regions. Admittedly, our cities do serve as our centers for "high art"; big cities are where we deposit, display, and boast the world's preeminent art, architecture, and music. But big-city culture has little to do anymore with one nation's distinct cultural traditions. After all, modern cities are essentially multicultural stew pots; accordingly, by assisting large cities, a government is actually helping to create a global culture as well to subsidize the traditions of other nations' cultures.

In the final analysis, government cannot philosophically justify assisting large cities for the purpose of either promoting or preserving the nation's cultural traditions; nor is government assistance necessary toward these ends. Moreover, assisting large cities would have little bearing on our distinct cultural traditions, which abide elsewhere.

Issue No. 21

Our Duty to Disobey Unjust Laws

According to this statement, each person has a duty to not only obey just laws but also to disobey unjust ones. In my view, this statement is too extreme, in two respects. First, it wrongly categorizes any law as either just or unjust; and secondly, it recommends an ineffective and potentially harmful means of legal reform.

First, whether a law is just or unjust is rarely a straightforward issue. The fairness of any law depends on one's personal value system. This is especially true when it comes to personal freedoms. Consider, for example, the controversial issue of abortion. Individuals with particular religious beliefs tend to view laws allowing women an abortion choice as unjust, while individuals with other value systems might view such laws as just.

The fairness of a law also depends on one's personal interest, or stake, in the legal issue at hand. After all, in a democratic society, the chief function of laws is to strike a balance among competing interests. Consider, for example, a law that regulates the toxic effluents a certain factory can emit into a nearby river. Such laws are designed chiefly to protect public health. But complying with the regulation might be costly for the company; the factory might be forced to lay off employees or shut down altogether or increase the price of its products to compensate for the cost of compliance. At stake are the respective interests of the company's owners, employees, and customers as well as the opposing interests of the region's residents whose health and safety are impacted. In short, the fairness of the law is subjective, depending largely on how one's personal interests are affected by it.

The second fundamental problem with the statement is that disobeying unjust laws often has the opposite effect of what was intended or hoped for. Most anyone would argue, for instance, that our federal system of income taxation is unfair in one respect or another. Yet the end result of widespread disobedience, in this case tax evasion, is to perpetuate the system. Free-riders only compel the government to maintain tax rates at high levels in order to ensure adequate revenue for the various programs in its budget.

Yet another fundamental problem with the statement is that by justifying a violation of one sort of law, we find ourselves on a slippery slope toward sanctioning all types of illegal behavior, including egregious criminal conduct. Returning to the abortion example mentioned above, a person strongly opposed to the freedom-of-choice position might maintain that the illegal blocking of access to an abortion clinic amounts to justifiable disobedience. However, it is a precariously short leap from this sort of civil disobedience to physical confrontations with clinic workers, then to the infliction of property damage, then to the bombing of the clinic and potential murder.

In sum, because the inherent function of our laws is to balance competing interests, reasonable people with different priorities will always disagree about the fairness of specific laws. Accordingly, radical action such as resistance or disobedience is rarely justified merely by one's subjective viewpoint or personal interests. And in any event, disobedience is never justifiable when the legal rights or safety of innocent people are jeopardized as a result.

Issue No. 25

What Should Be the Focus of Media?

The speaker asserts that rather than merely highlighting certain sensational events, the media should provide complete coverage of more important events. While the speaker's assertion has merit from a normative standpoint, in the final analysis, I find this assertion indefensible.

Upon first impression, the speaker's claim seems quite compelling, for two reasons. First, without the benefit of a complete, unfiltered, and balanced account of current events, it is impossible to develop an informed and intelligent opinion about important social and political issues and, in turn, to contribute meaningfully to our democratic society, which relies on broad participation in an ongoing debate about such issues to steer a proper course. The end result of our being a largely uninformed people is that we relegate the most important decisions to a handful of legislators, jurists, and executives who may or may not know what is best for us.

Second, by focusing on the "sensational"—by which I take the speaker to mean comparatively shocking, entertaining, and titillating events that easily catch one's attention—the media appeal to our emotions and baser instincts, rather than to our intellect and reason. Any observant person could list many examples aptly illustrating the trend in this direction—from trashy talk shows and local news broadcasts to *The National Enquirer* and *People Magazine*. This trend clearly serves to undermine a society's collective sensibilities and renders a society's members more vulnerable to demagoguery; thus, we should all abhor and resist the trend.

However, for several reasons, I find the media's current trend toward highlights and the sensational to be justifiable. First, the world is becoming an increasingly eventful place; thus, with each passing year, it becomes a more onerous task for the media to attempt full news coverage. Second, we are becoming an increasingly busy society. The average person spends 50 percent more time at work now than a generation ago. Since we have far less time today for news, highlights must often suffice. Third, the media does in fact provide full coverage of important events; anyone can find such coverage beyond their newspaper's front page, on daily PBS news programs, and on the Internet. I would wholeheartedly agree with the speaker if the sensational highlights were all the media were willing or permitted to provide; this scenario would be tantamount to thought control on a mass scale and would serve to undermine our free society. However, I am aware of no evidence of any trend in this direction. To the contrary, in my observation, the media are informing us more fully than ever before; we just need to seek out that information.

On balance, then, the speaker's claim is not defensible. In the final analysis, the media serves its proper function by merely providing what we in a free society demand. Thus, any argument about how the media should or should not behave—regardless of its merits from a normative standpoint—begs the question.

ISSUE No. 39

Imaginative Works vs. Factual Accounts

Do imaginative works hold more lasting significance than factual accounts, for the reasons the speaker cites? To some extent, the speaker overstates fiction's comparative significance. On balance, however, I tend to agree with the speaker. By recounting various dimensions of the human experience, a fictional work can add meaning to and appreciation of the times in which the work is set. Even where a fictional work amounts to pure fantasy, with no historical context, it can still hold more lasting significance than a factual account. Examples from literature and film serve to illustrate these points.

I concede that most fictional works rely on historical settings for plot, thematic, and character development. By informing us about underlying political, economic, and social conditions, factual accounts provide a frame of reference needed to understand and appreciate imaginative works. Fact is the basis for fiction, and fiction is no substitute for fact. I would also concede that factual accounts are more "accurate" than fictional ones—insofar as they are more objective. But this does not mean that factual accounts provide a "more meaningful picture of the human experience." To the contrary, only imaginative works can bring a historical period alive—by way of creative tools such as imagery and point of view. And, only imaginative works can provide meaning to historical events—through the use of devices such as symbolism and metaphor.

Several examples from literature serve to illustrate this point. Twain's novels afford us a sense of how nineteenth-century Missouri would have appeared through the eyes of 10-year-old boys. Melville's *Billy Budd* gives the reader certain insights into what travel on the high seas might have been like in earlier centuries, through the eyes of a crewman. And the epic poems *Beowulf* and *Sir Gawain and the Green Knight* provide glimpses of the relationships between warriors and their kings in medieval times. Bare facts about these historical eras are easily forgettable, whereas creative stories and portrayals such as the ones mentioned above can be quite memorable indeed. In other words, what truly lasts are our impressions of what life must have been like in certain places, at certain times, and under certain conditions. Only imaginative works can provide such lasting impressions.

Examples of important films underscore the point that creative accounts of the human experience hold more lasting significance than bare factual accounts. Consider four of our most memorable and influential films: *Citizen Kane, Schindler's List, The Wizard of Oz,* and *Star Wars.* Did Welles' fictional portrayal of publisher William Randolph Hearst or Spielberg's fictional portrayal of a Jewish sympathizer during the holocaust provide a more "meaningful picture of human experience" than a history textbook? Did these accounts help give "shape and focus" to reality more so than newsreels alone could? If so, will these works hold more "lasting significance" than bare factual accounts of the same persons and events? I think anyone who has seen these films would answer all three questions affirmatively. Or consider *The Wizard of Oz* and *Star Wars.* Both films, and the novels from which they were adapted, are pure fantasy. Yet both teem with symbolism and metaphor relating to life's journey, the human spirit, and our hopes, dreams, and ambitions—in short, the human experience. Therein lies the reason for their lasting significance.

In sum, without prior factual accounts, fictional works set in historical periods lose much of their meaning. Yet only through the exercise of artistic license can we convey human experience in all its dimensions and thereby fully understand and appreciate life in other times and places. And it is human experience, and not bare facts and figures, that endures in our minds and souls.

Issue No. 43

What Is Required to Become "Truly Educated"?

I fundamentally agree with the proposition that students must take courses outside their major field of study to become "truly educated." A contrary position would reflect a too-narrow view of higher education and its proper objectives. Nevertheless, I would caution that extending the proposition too far might risk undermining those objectives.

The primary reason why I agree with the proposition is that "true" education amounts to far more than gaining the knowledge and ability to excel in one's major course of study and in one's professional career. True education also facilitates an understanding of oneself and tolerance and respect for the viewpoints of others. Courses in psychology, sociology, and anthropology all serve these ends. "True" education also provides insight and perspective regarding one's place in society and in the physical and metaphysical worlds. Courses in political science, philosophy, theology, and even sciences such as astronomy and physics can help a student gain this insight and perspective. Finally, no student can be truly educated without having gained an aesthetic appreciation of the world around us—through course work in literature, the fine arts, and the performing arts.

Becoming truly educated also requires sufficient mastery of one academic area to permit a student to contribute meaningfully to society later in life. Yet, mastery of any specific area requires some knowledge about a variety of others. For example, a political-science student can fully understand that field only by understanding the various psychological, sociological, and historical forces that shape political ideology. An anthropologist cannot excel without understanding the social and political events that shape cultures and without some knowledge of chemistry and geology for performing field work. Even computer engineering is intrinsically tied to other fields, even non-technical ones such as business, communications, and media.

Nevertheless, the call for a broad educational experience as the path to becoming truly educated comes with one important caveat. A student who merely dabbles in a hodgepodge of academic offerings, without special emphasis on any one, becomes a dilettante—lacking enough knowledge or experience in any single area to come away with anything valuable to offer. Thus, in the pursuit of true education students must be careful not to overextend themselves—or risk defeating an important objective of education.

In the final analysis, to become truly educated, one must strike a proper balance in one's educational pursuits. Certainly, students should strive to excel in the specific requirements of their major course of study. However, they should complement those efforts by pursuing course work in a variety of other areas as well. By earnestly pursuing a broad education, one gains the capacity not only to succeed in a career, but also to find purpose and meaning in that career as well as to understand and appreciate the world and its peoples. To gain these capacities is to become "truly educated."

Issue No. 47

Pragmatism vs. Idealism

I agree with the speaker insofar as a practical, pragmatic approach toward our endeavors can help us survive in the short term. However, idealism is just as crucial—if not more so—for long-term success in any endeavor, whether it be in academics, business, or political and social reform.

When it comes to academics, students who we would consider pragmatic tend not to pursue an education for its own sake. Instead, they tend to cut whatever corners are needed to optimize their grade average and survive the current academic term. But is this approach the only way to succeed academically? Certainly not. Students who earnestly pursue intellectual paths that truly interest them are more likely to come away with a meaningful and lasting education. In fact, a sense of mission about one's area of fascination is strong motivation to participate actively in class and to study earnestly, both of which contribute to better grades in that area. Thus, although the idealist-student might sacrifice a high overall grade average, the depth of knowledge, academic discipline, and sense of purpose the student gains will serve that student well later in life.

In considering the business world, it might be more tempting to agree with the speaker; after all, isn't business fundamentally about pragmatism—that is, "getting the job done" and paying attention to the "bottom line"? Emphatically, no. Admittedly, the everyday machinations of business are very much about meeting mundane short-term goals: deadlines for production, sales quotas, profit margins, and so forth. Yet underpinning these activities is the vision of the company's chief executive—a vision that might extend far beyond mere profit maximization to the ways in which the firm can make a lasting and meaningful contribution to the community, to the broader economy, and to the society as a whole. Without a dream or vision—that is, without strong idealist leadership—a firm can easily be cast about in the sea of commerce without clear direction, threatening not only the firm's bottom line but also its very survival.

Finally, when it comes to the political arena, again at first blush, it might appear that pragmatism is the best, if not the only, way to succeed. Most politicians seem driven by their interest in being elected and reelected—that is, in surviving—rather than by any sense of mission or even obligation to their constituency or country. Diplomatic and legal maneuverings and negotiations often appear intended to meet the practical needs of the parties involved—minimizing costs, preserving options, and so forth. But, it is idealists—not pragmatists—who sway the masses, incite revolutions, and make political ideology reality. Consider idealists such as America's founders, Mahatma Gandhi, and Martin Luther King. Had these idealists concerned themselves with short-term survival and immediate needs rather than with their notions of an ideal society, the United States and India might still be

British colonies, and African Americans might still be relegated to the backs of buses.

In short, the statement fails to recognize that idealism—keeping one's eye on an ultimate prize—is the surest path to long-term success in any endeavor. Meeting one's immediate needs, while arguably necessary for short-term survival, accomplishes little without a sense of mission, a vision, or a dream for the long term.

Issue No. 48
Is History Relevant to Our Daily Lives?

The speaker alleges that studying history is valuable only insofar as it is relevant to our daily lives. I find this allegation to be specious. It wrongly suggests that history is not otherwise instructive and that its relevance to our everyday lives is limited. To the contrary, studying history provides inspiration, innumerable lessons for living, and useful value-clarification and perspective—all of which help us decide how to live our lives.

To begin with, learning about great human achievements of the past provides inspiration. For example, a student inspired by the courage and tenacity of history's great explorers might decide as a result to pursue a career in archeology, oceanography, or astronomy. This decision can, in turn, profoundly affect that student's everyday life—in school and beyond. Even for students not inclined to pursue these sorts of careers, studying historical examples of courage in the face of adversity can provide motivation to face their own personal fears in life. In short, learning about grand accomplishments of the past can help us get through the everyday business of living, whatever that business might be, by emboldening us and lifting our spirits.

In addition, mistakes of the past can teach us as a society how to avoid repeating those mistakes. For example, history can teach us the inappropriateness of addressing certain social issues, particularly moral ones, on a societal level. Attempts to legislate morality invariably fail, as aptly illustrated by the Prohibition experiment in the U.S. during the 1930s. Hopefully, as a society, we can apply this lesson by adopting a more enlightened legislative approach toward such issues as free speech, criminalization of drug use, criminal justice, and equal rights under the law.

Studying human history can also help us understand and appreciate the mores, values, and ideals of past cultures. A heightened awareness of cultural evolution, in turn, helps us formulate informed and reflective values and ideals for ourselves. Based on these values and ideals, students can determine their authentic life path as well as how they should allot their time and interact with others on a day-to-day basis.

Finally, it might be tempting to imply from the speaker's allegation that studying history has little relevance even for the mundane chores that occupy so much of our time each day and therefore is of little value.

However, from history, we learn not to take everyday activities and things for granted. By understanding the history of money and banking, we can transform an otherwise routine trip to the bank into an enlightened experience or a visit to the grocery store into an homage to the many inventors, scientists, engineers, and entrepreneurs of the past who have made such convenience possible today. And, we can fully appreciate our freedom to go about our daily lives largely as we choose only by understanding our political heritage. In short, appreciating history can serve to elevate our everyday chores to richer, more interesting, and more enjoyable experiences.

In sum, the speaker fails to recognize that in all our activities and decisions—from our grandest to our most rote—history can inspire, inform, guide, and nurture. In the final analysis, to study history is to gain the capacity to be more human—and I would be hard-pressed to imagine a worthier end.

Issue No. 55

Has Technology Failed to Help Humanity Progress?

Have technological innovations of the last century failed to bring about true progress for humanity, as the statement contends? Although I agree that technology cannot ultimately prevent us from harming one another, the statement fails to account for the significant positive impact that the modern-industrial and computer revolutions have had on the quality of life—at least in the developed world.

I agree with the statement insofar as there is no technological solution to the enduring problems of war, poverty, and violence, for the reason that they stem from certain aspects of human nature—such as aggression and greed. Although future advances in biochemistry might enable us to "engineer away" those undesirable aspects, in the meantime, it is up to our economists, diplomats, social reformers, and jurists—not our scientists and engineers—to mitigate these problems.

Admittedly, many technological developments during the last century have helped reduce human suffering. Consider, for instance, technology that enables computers to map Earth's geographical features from outer space. This technology allows us to locate lands that can be cultivated for feeding malnourished people in third-world countries. And few would disagree that humanity is the beneficiary of the myriad of twentieth-century innovations in medicine and medical technology—from prostheses and organ transplants to vaccines and lasers.

Yet for every technological innovation helping to reduce human suffering is another that has served primarily to add to it. For example, while some might argue that nuclear weapons serve as invaluable "peace-keepers," this argument flies in the face of the hundreds of thousands of innocent people murdered and maimed by atomic blasts. More recently, the increasing use of chemical weapons for human slaughter points out that so-called "advances" in biochemistry can amount to net losses for humanity.

Notwithstanding technology's limitations in preventing war, poverty, and violence, twentieth-century technological innovation has enhanced the overall standard of living and comfort level of developed nations. The advent of steel production and assembly-line manufacturing created countless jobs, stimulated economic growth, and supplied a plethora of innovative conveniences. More recently, computers have helped free up our time by performing repetitive tasks; have aided in the design of safer and more attractive bridges, buildings, and vehicles; and have made universal access to information possible.

Of course, such progress has not come without costs. One harmful byproduct of industrial progress is environmental pollution and its threat to public health. Another is the alienation of assembly-line workers from their work. And the Internet breeds information overload and steals our time and attention away from family, community, and coworkers. Nevertheless, on balance, both the modern-industrial and computer revolutions have improved our standard of living and comfort level; and both constitute progress by any measure.

In sum, enduring problems such as war, poverty, and violence ultimately spring from human nature, which no technological innovation short of genetic engineering can alter. Thus, the statement is correct in this respect. However, if we define "progress" more narrowly—in terms of economic standard of living and comfort level—recent technological innovations have indeed brought about clear progress for humanity.

Issue No. 66

Are Mistakes Necessary for Discovery and Progress?

The speaker contends that discovery and progress are made only through mistakes. I strongly agree with this contention, for two reasons. First, it accords with our personal experiences. Secondly, history informs us that on a societal level, trial-and-error provides the very foundation for discovery and true progress, in all realms of human endeavor.

To begin with, the contention accords with our everyday experience as humans from early childhood through adulthood. As infants, we learn how to walk by falling down again and again. As adolescents, we discover our social niche and develop self-confidence and assertiveness, only by way of the sorts of awkward social encounters that are part and parcel of adolescence. Through failed relationships, not only do we discover who we are and are not compatible with, but we also discover ourselves in the process. And, most of us find the career path that suits us only through trying jobs that don't.

This same principle also applies on a societal level. Consider, for example, how we progress in our scientific knowledge. Our scientific method is essentially a call for progress through trial and error. Any new theory must be tested by empirical observation and must withstand rigorous scientific scrutiny. Moreover, the history of theoretical science is essentially a history of trial and error. One modern example involves two contrary theories of physics: wave theory and quantum theory. During the last quarter-century, scientists have been struggling to disprove one or the other—or to reconcile them. As it turns out, a new so-called "string" theory shows that the quantum and wave theories are mistakes in the sense that each one is inadequate to explain the behavior of all matter; yet both so-called "mistakes" were necessary for physics to advance, or progress, to this newer theory.

The value of trial and error is not limited to the sciences. In government and politics, progress usually comes about through dissension and challenge—that is, when people point out the mistakes of those in power. In fact, without our challenging the mistaken notions of established institutions, political oppression and tyranny would go unchecked. Similarly, in the fields of civil and criminal law, jurists and legislators who uphold and defend legal precedent must face continual opposition from those who question the fairness and relevance of current laws. This ongoing challenge is critical to the vitality and relevance of our system of laws.

In sum, the speaker correctly asserts that it is through mistakes that discovery and true progress are made. Indeed, our personal growth as individuals, as well as advances in science, government, and law, depends on making mistakes.

Issue No. 73

Must We Choose Between Tradition and Modernization?

Must we choose between tradition and modernization, as the speaker contends? I agree that in certain cases, the two are mutually exclusive. For the most part, however, modernization does not reject tradition; in fact, in many cases, the former can and does embrace the latter.

In the first place, oftentimes, so-called "modernization" is actually an extension or new iteration of tradition or a variation on it. This is especially true in language and in law. The modern English language, in spite of its many words that are unique to modern Western culture, is derived from, and builds upon, a variety of linguistic traditions—and ultimately from the ancient Greek and Latin languages. Were we to insist on rejecting traditional in favor of purely modern language, we would have essentially nothing to say. Perhaps an even more striking marriage of modernization and tradition is our system of laws in the U.S., which is deeply rooted in English common-law principles of equity and justice. Our system requires that new, so-called "modern" laws be consistent with, and in fact build upon, those principles.

In other areas, modernization departs from tradition in some respects while embracing it in others. In the visual arts, for example, "modern" designs, forms, and elements are based on certain timeless aesthetic ideals—such as symmetry, balance, and harmony. Modern art that violates these principles might hold ephemeral appeal due to its novelty and brashness, but its appeal lacks staying power. An even better example from the arts is modern rock-and-roll music, which upon first listening might seem to bear no resemblance to classical music traditions. Yet both genres rely on the same twelve-note scale, the same notions of what harmonies are pleasing to the ear, the same forms, the same rhythmic meters, and even many of the same melodies.

I concede that, in certain instances, tradition must yield entirely to the utilitarian needs of modern life. This is true especially when it comes to architectural traditions and the value of historic and archeological artifacts. A building of great historic value might be located in the only place available to a hospital desperately needing additional parking area. An old school that is a prime example of a certain architectural style might be so structurally unsafe that the only practicable way to remedy the problem would be to raze the building to make way for a modern, structurally sound one. And when it comes to bridges whose structural integrity is paramount to public safety, modernization often requires no less than replacement of the bridge altogether. However, in other such cases, architecturally appropriate retrofits can solve structural problems without sacrificing history and tradition, and alternative locations for new buildings and bridges can be found in order to preserve the tradition associated with our historic structures. Thus, even in architecture, tradition and modernization are not necessarily mutually exclusive options.

To sum up, in no area of human endeavor need modernization supplant, reject, or otherwise exclude tradition. In fact, in our modern structures, architecture, and other art, and especially languages and law, tradition is embraced, not shunned.

ISSUE No. 81

Will Humans Always Be Superior to Machines?

This statement actually consists of a series of three related claims: (1) machines are tools of human minds; (2) human minds will always be superior to machines; and (3) it is because machines are human tools that human minds will always be superior to machines. While I concede the first claim, whether I agree with the other two claims depends partly on how one defines "superiority" and partly on how willing one is to humble oneself to the unknown future scenarios.

The statement is clearly accurate insofar as machines are tools of human minds. After all, would any machine even exist unless a human being invented it? Of course not. Moreover, I would be hard-pressed to think of any machine that cannot be described as a tool. Even machines designed to entertain or amuse us—for example, toy robots, cars, video games, and novelty items—are in fact tools, which their inventors and promoters use for engaging in commerce and the business of entertainment and amusement. And the claim that a machine can be an end in itself, without purpose or utilitarian function for humans whatsoever, is dubious at best, since I cannot conjure up even a single example of any such machine. Thus, when we develop any sort of machine, we always have some sort of end in mind—a purpose for that machine.

As for the statement's second claim, in certain respects, machines are superior. We have devised machines that perform number-crunching and other rote cerebral tasks with greater accuracy and speed than human minds ever could. In fact, it is because we can devise machines that are superior in these respects that we devise them—as our tools—to begin with. However, if one defines superiority not in terms of competence in performing rote tasks but rather in other ways, human minds are superior. Machines have no capacity for independent thought, for making judgments based on normative considerations, or for developing emotional responses to intellectual problems.

Up until now, the notion of human-made machines that develop the ability to think on their own and to develop so-called "emotional intelligence" has been pure fiction. Besides, even in fiction, we humans ultimately prevail over such machines—as in the cases of Frankenstein's monster and Hal, the computer in *2001: A Space Odyssey*. Yet it seems presumptuous to assert with confidence that humans will always maintain their superior status over their machines. Recent advances in biotechnology, particularly in the area of human genome research, suggest that within the twenty-first century, we'll witness machines that can learn to think on their own, to repair and nurture themselves, to experience visceral sensations, and so forth. In other words, machines will soon exhibit the traits to which we humans attribute our own superiority.

In sum, because we devise machines in order that they may serve us, it is fair to characterize machines as "tools of human minds." And insofar as humans have the unique capacity for independent thought, subjective judgment, and emotional response, it also seems fair to claim superiority over our machines. Besides, should we ever become so clever a species as to devise machines that can truly think for themselves and look out for their own well-being, then consider whether these machines of the future would be "machines" anymore.

ISSUE No. 85

From Whom Do Our Leading Voices Come?

I agree with the statement insofar as our leading voices tend to come from people whose ideas depart from the status quo. However, I do not agree that what motivates these iconoclasts is a mere desire to be different; in my view, they are driven primarily by their personal convictions. Supporting examples abound in all areas of human endeavor—including politics, the arts, and the physical sciences.

When it comes to political power, I would admit that a deep-seated psychological need to be noticed or to be different sometimes lies at the heart of a person's drive to political power and fame. For instance, some astute presidential historians have described Clinton as a man motivated more by a desire to be great than to accomplish great things. And many psychologists attribute Napoleon's and Mussolini's insatiable lust for power to a so-called "short-man complex"—a need to be noticed and admired in spite of one's small physical stature.

Nevertheless, for every leading political voice driven to new ideas by a desire to be noticed or to be different, one can cite many other political leaders clearly driven instead by the courage of their convictions. Iconoclasts Mahatma Gandhi and Martin Luther King, for example, secured prominent places in history by challenging the status quo through civil disobedience. Yet no reasonable person could doubt that it was the conviction of their ideas that drove these two leaders to their respective places.

Turning to the arts, mavericks such as Dali, Picasso, and Warhol, who departed from established rules of composition, ultimately emerge as the leading artists. And our most influential popular musicians are the ones who are flagrantly "different." Consider, for example, jazz pioneers Thelonius Monk and Miles Davis, who broke all the harmonic rules, or folk musician-poet Bob Dylan, who established a new standard for lyricism. Were all these leading voices driven simply by a desire to be different? Perhaps, but my intuition is that creative urges are born not of ego but rather of some intensely personal commitment to an aesthetic ideal.

As for the physical sciences, innovation and progress can only result from challenging conventional theories—that is, the status quo. Newton and Einstein, for example, both refused to blindly accept what were perceived to be the rules of physics. As a result, both men redefined those rules. Yet it would be patently absurd to assert that these two scientists were driven by a mere desire to conjure up "different" theories than those of their contemporaries or predecessors. Surely it was a conviction that their theories were better that drove these geniuses to their places in history.

To sum up, when one examines history's leading voices, it does appear that they typically bring to the world something radically different than the status quo. Yet in most cases, this sort of iconoclasm is a byproduct of personal conviction, not iconoclasm for its own sake.

Issue No. 87

Are War and Crime Products of the Human Condition?

Are products of human nature such as war and crime actually products of the human condition—specifically, lack of resources and territory? The speaker claims so. I strongly disagree, however. Whether we look at science and history or simply look around us in our daily lives, we see ample evidence that human aggression is the product of our nature as humans—and not of our circumstances.

First of all, the claim runs contrary to my personal observation about individual behavior—especially when it comes to males. One need look no further than the local school ground or kindergarten playroom to see the roots of crime and war. Every school yard has its bully who delights in tormenting meeker schoolmates; and in every kindergarten classroom, there is at least one miscreant whose habit is to snatch away the favorite toys of classmates—purely for the enjoyment of having seized property from another. And these behaviors are clearly not for want of resources or territory. Thus, the only reasonable explanation is that they are products of human nature—not of the human condition.

Secondly, the claim flies in the face of what scientists have learned about genetically determined human traits. Many human traits—not just physical ones but psychological ones as well—are predetermined at birth. And to a great extent, we have inherited our genetic predisposition from our nonhuman ancestors. One might argue that lower animal species engage in warlike behavior for the main reason that they must do so to protect their territory or their clan or for food—not because of their nature. Yet, this point begs the question; for we humans have been genetically programmed, through the evolutionary process, to behave in similar ways. In other words, doing so is simply our nature.

Thirdly, the claim makes little sense in the context of human history. Prior to the last few centuries, the inhabitable regions of our planet provided ample territory and resources—such as food and cultivable land—to accommodate every human inhabitant. Yet our distant ancestors engaged in war and crime anyway. What else explains this, except that it is part of our inherent nature to engage in aggressive behavior toward other humans? Moreover, if we consider the various experiments with Marx's Communism, it becomes clear that the pure Marxist State in which all territory and resources are shared according to the needs of each individual does not work in practice. Every attempt, whether on the macro or micro level, has failed at the hands of a few demagogues or despots, who aggress and oppress like playground bullies.

In sum, the author of this statement misunderstands the roots of such phenomena as war and crime. The statement runs contrary to my personal observations of human behavior, to the scientific notions of genetic predisposition and evolution of species, and to the overwhelming lack of evidence that providing ample resources to people solves these problems.

ISSUE No. 97

The Function and Value of Art and Science

The speaker maintains that the function of art is to "upset" while the function of science is to "reassure" and that it is in these functions that the value of each lies. In my view, the speaker unfairly generalizes about the function and value of art while completely missing the point about the function and value of science.

Consider first the intent and effect of art. In many cases, artists set about to reassure, not to upset. Consider Fra Angelico and others monks and nuns of the late medieval period, who sought primarily through their representations of the Madonna and Child to reassure and be reassured about the messages of Christian redemption and salvation. Or consider the paintings of impressionist and realist painters of the late nineteenth century. Despite the sharp contrast in the techniques employed by these two schools, in both genres, we find soothing, genteel, and pastoral themes and images—certainly nothing to upset the viewer.

In other cases, artists set about to upset. For example, the painters and sculptors of the Renaissance period, like the artists who preceded them, approached their art as a form of worship. Yet Renaissance art focuses on other Christian images and themes—especially those involving the crucifixion and apocalyptic notions of judgment and damnation—that are clearly "upsetting" and disconcerting and clearly not reassuring. Or consider the works of two important twentieth-century artists; few would argue that the surrealistic images by Salvador Dali or the jarring, splashy murals by abstract painter Jackson Pollock serve to "upset," or at the very least disquiet, the viewer on a visceral level.

When it comes to the function and value of science, in my view, the speaker's assertion is simply wrong. The final objective of science, in my view, is to discover truths about our world, our universe, and ourselves. Sometimes, these discoveries serve to reassure, and other times, they serve to upset. For example, many would consider reassuring the various laws and principles of physics that provide unifying explanations for what we observe in the physical world. These principles provide a reassuring sense of order, even simplicity, to an otherwise mysterious and perplexing world.

On the other hand, many scientific discoveries have clearly "upset" conventional notions about the physical world and the universe. The notions of a sun-centered universe, that humans evolved from lower primate forms, and that time is relative to space and motion are all disquieting notions to anyone whose belief system depends on contrary assumptions. And more recently, researchers have discovered that many behavioral traits are functions of individual neurological brain structure, determined at birth. This notion has "upset" many professionals in fields such as behavioral psychology, criminology, mental health, and law, whose work is predicated on the notion that undesirable human behavior can be changed—through various means of reform and behavior modification.

In sum, the speaker overgeneralizes when it comes to the function and value of art and science—both of which serve in some cases to reassure and in other cases to upset. In any event, the speaker misstates the true function and value of science, which is to discover truths, whether reassuring or upsetting.

ISSUE No. 103

Is It a Mistake to Theorize Without Data?

Is it a "grave mistake" to theorize without data, as the speaker contends? I agree insofar as to theorize before collecting sufficient data is to risk tainting the process of collecting and interpreting further data. However, in a sense, the speaker begs the question by overlooking the fact that every theory requires some data to begin with. Moreover, the claim unfairly ignores equally grave consequences of waiting to theorize until we obtain too much data.

In one important respect, I agree with the speaker's contention. A theory conjured up without the benefit of data amounts to little more than the theorist's hopes and desires—what he or she wants to be true and not be true. Accordingly, this theorist will tend to seek out evidence that supports the theory and overlook or avoid evidence that refutes it. One telling historical example involves theories about the center of the universe. Understandably, we ego-driven humans would prefer that the universe revolve around us. Early theories presumed so for this reason, and subsequent observations that ran contrary to this ego-driven theory were ignored, while the observers were scorned and even vilified.

By theorizing before collecting data, the theorist also runs the risk of interpreting that data in a manner that makes it appear to lend more credence to the theory than it actually does. Consider the theory that Earth is flat. Any person with a clear view of the horizon must agree in all honesty that the evidence does not support the theory. Yet prior to Newtonian physics, the notion of a spherical Earth was so unsettling to people that they interpreted the arc-shaped horizon as evidence of a convex, yet nevertheless "flattish," Earth.

Despite the merits of the speaker's claim, I find it problematic in two crucial respects. First, common sense informs me that it is impossible to theorize in the first place without at least some data. How can theorizing without data be dangerous, as the speaker contends, if it is not even possible? While a theory based purely on fantasy might ultimately be born out by empirical observation, it is equally possible that it won't. Thus, without prior data, a theory is not worth our time or attention.

Secondly, the speaker's claim overlooks the inverse problem: the danger of continuing to acquire data without venturing a theory based on that data. To postpone theorizing until all the data is in might be to postpone it forever. The danger lies in the reasons we theorize and test our theories: to solve society's problems and to make the world a better place to live. Unless we act timely based on our data, we render ourselves impotent. For example, governments tend to respond to urgent social problems by establishing agencies to collect data and think tanks to theorize about causes and solutions. These agencies and think tanks serve no purpose unless they admit that they will never have all the data and that no theory is foolproof and unless timely action is taken based on the best theory currently available—before the problem overwhelms us.

To sum up, I agree with the speaker insofar as a theory based on no data is not a theory but mere whimsy and fancy and insofar as by theorizing first, we tend to distort the extent to which data collected thereafter supports our own theory. Nevertheless, we put ourselves in equal peril by mistaking data for knowledge and progress, which require us not only to theorize but also to act upon our theories with some useful end in mind.

Issue No. 114

Do a Society's Heroes Reflect Its Character?

The speaker claims that the character of a society's heroes and heroines ('heroes' hereafter) reflects the character of that society. I tend to disagree. In my observation, a society chooses as its heroes not people who mirror the society but rather people whose character society's members wish they could emulate but cannot—for want of character. Nevertheless, I concede that one particular type of hero—the sociopolitical hero—by definition mirrors the character of the society whose causes the hero champions.

First, consider the sports hero, whom in my observation society chooses not merely by virtue of athletic prowess. We consider some accomplished athletes heroes because they have overcome significant obstacles to achieve their goals. For example, Lance Armstrong was not the first Tour de France cycling champion from the U.S.; yet he was the first to overcome a life-threatening illness to win the race. We consider other accomplished athletes heroes because they give back to the society that lionize them. As Mohammed Ali fought not just for boxing titles but also for racial equality, so baseball hero Mark McGuire fights now for disadvantaged children, while basketball hero Magic Johnson fights for AIDS research and awareness. Yet, do the character traits and resulting charitable efforts of sports heroes reflect similar traits and efforts among our society at large? No, they simply reveal that we admire these traits and efforts in other people and wish we could emulate them—but for our own personal failings.

Next consider the military hero, who gains heroic stature by way of courage in battle or by otherwise facing certain defeat and emerging victorious. Consider former presidential hopeful John McCain, whom even his political opponents laud as a war hero for having not only endured years of torture as a prisoner of war but also for continuing to serve his country afterward. Do his patriotism and mettle reveal our society's true character? Certainly not. They reveal only that we admire his courage, fortitude, and strength.

On the other hand, consider a third type of hero: the champion of social causes who inspires and incites society to meaningful political and social change. Such luminaries as India's Mahatma Gandhi, America's Martin Luther King, South Africa's Nelson Mandela, and Poland's Lech Lawesa come immediately to mind. This unique brand of hero does reflect, and indeed must reflect, the character of the hero's society. After all, it is the function of the social champion to call attention to the character of society, which having viewed its reflection in the hero is incited to act bravely—in accordance with its collective character.

In sum, I agree with the speaker's claim only with respect to champions of society's social causes. Otherwise, what society deems heroic reflects instead a basic and universal human need for paragons—to whom we can refer as metaphors for the sorts of virtues that for lack of character, we cannot ourselves reflect.

Issue No. 115

Rituals, Ceremonies, and Cultural Identity

The speaker asserts that rituals and ceremonies are needed for any culture or group of people to retain a strong sense of identity. I agree that one purpose of ritual and ceremony is to preserve cultural identity, at least in modern times. However, this is not their sole purpose; nor are ritual and ceremony the only means of preserving cultural identity.

I agree with the speaker insofar as one purpose of ritual and ceremony in today's world is to preserve cultural identity. Native American tribes, for example, cling tenaciously to their traditional ceremonies and rituals, which typically tell a story about tribal heritage. The reason for maintaining these rituals and customs lies largely in the tribes' 500-year struggle against assimilation, even extinction, at the hands of European intruders. An outward display of traditional customs and distinct heritage is needed to put the world on notice that each tribe is a distinct and autonomous people, with its own heritage, values, and ideas. Otherwise, the tribe risks total assimilation and loss of identity.

The lack of meaningful ritual and ceremony in homogenous mainstream America underscores this point. Other than a few gratuitous ceremonies such as weddings and funerals, we maintain no common rituals to set us apart from other cultures. The reason for this is that, as a whole, America has little cultural identity of its own anymore. Instead, it has become a patchwork quilt of many subcultures, such as Native Americans, Hasidic Jews, Amish, and urban African Americans—each of which resorts to some outward demonstration of its distinctiveness in order to establish and maintain a unique cultural identity.

Nevertheless, preserving cultural identify cannot be the only purpose of ritual and ceremony. Otherwise, how would one explain why isolated cultures that don't need to distinguish themselves to preserve their identity nevertheless engage in their own distinct rituals and ceremonies? In fact, the initial purpose of ritual and ceremony is rooted not in cultural identity but rather superstition and spiritual belief. The original purpose of a ritual might have been to frighten away evil spirits, to bring about weather conditions favorable to bountiful harvests, or to entreat the gods for a successful hunt or for victory in battle. Even today, some primitive cultures engage in rituals primarily for such reasons.

Nor are ritual and ceremony the only means of preserving cultural identity. For example, the Amish culture demonstrates its distinctiveness through dress and lifestyle. Hasidic Jews set themselves apart by their dress, vocational choices, and dietary habits. And African Americans distinguish themselves today by their manner of speech and gesture. Of course, these subcultures have their own distinct ways of celebrating events such as weddings, coming of age, and so forth. Yet ritual and ceremony are not the primary means by which these subcultures maintain their identity.

In sum, to prevent total cultural assimilation into our modern-day homogenous soup, a subculture with a unique and proud heritage must maintain an outward display of that heritage—by way of ritual and ceremony. Nevertheless, ritual and ceremony serve a spiritual function as well—one that has little to do with preventing cultural assimilation. Moreover, rituals and ceremonies are not the only means of preserving cultural identity.

Issue No. 119

Do Worthy Ends Justify Any Means?

The speaker asserts that if a goal is worthy, then any means of attaining that goal is justifiable. In my view, this extreme position misses the point entirely. Whether certain means are justifiable in reaching a goal must be determined on a case-by-case basis, by weighing the benefits of attaining the goal against the costs, or harm, that might accrue along the way. This applies equally to individual goals and to societal goals.

Consider the goal of completing a marathon running race. If I need to reduce my working hours to train for the race, thereby jeopardizing my job, or if I run a high risk of incurring a permanent injury by training enough to prepare adequately for the event, then perhaps my goal is not worth attaining. Yet if I am a physically challenged person with the goal of completing a highly publicized marathon, risking financial hardship or long-term injury might be worthwhile, not only for my own personal satisfaction but also for the inspiration that attaining the goal would provide many others.

Or consider the goal of providing basic food and shelter for an innocent child. Anyone would agree that this goal is highly worthy—considered apart from the means used to achieve it. But what if those means involve stealing from others? Or what if they involve employing the child in a sweatshop at the expense of educating the child? Clearly, determining the worthiness of such goals requires that we confront moral dilemmas, which we each solve individually—based on our own conscience, value system, and notions of fairness and equity.

On a societal level, we determine the worthiness of our goals in much the same way—by weighing competing interests. For instance, any thoughtful person would agree that reducing air and water pollution is a worthy societal goal; clean air and water reduce the burden on our health-care resources and improve the quality of life for everyone in society. Yet to attain this goal, would we be justified in forcing entire industries out of business, thereby running the risk of economic paralysis and widespread unemployment? Or consider America's intervention in Iraq's invasion of Kuwait. Did America's dual interest in a continuing flow of oil to the West and in deterring a potential threat against the security of the world justify our committing resources that could have been used instead for domestic social-welfare programs—or a myriad of other productive purposes? Both issues underscore the fact that the worthiness of a societal goal cannot be considered apart from the means and adverse consequences of attaining that goal.

In sum, the speaker begs the question. The worthiness of any goal, whether it be personal or societal, can be determined only by weighing the benefits of achieving the goal against its costs—to us as well as others.

Part 6

SAMPLE ESSAYS FOR 20 OFFICIAL GRE ARGUMENTS

Part 6 contains my responses to 20 of the Arguments in the test maker's official pool. You can obtain the entire list of official Arguments via my GRE Analytical Writing Web site (www.west.net/~stewart/grewa). As you study the responses here in Part 6, keep in mind the following:

- I did not compose these essays under timed conditions. Also, I did quite a bit of fine-tuning to make them better models for you to study. So, don't be concerned if your essays aren't as polished as mine. Be realistic about what *you* can produce in 30 minutes.

- In the first paragraph of each essay I've recapitulated the official Argument, for your reference. Keep in mind, however, that the readers do not expect you to restate the Argument in your essay.

- These essays are intended to provide you with substantive, organizational, and style ideas for composing your GRE Argument essay; but they are not for copying word-for-word. Be forewarned: GRE readers will be on the lookout for plagiarism.

> **IMPORTANT!** From time to time, ETS changes the sequence of Arguments in its pool; so be sure to check my online updates (www.west.net/~stewart/ws) for the current sequence. Preceding each essay here in Part 6 is a brief phrase that describes the Argument's topic; this description should help you match the essay to the corresponding Argument in the official pool.

ARGUMENT No. 1

Does Small-town Life Promote Health and Longevity?

This newspaper story concludes that living in a small town promotes health and longevity. The story's author bases this conclusion on a comparison between the small town of Leeville and nearby Mason City, a much larger town. However, careful scrutiny of the author's evidence reveals that it lends no credible support to the author's conclusion.

A threshold problem with the argument is that the author draws a general conclusion about the effect of a town's size on the health and longevity of its residents based only on characteristics of two towns. The author provides no evidence that these two towns (or their residents) are representative of other towns their size. In other words, this limited sample simply does not warrant any general conclusions about the effect of a town's size on the health and longevity of its residents.

Next, the author cites the fact that the incidence of sick leave in Leeville is less than in Mason City. This evidence would lend support to the argument only if the portion of local residents employed by local businesses were nearly the same in both towns and only if the portion of employees who are local residents were nearly the same in both towns. Moreover, in relying on this evidence, the author assumes that the portion of sick employees who actually take sick leave is nearly the same in both towns. In short, without showing that the two towns are similar in these ways, the author cannot draw any reliable comparisons about the overall health of the towns' residents—or about the impact of town size on health.

The author also cites the fact that Mason City has five times as many physicians per resident than Leeville. However, any number of factors besides the health of the towns' residents might explain this disparity. For example, perhaps Leeville residents choose to travel to Mason City for physician visits. Without ruling out such explanations, these physician-resident ratios prove nothing about the comparative health of Leeville and Mason City residents—or about the impact of town size on health.

Finally, the author cites the fact that the average age of Leeville residents is higher than that of Mason City residents. However, any number of factors might explain this disparity. For example, perhaps Leeville is a retirement community, while Mason City attracts younger working people. For that matter, perhaps Leeville is comprised mainly of former Mason City residents whose longevity is attributable chiefly to their former lifestyle in Mason City. In any event, the author cannot justify the conclusion that this disparity in average age is due to the difference in size between the two towns.

In conclusion, the argument that small-town living promotes good health and longevity is unpersuasive as it stands. To strengthen the argument, the author must provide clear evidence that the overall population of Leeville, not just employees in Leeville, is healthier than that of

Mason City. The author must also provide strong evidence that Leeville and Mason City residents visit local physicians whenever they become sick. Finally, to better evaluate the argument, we would need more information about why the average age of Leeville residents exceeds that of Mason City residents.

ARGUMENT No. 9

Cheating at Groveton College

In this editorial, the author concludes that colleges should adopt an honor code for detecting academic cheating. To support this conclusion, the author points out that the first year after switching from a monitoring system to an honor system, the annual number of reported cheating incidents at Groveton College decreased from 30 to 21 and that five years later, the number was only 14. The author also cites a survey in which most students indicated they would be less likely to cheat under an honor system than if they are closely monitored. This argument is unconvincing for several reasons.

First and foremost, the argument relies on the assumptions that Groveton students are just as capable of detecting cheating as faculty monitors and that these students are just as likely to report cheating whenever they observe it. However, without evidence to substantiate these assumptions, one cannot reasonably conclude that the honor code has in fact resulted in a decline in the incidence of cheating at Groveton. Besides, common sense tells me that these assumptions are dubious at best; an impartial faculty observer is more likely to detect and report cheating than a preoccupied student under peer pressure not to report cheating among classmates.

The argument also assumes that during the five-year period, all other conditions possibly affecting the reported incidence of cheating at Groveton remained unchanged. Such conditions include the number of Groveton students and the overall integrity of the student body. After five years, it is entirely possible that these conditions have changed and that the reported decrease in cheating is attributable to one or more such changes. Thus, without ruling out such alternative explanations for the reported decrease, the author cannot convince me that the honor code has in fact contributed to a decline in the incidence of cheating at Groveton.

The author's recommendation that other colleges follow Groveton's example depends on the additional assumption that Groveton is typical in ways relevant to the incidence of cheating. However, this is not necessarily the case. For instance, perhaps Groveton students are more or less likely to report cheating, or to cheat under an honor system, than typical college students. Lacking evidence that Groveton students are typical in these respects, the argument is indefensible.

Finally, the survey that the author cites might be unreliable in any of three respects. First, the author fails to assure us that the survey's respondents are representative of all college students. Second, the survey results depend on the honesty and integrity of the respondents. Third, hypothetical predictions about one's future behavior are inherently less reliable than reports of proven behavior. Lacking evidence that the survey is reliable, the author cannot reasonably rely on the survey in recommending that other colleges adopt an honor code.

In conclusion, to persuade me that other colleges should adopt an honor code in order to reduce cheating, the author must supply clear evidence that cheating at Groveton in fact decreased after the honor code was instituted there and that it is this code that was responsible for the decrease. Finally, to better assess the usefulness of the survey, I would need specific information about the survey's sampling methodology.

ARGUMENT No. 14

A Jazz Club for Monroe

This loan applicant claims that a jazz club in Monroe would be a profitable venture. To support this claim, the applicant points out that Monroe has no other jazz clubs. He also cites various other evidence that jazz is popular among Monroe residents. Careful examination of this supporting evidence, however, reveals that it lends little credible support to the applicant's claim.

First of all, if the demand for a live jazz club in Monroe were as great as the applicant claims, it seems that Monroe would already have one or more such clubs. The fact that the closest jazz club is 65 miles away suggests a lack of interest among Monroe residents in a local jazz club. Since the applicant has not adequately responded to this concern, his claim that the proposed club would be profitable is untenable.

The popularity of Monroe's annual jazz festival and of its nightly jazz radio show might appear to lend support to the applicant's claim. However, it is entirely possible that the vast majority of festival attendees are out-of-town visitors. Moreover, the author provides no evidence that radio listeners would be interested in going out to hear live jazz. For that matter, the radio program might actually pose competition for the C-Note club, especially considering that the program airs during the evening.

Nor does the mere fact that several well-known jazz musicians live in Monroe lend significant support to the applicant's claim. It is entirely possible that these musicians perform elsewhere, perhaps at the club located 65 miles away. This would go a long way toward explaining why Monroe does not currently have a jazz club, and it would weaken the applicant's assertion that the C-Note would be profitable.

Finally, the nationwide study showing that the average jazz fan spends $1,000 each year on jazz entertainment would lend support to the applicant's claim only if Monroe residents typify jazz fans nationwide. However, the applicant provides no credible evidence that this is the case.

In conclusion, the loan applicant's argument is not persuasive. To bolster it, he must provide clearer evidence that Monroe residents would patronize the C-Note on a regular basis. Such evidence might include the following: statistics showing that a significant number of Monroe residents attend the jazz festival each year, a survey showing that fans of Monroe's jazz radio program would go out to hear live jazz if they had the chance, and assurances from well-known local jazz musicians that they would play at the C-Note if given the opportunity.

ARGUMENT NO. 20

Worker Safety at Alta Manufacturing

This editorial recommends that Alta Manufacturing reduce its work shifts by 1 hour each in order to reduce its on-the-job accident rate and thereby increase Alta's productivity. To support this recommendation, the author points out that last year, the number of accidents at Alta was 30 percent greater than at Panoply Industries, where work shifts were 1 hour shorter. The author also cites certain experts who believe that many on-the-job accidents are caused by fatigue and sleep deprivation. I find this argument unconvincing for several reasons.

First and foremost, the author provides absolutely no evidence that overall worker productivity is attributable in part to the number of on-the-job accidents. Although common sense informs me that such a relationship exists, the author must provide some evidence of this cause-and-effect relationship before I can accept the author's final conclusion that the proposed course of action would in fact increase Alta's productivity.

Secondly, the author assumes that some accidents at Alta are caused by fatigue or sleep deprivation. However, the author overlooks other possible causes, such as inadequate equipment maintenance or worker training or the inherent hazards of Alta's manufacturing processes. By the same token, Panoply's comparatively low accident rate might be attributable not to the length of its work shifts but rather to other factors, such as superior equipment maintenance or worker training. In other words, without ruling out alternative causes of on-the-job accidents at both companies, the author cannot justifiably conclude that merely by emulating Panoply's work-shift policy, Alta would reduce the number of such accidents.

Thirdly, even assuming that Alta's workers are fatigued or sleep-deprived and that this is the cause of some of Alta's on-the-job accidents, in order to accept the author's solution to this problem, we must assume that Alta's workers would use the additional hour of free time to sleep or rest. However, the author provides no evidence that they would use the time in this manner. It is entirely possible that Alta's workers would use that extra hour to engage in some other fatiguing activity. Without ruling out this possibility, the author cannot convincingly conclude that reducing Alta's work shifts by 1 hour would reduce Alta's accident rate.

Finally, a series of problems with the argument arise from the scant statistical information on which it relies. In comparing the number of accidents at Alta and Panoply, the author fails to consider that the per-worker accident rate might reveal that Alta is actually safer than Panoply, depending on the total number of workers at each company. Second, perhaps accident rates at the two companies last year were aberrations, and during other years, Alta's accident rate was no greater, or even lower, than Panoply's rate. Or perhaps Panoply is not representative of industrial companies generally, and other companies with shorter work shifts have even higher accident rates. In short, since the argument relies on very limited statistical information, I cannot take the author's recommendation seriously.

In conclusion, the recommendation for emulating Panoply's work-shift policy is not well supported. To convince me that shorter work shifts would reduce Alta's on-the-job accident rate, the author must provide clear evidence that work-shift length is responsible for some of Alta's accidents. The author must also supply evidence to support her final conclusion that a lower accident rate would in fact increase overall worker productivity.

ARGUMENT No. 22

Investing in Old Dairy Stock

This excerpt from an investment newsletter cites a recent study in which 80 percent of respondents indicated a desire to reduce their consumption of high-fat and high-cholesterol foods, then points out that food stores are well-stocked with low-fat food products. Based on this evidence, the newsletter predicts a significant decline in sales and profits for Old Dairy (OD), a producer of dairy products high in fat and cholesterol, and advises investors not to own OD stock. I find this advice specious, on several grounds.

First, the excerpt fails to assure me that the survey results accurately reflect the desires of most consumers or that the results accurately predict consumer behavior. Without evidence that the respondents' desires are representative of those of the overall population where OD products are sold, it is hasty to draw any conclusions about future food-buying habits from the survey. Moreover, common sense informs me that consumers do not necessarily make food-purchase decisions in strict accordance with their expressed desires. Thus, as it stands, the statistic that the newsletter cites amounts to scant evidence that OD sales and profits will decline in the future.

Secondly, the fact that low-fat foods are in abundant supply in food stores does not necessarily indicate an increasing demand for low-fat dairy products or a diminishing demand for high-fat dairy products. Absent evidence to the contrary, it is quite possible that consumers are buying other types of low-fat foods but are still demanding high fat in their dairy products. For that matter, it is entirely possible that food stores are well-stocked with low-fat foods because actual demand has not met the demand anticipated by the stores.

Thirdly, even assuming an indisputable consumer trend toward purchasing more low-fat dairy products and fewer high-fat dairy products, the newsletter concludes too hastily that OD profits will decline as a result. OD can always raise the price of its dairy products to offset declining sales, and given a sufficient demand, OD might still turn a profit, despite the general consumer trend. Besides, profit is a function of not just revenue but also expenses. Perhaps OD expenses will decline by a greater amount than its revenue; if so, then OD profits will increase despite falling revenues.

In sum, without additional information, prudent investors should refrain from following the newsletter's advice. To better assess the soundness of this advice, it would be helpful to know the following: (1) the demographic profile of the survey's respondents, (2) the extent to which consumer desires regarding food intake accord with their subsequent behavior, (3) the extent of OD's loyalty among its regular retail customers who might continue to prefer OD products over low-fat products even at higher prices, and (4) the extent to which OD might be able to reduce expenses to offset any revenue loss resulting from diminishing sales of OD products.

ARGUMENT No. 31

The Best Location for Viva-Tech's New Plant

In this memo, the president of Viva-Tech, a high-tech medical equipment firm, recommends closing its small assembly plants and centralizing its operations at one location—in the city of Grandview. To support this recommendation, the president points out certain attractive demographic features as well as the town's willingness to allow Viva-Tech to operate there without paying property taxes for the first three years. However, careful scrutiny of the evidence reveals that it provides little credible support for the president's recommendation.

To begin with, the fact that Grandview's adult population is larger than that of any other locale under consideration is scant evidence in itself that Grandview would be the best location for Viva-Tech. Perhaps Grandview's adult residents are not skilled to work in the medical equipment industry. Or perhaps a large portion of its residents are retired. Or, perhaps virtually all of its residents are already employed in jobs that they would be unwilling or unable to leave to work at Viva-Tech. Without considering and eliminating these and other possible reasons why Viva-Tech might have difficulty finding enough suitable employees in Grandview, the president cannot rely on the fact that Grandview has a large adult population to bolster the recommendation.

Furthermore, the fact that the earnings of the average Grandview worker are comparatively low does not necessarily mean that Viva-Tech could minimize labor costs by employing Grandview residents, as the president suggests. It is entirely possible that this low average wage is attributable to a high percentage of jobs requiring low-level skills. This scenario would be particularly likely if a large portion of Grandview's workers are teenagers and college students. In fact, the low average wage in Grandview is further evidence that Grandview residents do not possess the sorts of high-tech skills that would command a higher wage and that Viva-Tech might require among its workforce.

A final problem with the argument involves Grandview's willingness to forego payment of property taxes for the first three years. Admittedly, this evidence lends some measure of support to the recommendation. However, the president ignores the possibility that other cities under consideration would be willing to make similar concessions or provide other equally attractive financial incentives. The president also overlooks the expense of property taxes over the longer term. Lacking evidence to the contrary, it is entirely possible that Grandview's property-tax rates are otherwise comparatively high and that in the longer term, Viva-Tech's property-tax liability would be greater in Grandview than in other locales. Until the president accounts for these two possibilities, I cannot be persuaded that Grandview is the best location for Viva-Tech from a property-tax standpoint.

In the final analysis, the recommendation of Viva-Tech's president is not well supported. To strengthen it, the president must provide detailed demographic evidence showing that a sufficient number of Grandview residents would be able and willing to work in Viva-Tech's high-tech environment. A proper evaluation of the recommendation requires more information about Grandview's property-tax rates vis-a-vis those of other locales under consideration and about the willingness of these other municipalities to provide their own financial or tax incentives to Viva-Tech.

ARGUMENT NO. 42
The Relationship Between Snoring and Weight Gain

In this argument, the speaker concludes that any person who snores should try to eat less and exercise more than the average person. To justify this conclusion, the speaker points out that many snorers awaken frequently during sleep—often so briefly that they are unaware that they are awake—in order to catch their breath (a condition called sleep apnea) and as a result are too tired during normal waking hours to exercise. The speaker also cites data collected during a recent study, suggesting that snorers are more likely to gain weight than other people. This argument is flawed in several critical respects.

First, the speaker provides no assurances that the recently collected data suggesting a correlation between snoring and weight gain are statistically reliable. Perhaps the study's subjects were unrepresentative of the overall population—in terms of other traits and habits that might affect body weight. Lacking such evidence, the speaker simply cannot draw any firm conclusions based on the study about the relationship between snoring and weight gain.

Even assuming a strong correlation between snoring and weight gain among the general population, the speaker has not adequately shown that sleep apnea causes weight gain. A correlation is one indication of a causal relationship, but in itself, it does not suffice to prove such a relationship. It is entirely possible that some other medical condition, or some other trait or habit, that causes snoring also causes weight gain. Without establishing clearly that snoring at least contributes to weight gain, the speaker cannot convince me that snorers should either eat less or exercise more than the average person.

Even if many snorers suffer from sleep apnea and tend to gain weight as a result, the speaker's advice that "anyone who snores" should try to eat less and to exercise is nevertheless unwarranted. It is entirely possible that some—or perhaps even most—snorers do not suffer from sleep apnea, are not too tired to exercise, or do not in any event tend to gain weight. Without ruling out these possibilities, the speaker must expressly limit the advice to those snorers whose snoring causes weight gain.

Even if the speaker's advice were modified as indicated above, the advice to exercise would still be logically unsound. If a person with sleep apnea is too tired to exercise, as a result, then simply advising that person to exercise begs the question: What should the person do to eliminate the cause of the tiredness? Thus, the speaker should determine the cause of sleep apnea and modify the advice so that it targets that cause. Of course, if it turns out that weight gain is one cause of snoring and sleep apnea, then the speaker's advice that snorers should try to eat less would have considerable merit. Yet, without any evidence that this is the case, the speaker's advice might be at least partially ineffective in counteracting a snorer's tendency to gain weight.

In sum, the speaker's advice for "any" snorer is ill-conceived and poorly supported. To lend credibility to this advice, the speaker should provide evidence that the recently collected data reflect the general population. To better assess the argument, it would be useful to know all the possible causes of snoring and of sleep apnea.

ARGUMENT No. 46

Aircraft Maintenance and Airline Profits

In this memorandum, Get-Away Airline's personnel director asserts that Get-Away mechanics should enroll in the Quality Care Seminar on proper maintenance procedures in order to increase customer satisfaction and, in turn, profits. The director reasons that because the performance of auto-racing mechanics improves after the seminar, so will that of Get-Away's mechanics. The director's argument relies on a number of dubious assumptions and is therefore unconvincing.

First of all, the argument unfairly assumes that because the performance of auto-racing mechanics improves after the seminar, so will the performance of aircraft mechanics. Common sense tells me that, even though aircraft and auto mechanics serve similar functions, aircraft repair and maintenance is far more involved than car repair and maintenance. Thus, a seminar that improves the performance of auto mechanics will not necessarily improve that of aircraft mechanics.

Secondly, the argument assumes that the performance of Get-Away mechanics is subject to improvement. However, it is entirely possible that their performance level is already very high and that the seminar will afford little or no improvement. Perhaps Get-Away's mechanics have already attended a similar seminar, or perhaps they meet higher standards than the ones imposed on auto-racing mechanics.

Thirdly, the argument concludes from the mere fact that the performance of auto-racing mechanics improved after the seminar that the seminar was responsible for this improvement. However, it is possible that some other factor, such as improved diagnostic technology or more stringent inspection requirements, was the reason for the improved performance. Without ruling out these and other such possibilities, I cannot accept the memo's final conclusion that enrolling in the seminar will improve the performance of Get-Away's mechanics as well.

Finally, the argument concludes without adequate evidence that improved performance on the part of Get-Away's mechanics will result in greater customer satisfaction and therefore greater profits for Get-Away. Admittedly, if a low performance level results in accidents, customer satisfaction and profits will in all probability decrease. Otherwise, however, improved mechanic performance will in all likelihood have no bearing on customer satisfaction; in other words, customers are unlikely to be aware of the level of performance of an aircraft's mechanics unless accidents occur.

In conclusion, the argument is unconvincing as it stands. To strengthen it, the director must provide more convincing evidence that the performance of Get-Away's mechanics will actually improve as a result of the seminar—perhaps by pointing out other airlines whose mechanics benefited from the seminar. The director must also show a strong causal nexus between improved mechanic performance and profit. In order to better evaluate the argument, I would need more information about the cost of the seminar compared to its expected benefits and about what factors other than the seminar might have been responsible for the improved performance of auto-racing mechanics.

ARGUMENT No. 52

Learning to Read by Listening to Audiotapes

This editorial concludes that the school board should invest in audiocassettes, because listening to audiocassettes makes elementary students more eager to learn and to read. To support this conclusion, the editorial cites studies showing the value of listening to someone else read. However, close scrutiny of this evidence and of the editorial's line of reasoning reveals that they provide little credible support for the editorial's conclusion.

To begin with, the argument claims that for a poor reader, the isolation of reading will provide a general disincentive to do schoolwork. However, the author provides no evidence to support this claim. It is just as possible that a child who has difficulty reading might excel at other subjects that do not require much reading, such as mathematics or music. Besides, this argument assumes that learning to read must be an isolated activity. Experience informs us, however, that this is not the case, especially for elementary school students who typically learn to read in a group environment.

The editorial goes on to cite studies that "attest to the value" of allowing students to hear books read aloud. However, as it stands, this evidence is far too vague to support the editorial's conclusion; we are not informed whether the "value" relates specifically to reading skills. Common sense tells me that, while audiocassettes can help any person learn facts and understand concepts, a skill such as reading can only be learned by practicing the skill itself.

Nor are we informed about the manner in which books were read aloud in the study; were they read directly by parents, or were they recorded on audiocassettes? Absent additional information about the cited studies, these studies lend no credible support to the conclusion that audiocassettes will help elementary school students to read and to learn.

The editorial continues by claiming that listening to audiocassettes will make children better readers because when parents read aloud to their children, these children become better readers. This argument by analogy is wholly unpersuasive. The latter allows for interaction between parent and child, while the former does not. The latter allows for the child to view written words as the parent reads—that is, to read—while the former does not. Besides, common sense and experience tell us that audiocassettes, which provide for passive listening, are likely to serve as crutches that dissuade children from active reading—instead of encouraging them to read.

In conclusion, the editorial is unconvincing as it stands. To strengthen the argument, the editorial's author must provide more compelling evidence that listening to audiocassettes will actually help and encourage elementary school students to read, not just to learn in general. In order to better evaluate the argument, we would need more information about whether the cited studies refer specifically to the value of audiocassettes and specifically to their value in terms of the reading and learning processes.

ARGUMENT No. 59
Eating Soy to Prevent Fatigue and Depression

This argument concludes that North Americans should eat soy on a regular basis as a means of preventing fatigue and depression. The argument cites a recent study showing that North Americans suffer far greater from these problems than people in Asia do, that Asians eat soy regularly whereas North Americans do not, and that soy is known to possess disease-preventing properties. The argument relies on several doubtful assumptions and is therefore unconvincing.

First, the argument assumes that depression and fatigue are just as readily diagnosed in Asia as in North America. However, it is entirely possible that Asians suffering from these problems do not complain about them or otherwise admit them. For that matter, perhaps Asian medical doctors view certain symptoms that North Americans would consider signs of fatigue and depression as signs of some other problem.

Secondly, the argument assumes that the difference in soy consumption is the only possible explanation for this disparity in the occurrence of fatigue and depression. Yet the argument fails to substantiate this assumption. Common sense informs me that any one of a myriad of other differences—environmental, dietary, and genetic—might explain why North Americans suffer from these problems to a greater extent than Asians do. Without considering and ruling out alternative reasons for this disparity, the argument's conclusion that soy is the key to the disparity is indefensible.

Thirdly, the argument unfairly infers from the fact that soy is known to possess disease-preventing properties that these properties help prevent fatigue and depression specifically. The argument supplies no evidence to substantiate this assumption. Moreover, whether fatigue and depression are appropriately classified as diseases in the first place is questionable.

Finally, even if the properties in soy can be shown to prevent fatigue and depression, the argument unfairly assumes that eating soy is the only means of ingesting the key substances. It is entirely possible that these same properties are found in other forms and therefore that North Americans need not increase soy consumption to help prevent fatigue and depression.

In sum, the argument is dubious at best. Before I can accept its conclusion, the argument's proponent must provide better evidence that people in Asia in fact suffer less from fatigue and depression than North Americans do. To better evaluate the argument, I would need to know what kinds of diseases the properties of soy are known to help prevent and whether they relate at all to fatigue and depression. I would also need to know what other foods contain the same properties as soy—to determine what alternatives, if any, are available for preventing fatigue and depression.

ARGUMENT No. 68
The Price of Oysters

This argument points out that ever since harmful bacteria were found in a few Gulf Coast oysters five years ago, California consumers have been willing to pay twice as much for northeastern Atlantic oysters as for Gulf oysters. The argument then notes that scientists have now developed a process for killing these bacteria. The argument concludes that once consumers become aware of this fact, they will be willing to pay as much for these oysters as for Atlantic oysters and that profits for Gulf oyster producers will thereby increase. The argument is flawed in three critical respects.

First, the argument assumes that the bacteria discovery is the reason for California consumers' unwillingness to pay as much for Gulf shrimp during the past five years. However, this is not necessarily so. Perhaps regional culinary tastes shifted during the last five years, and perhaps Atlantic oysters have a distinct taste, texture, size, or other quality that has made them more popular among California consumers. Since the argument fails to rule out this and other alternative explanations for the willingness of California consumers to pay more for Atlantic oysters, the argument's conclusion is unwarranted.

Secondly, the argument assumes too hastily that consumer awareness of the process that kills the bacteria will necessarily result in the behavior that the argument predicts. Perhaps after five years of favoring Atlantic oysters, consumer oyster tastes and habits have become so well entrenched that consumers will continue to favor Atlantic oysters and will happily pay a premium for them. Moreover, in my observation, consumers often act unpredictably and irrationally, and therefore, any prediction about consumer preferences is dubious at best. Besides, it is entirely possible that Gulf oyster producers will be unwilling to employ the new bacteria-killing process; if so, and if consumers are aware of this fact, then in all likelihood, consumers will continue to favor Atlantic oysters.

Thirdly, even if consumers begin paying as much for Gulf oysters once they become aware of the bacteria-killing process, the argument's conclusion that Gulf oyster producers will enjoy increased profits as a result is unwarranted. Profit is a factor of not only revenue but also costs. It is entirely possible that the costs of employing this new process for killing bacteria, or other costs associated with producing Gulf oysters, will offset additional revenue. Besides, a myriad of other possible occurrences, such as unfavorable regional weather or economic conditions, might prevent the Gulf oyster producers from being as profitable in the foreseeable future as the argument predicts.

In sum, the argument is unpersuasive as it stands. To strengthen it, the argument's proponent must consider and rule out all other possible explanations for the willingness of California consumers to pay a premium for Atlantic oysters and must convince me that with consumer awareness of the bacteria-killing process, Gulf oysters will become just as desirable as Atlantic oysters. To better assess the argument's claim that profits for Gulf oyster producers will increase as an end result, I would need to know whether Gulf oyster producers will incur the expenses involved in killing the bacteria and, if so, the extent to which these expenses will impinge on the producers' profits.

Argument No. 76

Employee Compensation at National Brush Company

In this report, the president of National Brush Company (NBC) concludes that the best way to ensure that NBC will earn a profit next year is for the company to pay its workers according to the number of brushes they produce—rather than hourly. To support this conclusion, the president claims that the new policy will result in the production of more and better brushes, which in turn will allow NBC to reduce its staff size and operating hours, thereby cutting expenses. This argument is fraught with dubious assumptions, which render it entirely unconvincing.

First of all, the argument relies on the unsubstantiated assumption that the new policy will motivate workers to produce brushes more quickly. Whether this is the case will depend, of course, on the amount earned per brush and the rate at which workers can produce brushes. It will also depend on the extent to which NBC workers are content with their current income level. Lacking evidence that the new policy would result in the production of more brushes, the president cannot convince me that this policy would be an effective means to ensure a profit for NBC in the coming year.

Even if the new policy does motivate NBC workers to produce more brushes, the president's argument depends on the additional assumption that producing brushes more quickly can be accomplished without sacrificing quality. In fact, the president goes further by predicting an increase in quality. Yet common sense informs me that if the production process otherwise remains the same, quicker production is likely to reduce quality—and in any event certainly not increase it. And a decline in quality might serve to diminish the value of NBC's brushes in the marketplace. Thus, the ultimate result of the new policy might be to reduce NBC's revenue and, in turn, profits.

Even assuming that as the result of the new policy, NBC's current workforce produces more brushes without sacrificing quality, reducing the size of the workforce and the number of operating hours would serve to offset those production gains. Admittedly, by keeping the most efficient employees, NBC would minimize the extent of this offset. Nevertheless, the president provides no evidence that the result would be a net gain in production. Without any such evidence, the president's argument that the new policy will help ensure profitability is highly suspect.

In sum, the president has failed to provide adequate evidence to support his claim that the new policy would serve to ensure a profit for NBC in the coming year. To strengthen the argument, NBC should conduct a survey or other study to demonstrate not only its workers' willingness to work more quickly but also their ability to maintain quality at a quicker pace. To better assess the argument, I would need detailed financial projections comparing current payroll and other operating costs with projected costs under the new policy—in order to determine whether NBC is likely to be more profitable under the proposed scheme.

ARGUMENT NO. 80

Should Happy Pancake House Serve Margarine or Butter?

In this argument, the speaker recommends that in order to save money, Happy Pancake House (HPH) should serve margarine instead of butter at all its restaurants. To support the argument, the speaker points out that HPH's Southwestern restaurants now serve margarine but not butter and that only 2 percent of these restaurants' customers have complained about the change. The speaker also cites reports from many servers that a number of customers asking for butter have not complained when given margarine instead. This argument is unconvincing for several reasons.

First of all, the speaker does not indicate how long these restaurants have been refusing margarine to customers. If the change is very recent, it is possible that insufficient data have been collected to draw any reliable conclusions. Lacking this information, I cannot assess the reliability of the evidence for the purpose of showing that HPH customers in the Southwest are generally happy with the change.

Secondly, the speaker fails to indicate what portion of HPH customers order meals calling for either butter or margarine. Presumably, the vast majority of meals served at any pancake restaurant call for one or the other. Yet it is entirely possible that a significant percentage of HPH customers do not order pancakes or prefer fruit or another topping instead. The greater this percentage, the less meaningful any statistic about the level of customer satisfaction among all of HPH's Southwestern customers as an indicator of preference for butter or margarine.

Thirdly, the speaker unfairly assumes that HPH customers unhappy with the change generally complain about it. Perhaps many such customers express their displeasure simply by not returning to the restaurant. The greater the percentage of such customers, the weaker the argument's evidence as a sign of customer satisfaction with the change.

Two additional problems specifically involve the reports from "many" servers that "a number" of customers asking for butter do not complain when served margarine instead. Since the speaker fails to indicate the percentage of servers reporting or customers who have not complained to servers, this evidence is far too vague to be meaningful. Also, the speaker omits any mention of reports from servers about customers who have complained. Since the anecdotal evidence is one-sided, it is inadequate to assess overall customer satisfaction with the change.

Finally, even if HPH's Southwest customers are happy with the change, the speaker unfairly assumes that customers in other regions will respond similarly to it. Perhaps Southwesterners are generally less concerned than other people about whether they eat margarine or butter. Or, perhaps Southwesterners actually prefer margarine to butter, in contrast to prevailing tastes elsewhere. Or, perhaps Southwesterners have relatively few choices when it comes to pancake restaurants.

In sum, the speaker's argument is weak. To better assess it, I would need to know (1) how long the change has been in effect in the Southwest, (2) what percentage of HPH servers and managers have received customer complaints about the change, and (3) the number of such complaints as a percentage of the total number of HPH customers who order meals calling for either butter or margarine. To strengthen the argument, the speaker must provide clear evidence—perhaps by way of a reliable survey—that HPH customers in other regions are likely to be happy with the change and continue to patronize HPH after the change.

ARGUMENT No. 88

Advance Ticket Sales for Glenville's Concerts

This letter recommends that Glenville feature modern music, especially the music of Richerts, at its summer concerts in order to boost advance ticket sales and attendance. To support this recommendation, the letter's author points out that advance-ticket sales have declined over the past few years, but unpredictable weather cannot be the reason for the decline because "many people attended the concerts even in bad weather." The author concludes that choice of music must be the reason for the decline, then reasons further that since Richerts' recordings are very popular among Glenville residents, featuring Richerts' music at the concerts would boost ticket sales and attendance. I find this argument to be logically unconvincing in several respects.

As a threshold matter, the author unfairly equates the number of ticket purchasers with the number of tickets purchased. The author ignores the possibility that the average number of tickets sold to each purchaser is increasing, and, as a result, the total number of tickets is not declining—or perhaps even increasing. Thus, the author cannot convincingly conclude that Glenville has a ticket-sale problem in the first place.

Even if the actual number of tickets sold in advance has been declining, the author concludes too hastily that unpredictable weather cannot be the reason for the decline. Perhaps concert attendees during the past few years have now learned from their experience with bad concert weather not to purchase advance tickets again. Besides, the mere fact that "many people" attended concerts in bad weather proves nothing unless the author can show that total attendance has been lower in bad weather than in good weather.

Even assuming unpredictable weather is not the reason for the decline in advance ticket sales, the author falsely assumes that the decline must be attributable to choice of music. This "either-or" argument is fallacious in that it ignores other possible causes of the decline. For example, perhaps during the last few years, Glenville has begun its promotional efforts unusually late. Or perhaps the number of outlets where tickets are available in advance has declined. For that matter, perhaps Glenville's demographics are in flux so that the total number of residents willing and able to attend summer concerts is declining.

Finally, even assuming that choice of music is the true cause of the decline in advance-ticket sales, the author fails to provide adequate evidence that choosing modern music, and Richerts' compositions in particular, will boost sales and attendance. The author unfairly assumes that people who purchase recordings are the same group that would be inclined to attend live concerts. Lacking evidence that this is the case, the author cannot convince me that the proposed course of action will bring about its intended result.

In sum, the argument is logically unconvincing as it stands. To strengthen it, the author must first establish a clear causal relationship between the number of people buying advance tickets and actual concert attendance. The author must also provide evidence—perhaps by way of a reliable survey—that the "many people" who have attended the concerts in bad weather are likely to do so again despite their experience. The author must then consider and eliminate all other possible explanations for the decline. Finally, to better assess the argument, I would need more information about the musical tastes of the Glenville residents who are most inclined to attend live concerts.

ARGUMENT No. 91

Homework Assignments and Academic Performance

The speaker argues that if the state board of education required that homework be assigned to high school students no more than twice per week, academic performance would improve. To support this assertion, the speaker cites a statewide survey of math and science teachers. According to the survey, students in the Marlee district, who are assigned homework no more than once per week, achieve better grades and are less likely to repeat a school year than students in the Sanlee district, who are assigned homework every night. Close scrutiny reveals, however, that this evidence provides little credible support for the speaker's assertion.

To begin with, the survey appears to suffer from two statistical problems, either of which renders the survey's results unreliable. First, the speaker relies on statistics from only two districts; however, it is entirely possible that these two districts are not representative of the state's school districts overall. Second, the survey involved only math and science teachers. Yet the speaker draws a broad recommendation for all teachers based on the survey's results.

In addition, the speaker's recommendation relies on the assumption that the amount of homework assigned to students is the only possible reason for the comparative academic performance between students in the two districts. However, in all likelihood, this is simply not the case. Perhaps Sanlee teachers are stricter graders then Marlee teachers. Or perhaps Sanlee teachers are less effective than Marlee teachers, and therefore, Sanlee students would perform more poorly, regardless of homework schedule. Or perhaps fewer Sanlee students than Marlee students actually do their assigned homework. In short, in order to properly conclude that fewer homework assignments results in better academic performance, the speaker must first rule out all other feasible explanations for the disparity in academic performance between the two districts.

Finally, the survey results as reported by the speaker are too vague to support any firm conclusion. The speaker reports that Sanlee students receive lower grades and are more likely to repeat a school year then Marlee students. Yet the speaker does not indicate whether this fact applies to Sanlee and Marlee students generally or just to math and science students. The speaker's recommendation for all high school students might be defensible in the former case but not in the latter case.

In conclusion, the recommendation that all high school students be assigned homework once per week at most is indefensible based on the evidence. To strengthen the argument, the speaker must show that the reported correlation in the areas of math and science is also found among most other academic subjects. The speaker must also rule out other factors that might determine the students' grades and their likelihood of repeating a year. Finally, to better assess the argument, we would need to know whether the reported disparity in academic performance between Sanlee and Marlee students involved only math and science students or all students.

ARGUMENT No. 96

Have Forsythe Citizens Adopted Healthier Lifestyles?

In this argument, the speaker concludes that Forsythe citizens have adopted healthier lifestyles. To justify this conclusion, the speaker cites a recent survey of Forsythe citizens suggesting that their eating habits now conform more closely to government nutritional recommendations than they did ten years ago. The speaker also points out that sales of kiran, a substance known to reduce cholesterol, have increased fourfold, while sales of sulia, which few of Forsythe's healthiest citizens eat regularly, have been declining. This argument is unpersuasive for several reasons.

First, the survey must be shown to be reliable before I can accept any conclusions based upon it. Specifically, the responses must be accurate, and the respondents must be statistically significant in number and representative of the overall Forsythe citizenry in terms of eating habits. Without evidence of the survey's reliability, it is impossible to draw any firm conclusions about the current dietary habits of Forsythe citizens based on the survey.

Second, the argument relies on the dubious assumption that following the government's nutrition recommendations promotes health to a greater extent than following any other nutrition regime. It is entirely possible that the dietary habits of Forsythe citizens were healthier ten years ago than they are now. Thus, without evidence to substantiate this assumption, the speaker cannot reasonably conclude that the diet of Forsythe's citizens has become more nutritional.

Third, the speaker assumes too hastily that increasing sales of products with kiran indicates healthier eating habits. Perhaps Forsythe citizens are eating these foods in amounts or at intervals that undermine the health benefits of kiran. Without ruling out this possibility, the speaker cannot reasonably conclude with any confidence that increased kiran consumption has resulted in improved health for Forsythe's citizens.

Fourth, the mere fact that few of Forsythe's healthiest citizens eat sulia regularly does not mean that sulia is detrimental to their health—as the speaker assumes. It is possible that sulia has no effect on their health or that it actually promotes health. Lacking firm evidence that sulia affects health adversely and that healthy people avoid sulia for this reason, the speaker cannot justify any conclusions about the health of Forsythe's citizens from the mere fact that sulia sales are declining.

Finally, even if the dietary changes to which the speaker refers are healthful ones, the speaker overlooks the possibility that Forsythe citizens have been making other changes in their dietary or other habits that offset these healthful changes. Unless all other habits affecting health have remained unchanged, the speaker cannot justifiably conclude that the overall lifestyle of Forsythe's citizenry has become healthier.

In sum, the argument is unconvincing as it stands. To strengthen it, the speaker must show that the survey accurately reflects the dietary habits of Forsythe's citizens and that by following the government's nutritional recommendations more closely, these citizens are in fact healthier. The speaker must also show that Forsythe's citizens have not made other dietary or other lifestyle changes that offset healthful changes. Finally, to better assess the argument, I would need more information about the manner and extent to which Forsythe's citizens now consume kiran and about the healthfulness of sulia.

ARGUMENT No. 105

A New President for the Fancy Toy Company

In this memo, a manager at Fancy Toy Company recommends replacing Pat Salvo, the company's current president, with Rosa Winnings, who is currently president of Starlight Jewelry. To support this recommendation, the manager points out that Fancy's profits have declined during the last three quarters under Pat's leadership, while Starlight's profits have been increasing dramatically. The manager's argument is unconvincing for several reasons.

First, the manager's recommendation relies partly on the assumption that Pat was the cause of Fancy Toy's declining profits. However, this need not be the case. Perhaps the toy business is seasonal, and the coming quarter is always the most profitable one. Or perhaps the cost of materials or labor have increased, and Pat has had no control over these increases. Without taking into account such possibilities, the manager simply cannot reasonably conclude that Pat is responsible for Fancy's declining profits and that replacing Pat will therefore enhance Fancy's profits.

Similarly, the manager's recommendation assumes that it is Rosa who has been primarily responsible for Starlight's profitability. However, the manager provides no evidence to affirm this assumption. It is entirely possible that all jewelry businesses have prospered recently, regardless of the abilities of the managers. Or perhaps the costs of precious metals and other materials have declined in recent years, thereby leading to increased profits for Starlight. Moreover, perhaps Rosa has only served as president of Starlight for a short while, and it was her predecessor who is to credit for Starlight's profitability. Without taking into account these possibilities, the manager cannot defend the conclusion that it is Rosa who is responsible for Starlight's increasing profitability.

Finally, the manager's recommendation to replace Pat with Rosa rests on the poor assumption that the two businesses are sufficiently similar that Rosa's experience and skill in one business will transfer to the other. Even if Starlight's increasing profitability is attributable to Rosa's leadership, she might nevertheless be unsuccessful leading a toy company, depending on how much experience in the toy business is required to successfully lead such a company.

In conclusion, the argument is unconvincing as it stands. To strengthen it, the manager must show that Pat, and not some other factor beyond Pat's control, is responsible for Fancy's declining profits. Similarly, the manager must show that it is Rosa who is primarily responsible for Starlight's profitability and that Rosa's abilities will transfer to the toy business. In order to better evaluate the argument, we would need more information about how long Pat and Rosa have served as presidents of their respective companies and what their long-term record is for leading their respective companies to profitability.

ARGUMENT No. 109

Boosting Armchair Video's Profits

In this memo, the owner of Armchair Video concludes that in order to boost sagging profits, Armchair's stores should eliminate evening operating hours and should stock only movies that are less than two years old. To support this conclusion, the owner points out that since Armchair's downtown Marston store implemented these changes, very few customers have complained. The owner's argument relies on several unsubstantiated assumptions and is therefore unconvincing as it stands.

In the first place, implicit in the argument is the assumption that no other means of boosting profits is available to Armchair. While the owner has explicitly ruled out the option of raising its rental rates, the owner ignores other means, such as selling videos or renting and selling compact discs, candy, and so forth. Without considering such alternatives, the owner cannot justifiably conclude that the proposed changes are the only ways Armchair can boost its profits.

A second problem with the argument is that it assumes that the proposed changes would in fact enhance profits. It is entirely possible that the lost revenue from reducing store hours would outweigh the savings in reduced operating costs. Perhaps Armchair customers are attracted to the stores' wide selection and variety of movies, and Armchair would lose their patronage should it reduce its inventory. Moreover, common sense informs me that video rental stores do most of their business during evening hours, and therefore, the proposed action would actually result in a further decline in profits.

Two additional problems involve the downtown Marston store. First, the owner implicitly assumes that the store has increased its profits as a result of eliminating evening operating hours and stocking only newer movies. Yet the owner provides no evidence to support this assumption. One cannot infer from the mere fact that the store's patrons have not complained that the store's business, and in turn profits, have increased as a result of these changes.

A second problem with Marston is that the owner assumes this store is representative of Armchair outlets generally. It is entirely possible that, due to its downtown location, the Marston store attracts a daytime clientele more interested in new movies, whereas other outlets depend on an evening clientele with different or more diverse tastes in movies. Or perhaps downtown Marston lacks competing video stores or movie theaters, whereas Armchair's other stores are located in areas with many competitors. Without accounting for such possibilities, the owner cannot convince me that the profits of other Armchair outlets would increase by following Marston's example.

In conclusion, the argument is unconvincing as it stands. To strengthen it, the owner must provide strong evidence that the cost savings of the proposed course of action would outweigh any loss in revenue and that no other viable means of boosting its profits is available to Armchair. To better evaluate the argument, we would need information enabling us to compare the Marston store's clientele and competition with that of other Armchair stores. We would also need more information about Marston's profitability before and after it implemented the new policies.

ARGUMENT No. 113

A Fitness-Gym Franchise Opportunity

This brochure for Power-Lift Gym claims that by investing in a Power-Lift franchise, an investor will earn a quick profit. To support this claim, the brochure cites a variety of statistics about the current popularity of physical fitness and of Power-Lift Gyms in particular. However, careful scrutiny of this evidence reveals that it lends no credible support to the claim.

One problem with the brochure's claim involves its reliance on the bare fact that revenue from last year's sales of health books and magazines totaled $50 million. This statistic in itself proves nothing. Health magazines do not all focus on weightlifting or even physical fitness; it is possible that very few sales were of those that do. Besides, it is entirely possible that in previous years, total sales were even higher and that sales are actually declining. Either scenario, if true, would serve to weaken the brochure's claim rather than support it.

Another problem with the brochure's claim involves the fact that more and more consumers are purchasing home gyms. It is entirely possible that consumers are using home gyms as a substitute for commercial gyms and that the number of Power-Lift memberships will decline as a result. Without ruling out this possibility, the brochure cannot convince me that a new Power-Lift franchise would be profitable.

A third problem with the brochure's claim involves its reliance on the fact that 500 Power-Lift franchises are now in existence. It is entirely possible that the market has become saturated and that additional Power-Lift gyms will not be as successful as current ones. Moreover, it is possible that the number of competing gyms has also increased in tandem with the general interest in health and fitness. Without addressing this supply-and-demand issue, the brochure cannot justify its conclusion that a new Power-Lift franchise would be a sound investment.

In conclusion, the brochure is unpersuasive as it stands. To strengthen its claim that a new Power-Lift franchise would be profitable, the brochure should provide stronger evidence that the general interest in physical fitness, and weightlifting in particular, will continue unabated in the foreseeable future. The brochure must also provide evidence that home gyms are not serving as substitutes for commercial gyms. Finally, to better evaluate the argument, we would need more information about the extent to which the fitness-gym market has become saturated, not only by Power-Lift franchises but by competing gyms as well.

ARGUMENT No. 122

The Benefits of a New Expressway

In this newsletter, the author concludes that in order to promote the economic health of the city's downtown area, voters should approve the construction of an expressway linking downtown to outlying suburbs. To support this conclusion, the author claims that the expressway would alleviate shortages of stock and materials among downtown businesses and manufacturers and would attract workers from elsewhere in the state. However, the argument relies on a series of unsubstantiated assumptions, which render it unconvincing.

The first problem with the argument involves the author's claim that the expressway would help prevent downtown merchants and manufacturers from experiencing shortages in stock and materials. This claim depends on three assumptions. One assumption is that such a problem exists in the first place. A second assumption is that the absence of an expressway is the cause of such shortages; yet common sense tells me that the availability of these commodities is probably the primary such factor. A third assumption is that stock and materials would be delivered primarily via the expressway. Yet it is entirely possible that these commodities are delivered directly to the downtown area by other means, such as rail or air transport. Without substantiating these assumptions, the author cannot justifiably conclude that the expressway would help prevent shortages of stock and materials.

Another problem with the argument involves the author's dual claim that because of the new expressway, workers from elsewhere in the state will be lured to work in this city's downtown area and at the same time will choose to live in the suburbs. The author provides no evidence that the existence of an expressway would suffice to entice people to work in this city's downtown area. Moreover, the author ignores the possibility that people who might want to work in the city's downtown area would generally prefer to live in that area as well. In this case, the expressway would be of no help in attracting qualified workers to this city's downtown area.

A third problem with the argument is that it unfairly assumes that the expressway will result in a net influx, rather than outflow, of workers to the downtown area. In fact, the expressway might make it easier for people who currently live and work downtown to commute to jobs in other areas or even relocate their businesses to outlying areas. Either scenario would serve to undermine the author's claim that the expressway would provide a boon to the downtown economy.

Finally, the argument rests on the assumption that funds used to build the expressway and to create jobs for construction workers cannot be applied to some other program instead—one that would be even more effective in promoting the health of the downtown economy. Without identifying and weighing such alternatives, the author cannot defend the conclusion that voters should approve the expressway project.

In conclusion, the argument is unconvincing as it stands. To strengthen it, the author must provide strong evidence that the expressway would help alleviate shortages of supply and materials among downtown businesses and manufacturers. The author must also show that the expressway would in fact result in a net influx of workers who would change jobs because of the availability of the expressway. Finally, to better evaluate the argument, we would need more information about possible alternatives to the proposal and whether any such alternative would be more effective in promoting the health of the downtown economy.

Part 7

SAMPLE ESSAYS FOR 20 OFFICIAL GMAT ISSUES

Part 7 contains my responses to 20 of the Issues in the test maker's official pool. You can obtain the entire list of official Issues via my GMAT Analytical Writing Web site (www.west.net/~stewart/awa). As you study the responses here in Part 7, keep in mind the following:

- Each essay provides merely one of many possible viewpoints on the issue at hand. Keep in mind: there is no single "correct" perspective on any GMAT Issue.

- I did not compose these essays under timed conditions. Also, I did quite a bit of fine-tuning to make them better models for you to study. So, don't be concerned if your essays aren't as polished as mine. Be realistic about what *you* can produce in 30 minutes.

- These essays are intended to provide you with substantive, organizational, and style ideas for composing your GMAT Issue essay; but they are not for copying word-for-word. Be forewarned: GMAT readers will be on the lookout for plagiarism.

IMPORTANT! From time to time, the test maker might change the sequence of Issues in the official pool; so be sure to check my online updates (www.west.net/~stewart/ws) for the current sequence. Preceding each essay here in Part 7 is a brief phrase that describes the Issue's topic; this description should help you match the essay to the corresponding Issue in the official pool.

▌▌▌▌ Issue No. 11

Personal Failings of Great Achievers

Are the personal failings of great achievers generally unimportant compared to the individual's achievements, as the speaker contends? In some cases, perhaps so. However, in my view, this contention amounts to an unfair generalization. The speaker overlooks that personal failings often play an integral role in the process of achieving great things—either as a catalyst for it or as part of the process.

Some personal failings can serve as catalysts for great achievement. A personal failing can test the would-be achiever's mettle; it might pose a challenge—necessary resistance that drives the individual to achieve despite the shortcoming. For example, poor academic or job performance can propel a gifted entrepreneur to start a business, which ultimately becomes the dominant player in its industry. Or serious illness or injury can spur an athlete on to attain world-class standing in a particular sport.

Other personal failings are symbiotically connected with achievement; that is, a personal failing might be a necessary ingredient or integral part of the achievement process itself. For instance, artists and musicians often produce their most creative works during periods of depression, addiction, or other distress; indeed, an artwork's greatness often lies in how it reflects and reveals the artist's own failings and foibles. And in the realms of business and politics, insensitivity to the human costs of success, which I consider to be a personal failing, has bred many grand achievements. History is replete with examples—from the use of "expendable" slaves by the ancient emperors in realizing our world's greatest monuments to the questionable labor practices of America's great late nineteenth-century industrialists.

Even personal failings that are unconnected with certain achievements lie at the heart of other, unintended ones. Consider, for example, two modern American presidents: Nixon and Clinton. Nixon's paranoia, which historians generally agree was his fatal flaw, resulted in the Watergate scandal—a watershed event in American politics. And more recently, Clinton's marital indiscretions and subsequent impeachment prompted a national reexamination of the requisites for legitimate political leadership. Were the personal failings of Nixon and Clinton less "important" than their achievements as statesman and social reformer, respectively? Perhaps not.

Admittedly, some types of personal failings pale in importance to the individual's achievements. For example, the people who we consider great artists, actors, and musicians are often notorious for their poor financial and business judgment. Yet, in our hearts and minds, this sort of failing only elevates them in greatness. Moreover, other types of personal failings are, in my view, patently more important than any achievement. For instance, many a male sports hero has found his name on a newspaper's police blotter after committing a violent crime. In my view, the importance of any violent crime outweighs that of any sports record.

In sum, the speaker's contention amounts to an overstatement. Current and historical events inform us that personal failings are often part and parcel of great achievements. And even where they are not, personal shortcomings of great achievers often make an important societal impact of their own.

Issue No. 20

The Role of Automation in Our Lives

In some respects, humans serve machines, while in other respects, machines serve us by enhancing our lives. While mechanical automation may have diminished our quality of life, on balance, digital automation is doing more to improve our lives than to undermine our autonomy.

Consider first mechanical automation, particularly assembly-line manufacturing. With automation came a loss of pride in and alienation from one's work. In this sense, automation both diminished our quality of life and rendered us slaves to machines in our inability to reverse "progress." Admittedly, mechanical automation spawned entire industries, creating jobs, stimulating economic growth, and supplying a plethora of innovative conveniences. Nevertheless, the sociological and environmental price of progress may have outweighed its benefits.

Without a doubt, digital automation has brought its own brand of alienation. Computer automation, and especially the Internet, breeds information overload and steals our time and attention away from family, community, and coworkers. In these respects, digital automation tends to diminish our quality of life and create its own legion of human slaves.

However, by relegating repetitive tasks to computers, digital technology has spawned great advances in medicine and physics, helping us to better understand the world, to enhance our health, and to prolong our lives. Digital automation has also emancipated architects, artists, designers, and musicians by opening up creative possibilities and by saving time. Perhaps most importantly, however, information technology makes possible universal access to information, thereby providing a democratizing influence on our culture.

In sum, while mechanical automation may have created a society of slaves to modern conveniences and unfulfilling work, digital automation holds more promise for improving our lives without enslaving us to the technology.

Issue No. 22

Government's Responsibility Regarding the Arts

The speaker here argues that government must support the arts but at the same time impose no control over what art is produced. The implicit rationale for government intervention in the arts is that without it, cultural decline and erosion of our social fabric will result. However, I find no empirical evidence to support this argument, which in any event is unconvincing in light of more persuasive arguments that government should play no part in either supporting or restricting the arts.

First, subsidizing the arts is neither a proper nor necessary job for government. Although public health is generally viewed as critical to a society's very survival and therefore an appropriate concern of government, this concern should not extend tenuously to our cultural "health" or well-being. A lack of private funding might justify an exception; in my observation, however, philanthropy is alive and well today, especially among the new technology and media moguls.

Secondly, government cannot possibly play an evenhanded role as arts patron. Inadequate resources call for restrictions, priorities, and choices. It is unconscionable to relegate normative decisions as to which art has "value" to a few legislators and jurists, who may be unenlightened in their notions about art. Also, legislators are all too likely to make choices in favor of the cultural agendas of those lobbyists with the most money and influence.

Thirdly, restricting artistic expression may in some cases encroach upon the constitutional right of free expression. In any case, governmental restriction may chill creativity, thereby defeating the very purpose of subsidizing the arts.

In the final analysis, government cannot philosophically or economically justify its involvement in the arts, either by subsidy or sanction. Responsibility lies with individuals to determine what art has value and to support that art.

ISSUE No. 26

Location: Still the Key to Business Success

In retail, or "storefront," business, location is still a key ingredient of business success. The extent to which this will continue to be true, given the inexorable growth of Internet commerce, will vary among industries.

In more traditional retail sectors, such as clothing, cosmetics, and home improvement, an in-person visit to a retail store is often necessary—to try on clothes for fit, compare fragrances, or browse among a full selection of textures, colors, and styles. Also, activities such as shopping and dining out are for many consumers enjoyable experiences in themselves as well as excuses to get out of the house and mingle with others in their community. Finally, shipping costs for large items such as appliances and home-improvement items render home shopping impracticable. Thus, burgeoning technologies pose no serious threat to Main Street, and location will continue to play a pivotal role in the fate of many retail businesses.

Nevertheless, technology-related industries are sure to move away from physical storefronts to virtual ones. Products that can be reduced to digital "bits and bites," such as books and magazines, recordings, and software applications, are more efficiently distributed electronically. Computer hardware will not disappear from Main Street quite so quickly, though, since its physical look and feel enters into the buying decision. Computer superstores should continue to thrive alongside companies such as Dell, which does not distribute through retail stores.

In conclusion, consumer demand for convenient location will continue with respect to certain tangible products, while for other products, alternative distribution systems will gradually replace the storefront, rendering location an obsolete issue.

ISSUE NO. 32
Advertisements as Reflections of a Nation's Ideas

In order to determine whether advertisements reflect a nation's ideas, it is necessary to determine whether advertisements present real ideas at all and, if so, whose ideas they actually reflect. On both counts, it appears that advertisements fail to accurately mirror a nation's ideas.

Indisputably, advertisements inform us as to a nation's values, attitudes, and priorities—what activities are worthwhile, what the future holds, and what is fashionable and attractive. For instance, a proliferation of ads for sport-utility vehicles reflects a societal concern more for safety and machismo than for energy conservation and frugality, while a plethora of ads for inexpensive online brokerage services reflects an optimistic and perhaps irrationally exuberant economic outlook. However, a mere picture of a social more, outlook, or fashion is not an "idea"—it does not answer questions such as "why" and "how."

Admittedly, public-interest advertisements do present ideas held by particular segments of society—for example, those of environmental and other public-health interest groups. However, these ads constitute a negligible percentage of all advertisements, and they do not necessarily reflect the majority's view. Consequently, to assert that advertisements reflect a nation's ideas distorts reality. In truth, they mirror only the business and product ideas of companies whose goods and services are advertised and the creative ideas of advertising firms. Moreover, advertisements look very much the same in all countries, Western and Eastern alike. Does this suggest that all nations have essentially identical ideas? Certainly not.

In sum, the few true ideas we might see in advertisements are those of only a few business concerns and interest groups; they tell us little about the ideas of a nation as a whole.

ISSUE NO. 43
The Importance of Studying History

Examining history makes us better people insofar as it helps us to understand our world. It would seem, therefore, that history would also provide useful clues for dealing with the same social ills that have plagued societies throughout history. On balance, however, the evidence suggests otherwise.

Admittedly, history has helped us learn the appropriateness of addressing certain issues, particularly moral ones, on a societal level. Attempts to legislate morality invariably fail, as illustrated by Prohibition in the 1930s and, more recently, failed federal legislation to regulate access to adult material via the Internet. We are slowly learning this lesson, as the recent trend toward legalization of marijuana for medicinal purposes and the recognition of equal rights for same-sex partners both demonstrate.

However, the overriding lesson from history about social ills is that they are here to stay. Crime and violence, for example, have troubled almost every society. All manner of reform, prevention, and punishment have been tried. Today, the trend appears to be away from reform toward a "tough-on-crime" approach. Is this because history makes clear that punishment is the most effective means of eliminating crime? No; rather, the trend merely reflects current mores, attitudes, and political climate.

Another example involves how we deal with the mentally-ill segment of the population. History reveals that neither quarantine, treatment, nor accommodation solves the problem, only that each approach comes with its own trade-offs. Also undermining the assertion that history helps us to solve social problems is the fact that, despite the civil-rights efforts of Martin Luther King and his progenies, the cultural gap today between African Americans and white Americans seems to be widening. It seems that racial prejudice is a timeless phenomenon.

To sum up, while history can teach us lessons about our social problems, more often than not, the lesson is that there are no panaceas or prescriptions for solving these problems—only alternate ways of coping with them.

Issue No. 46

Bureaucracy's Impact in Business and Government

Contrary to the statement's premise, my view is that businesses are less likely than government to establish large bureaucracies, because businesses know that they are more vulnerable than government to damage resulting from bureaucratic inefficiencies. My position is well supported by common sense and by observation.

First, public administrators lack the financial incentives to avoid bureaucratic waste. In contrast, inefficiencies in a private corporation will reduce profits, inflicting damage in the form of job cuts, diminishing common-stock value, and reducing employee compensation. These are ample incentives for the private firm to minimize bureaucratic waste.

Secondly, there is almost no accountability among government bureaucrats. The electorate's voting power is too indirect to motivate mid-level administrators, whose salaries and jobs rarely depend on political elections. In contrast, private corporations must pay strict attention to efficiency, since their shareholders hold an immediate power to sell their stock, thereby driving down the company's market value.

Thirdly, government is inherently monopolistic, large, and unwieldy; these features breed bureaucracy. Admittedly, some corporations rival state governments in size. Yet even among the largest companies, the profit motive breeds a natural concern for trimming waste, cutting costs, and streamlining operations. Even virtual monopolies strive to remain lean and nimble in order to maintain a distance from upstart competitors. When government pays lip service to efficiency, shrewd listeners recognize this as political rhetoric designed only to pander to the electorate.

In the final analysis, financial incentives, accountability, and competition all distinguish private business from government, both in terms of their likelihood of establishing large bureaucracies and in terms of the damage that these bureaucracies can inflict on the organization.

ISSUE No. 53

User-Unfriendly Systems in Today's Society

If one focuses on systems such as financial services and telecommunications, where emerging technologies have the greatest impact, one sees increasing user-friendliness. However, in other systems—public and private alike—inefficiencies, roadblocks, and other "unfriendly" features still abound. One such example is the U.S. health-care delivery system.

To a large extent, the user-unfriendly nature of health-care delivery stems from its close tie to the insurance industry. Service providers and suppliers inflate prices, knowing that insurance companies can well afford to pay by passing on inflated costs to the insured. Hospital patients are often discharged prematurely merely because insurance fails to cover in-patient care beyond a certain amount or duration. In the extreme, patients are sometimes falsely informed that they are well or cured, just so that the facility can make room for insured patients.

Meanwhile, the insurance companies often reject claims and coverage intentionally and in bad faith when the insured has suffered or is statistically likely to suffer from a terminal or other long-term—and costly—illness. Insurance companies also impose extreme coverage exceptions for preexisting conditions. Both tactics are designed, of course, to maximize insurance company profits at the expense of the system's user. Moreover, new medical technologies that provide more effective diagnosis and treatment are often accessible only to the select few who can afford the most comprehensive insurance coverage.

The consequences of these user-unfriendly features can be grave indeed for the individual, since this system relates directly to a person's physical well-being and very life. For example, when a claim or coverage is wrongfully denied, lacking financial resources to enforce their rights, an individual customer has little practical recourse. The end result is to render health care inaccessible to the very individuals who need it most. These user-unfriendly features can be deleterious on a societal scale as well. An unhealthy populace is an unproductive one. Also, increased health-care costs place an undue burden on bread-winning adults who feel the squeeze of caring for aging parents and for children. Finally, these features foster a pervasive distrust of government, big business, and bureaucracy.

In sum, today's "point-and-click" paradigm inaccurately portrays the actual functionality of many systems, including our health-care delivery system, which is well-entrenched in self-interest and insensitivity to the needs of its users.

ISSUE No. 54

Commercial Success of Films and Television Programs

Clearly, most popular films and television shows are superficial and/or include a certain amount of violence or obscenity. Just as clearly, popularity leads to commercial success. But can we conclude that these productions are overly influenced by commercial interests? Perhaps not, since some popular films and television shows are neither superficial, obscene, nor violent. Closer scrutiny, however, reveals that most such productions actually support, not disprove, the thesis that commercial interests dictate movie and television content.

One would-be threat to the thesis can be found in lower-budget independent films, which tend to focus more on character development and topical social issues than on sensationalism. Recently, a few such films have supplanted Hollywood's major studio productions as top box-office hits. Does this mean that profit potential no longer dictates the content of films? No, it simply suggests that the tastes and preferences of the movie-going public are shifting.

A second ostensible threat to the thesis resides in companies such as Disney, whose productions continue to achieve great popularity and commercial success, without resort to an appeal to baser interests. Yet it is because these productions are commercially successful that they proliferate.

A third, and the only cogent, challenge to the thesis is found in perennial television favorites such as Nova, a public television show that is neither commercially supported nor influenced. However, such shows are more in the nature of education than entertainment, and for every one program like Nova, there are several equally popular—and highly superficial—programs.

With few exceptions, then, commercial success of certain films and television shows is no accidental byproduct of popularity; it is the intentional result of producers' efforts to maximize profits.

Issue No. 59

Business' Social Duty Regarding Juvenile Crime

Juvenile delinquency is clearly a serious social problem. Whether businesses must become more involved in helping to prevent the problem depends, however, on the specific business—whether it is culpable in creating the problem and whether its owners' collective conscience calls for such involvement.

Although parents and schools have the most direct influence on children, businesses nonetheless exert a strong, and often negative, influence on juveniles by way of their advertisements and of the goods they choose to produce. For example, cigarette advertisements aimed at young people, music and clothing that legitimize "gang" sub-culture, and toys depicting violence all sanction juvenile delinquency. In such cases, perhaps the business should be obligated to mitigate its own harmful actions—for example, by sponsoring community youth organizations or by producing public-interest ads.

In other cases, however, imposing on a business a duty to help solve juvenile delinquency or any other social problem seems impractical and unfair. Some would argue that because business success depends on community support, businesses have an ethical duty to give back to the community—by donating money, facilities, or services to social programs. Many successful businesses—such as Mrs. Field's, Ben & Jerry's, and Timberland—have embraced this philosophy. But how far should such a duty extend, and is it fair to impose a special duty on businesses to help prevent one specific problem, such as juvenile delinquency? Moreover, businesses already serve their communities by enhancing the local tax base and by providing jobs, goods, and services.

In the final analysis, while businesses are clearly in a position to influence young people, whether they should help solve juvenile delinquency is perhaps a decision best left to the collective conscience of each business.

Issue No. 60

Access to Personal Information About Employees

Determining whether employers should have access to personal information about employees requires that the interests of businesses in ensuring productivity and stability be weighed against concerns about equity and privacy interests. My view is that, on balance, employers should have the right to obtain personal information about current employees without their consent.

Admittedly, prior to hiring a job candidate, the firm's interest in maintaining a stable, productive, and safe workforce well justifies right of access to certain personal information about the candidate, without consent.

After all, an applicant can easily conceal personal information that might adversely affect job performance, thereby damaging the employer in terms of low productivity and high turnover. Moreover, an applicant might pose a potential security threat, in terms of the company's trade secrets or even the physical safety of the firm's employees. A thorough check of the applicant's personal background might reveal a potential threat.

During employment, however, the employee's interests are far more compelling than those of the employer, for three reasons. First, the employer has every opportunity to monitor ongoing job performance and to replace workers who fail to meet standards, regardless of the reason for that failure. Second, allowing free access to personal information about employees might open the floodgates to discriminatory promotions and salary adjustments. Current federal laws protecting employees from unfair treatment based on gender, race, and marital status may not adequately guard against an employer's searching for an excuse to treat certain employees unfairly. Third, access to personal information without consent raises serious privacy concerns, especially where multiple individuals have access to the information. Heightening this concern is the ease of access to information that our burgeoning electronic Intranets make possible.

In sum, ready access to certain personal information about prospective employees is necessary to protect businesses. However, once hired, an employee's interest in equitable treatment and privacy far outweighs the employer's interest in ensuring a productive and stable workforce.

Issue No. 63

Government Bureaucracy

At first glance, it would seem that increased bureaucracy creates obstacles between the citizens and those who govern, thereby separating the two groups. Closer examination reveals, however, that in many ways, government bureaucracy actually bridges this gap, and that new technologies now allow for ways around the gap.

Many government bureaucracies are established as a response to the needs of the citizenry. In a sense, they manifest a nexus between citizens and government, providing a means of communication and redress for grievances that would not otherwise be available. For example, does the FDA, by virtue of its ensuring the safety of our food and drugs, separate us from the government? Or does the FHA, by helping to make home ownership more viable to ordinary citizens, thereby increase the gap between citizens and the government? No, these agencies serve our interests and enhance the accessibility of government resources to citizens.

Admittedly, agencies such as these are necessary proxies for direct participation in government, since our societal problems are too large and complex for individuals to solve. However, technology is coming forward to bridge some of the larger gaps. For example, we can now communicate directly with our legislators by e-mail, visit our lawmakers on the Web, and engage in electronic town hall meetings. In addition, the fact that government bureaucracies are the largest employers of citizens should not be overlooked. In this sense, bureaucracies bridge the gap by enabling more citizens to become part of the government.

In the final analysis, one can view bureaucracies as surrogates for individual participation in government; however, they are more accurately viewed as a manifestation of the symbiotic relationship between citizens and the government.

Issue No. 65
Multinational Corporations and Global Homogeneity

Although global homogeneity in a broader sense may not be as inexorable as the speaker here suggests, I agree that multinational corporations are indeed creating global sameness in consumer preferences. This homogeneity is manifested in two concurrent megatrends: (1) the embracing of American popular culture throughout the world and (2) a synthesis of cultures, as reflected in consumer preferences.

The first trend is toward Americanization of popular culture throughout the world. In food and fashion, once a nation's denizens "fall into the Gap" or get a taste of a Coke or Big Mac, their preferences are forever Westernized. The ubiquitous Nike "swoosh," which nearly every soccer player in the world will soon don, epitomizes this phenomenon. In media, the cultural agendas of giants such as Time-Warner now drive the world's entertainment preferences. The Rolling Stones and the stars of America's prime-time television shows are revered among young people worldwide, while Mozart's music, Shakespeare's prose, and Gandhi's ideology are largely ignored.

A second megatrend is toward a synthesis of cultures into a homogenous stew. The popularity of so-called "world music" and of "New Age" health care and leisure-time activities aptly illustrate this blending of Eastern, Western, and third-world cultures. Perhaps nowhere is the cultural-stew paradigm more striking, and more bland, than at the international food courts now featured in malls throughout the developed world.

These trends appear inexorable. Counterattacks, such as Ebonics, rap music, and bilingual education, promote the distinct culture of minority groups but not of nations. Further homogenization of consumer preferences is all but ensured by falling trade barriers, coupled with the global billboard that satellite communications and the Internet provide.

In sum, American multinationals have indeed instigated a homogeneous global, yet American-style, consumerism—one that in all likelihood will grow in extent along with free-market capitalism and global connectivity.

Issue No. 74

Rule-Breakers: The Most Memorable People

I strongly agree that rule-breakers are the most memorable people. By departing from the status quo, iconoclasts call attention to themselves, some providing conspicuous mirrors for society, others serving as our primary catalysts for progress.

In politics, for example, rule-breakers Mahatma Gandhi and Martin Luther King secured prominent places in history by challenging the status quo through civil disobedience. Renegades such as Ghengus Khan, Stalin, and Hussein broke all the human-rights "rules," thereby leaving indelible marks in the historical record. And future generations will probably remember Nixon and Kennedy more clearly than Carter or Reagan, by way of their rule-breaking activities—specifically, Nixon's Watergate debacle and Kennedy's extramarital trysts.

In the arts, mavericks such as Dali, Picasso, and Warhol, who break established rules of composition, ultimately emerge as the greatest artists, while the names of artists with superior technical skills are relegated to the footnotes of art-history textbooks. Our most influential popular musicians are the flagrant rule-breakers—for example, bebop musicians such as Charlie Parker and Thelonius Monk, who broke all the harmonic rules, and folk musician-poet Bob Dylan, who broke the rules for lyrics.

In the sciences, innovation and progress can only result from challenging conventional theories—i.e., by breaking rules. Newton and Einstein, for example, both refused to blindly accept what were perceived at their time as certain "rules" of physics. As a result, both men redefined those rules, and both men emerged as two of the most memorable figures in the field of physics.

In conclusion, it appears that the deepest positive and negative impressions appear on either side of the same iconoclastic coin. Those who leave the most memorable imprints in history do so by challenging norms, traditions, cherished values, and the general status quo—that is, by breaking the rules.

Issue No. 79

Social Skills as Purchasable Commodities

This first part of this statement means that interpersonal, or social, skills can be marketed as part of a bundle of assets that one might tout to a prospective client, customer, or especially employer. Presumably, the extent and value of these skills can be gauged by one's previous experience with clients and customers or at jobs requiring a significant amount of teamwork and cooperation among workers—as measured by factors such as one's tenure in such a job and letters of reference from supervisors. While this claim seems plausible in the abstract, it ignores critical valuation problems.

Furthermore, the claim that the ability to deal with people exceeds the value of all other commodities is an overgeneralization, since relative values depend on particular circumstances.

The first problem with this claim is that it is far more difficult to quantify the value of interpersonal skills, or other human qualities, than the value of commodities such as coffee or sugar, which can be measured, weighed, or otherwise examined prior to purchase. To a large extent, the ability to work with people is a quality whose true value can be determined only after it is purchased, then tried and tested for a period of time. In addition, its value may vary depending on the idiosyncrasies of the job. For example, a technically-oriented programmer or researcher might function well with a team of like-minded workers yet have trouble dealing with management or marketing personnel.

The second problem with this claim is that it overgeneralizes in asserting that the ability to work with people is "worth more than any other commodity." The relative value of this ability depends on the peculiarities of the job. In some jobs, especially sales, ambition and tenacity are more valuable. In other areas, such as research and development, technical skills and specific knowledge are paramount. Moreover, in some businesses, such as mining or oil drilling, the value of raw materials and capital equipment might be far more important a commodity than the social skills, or most other skills, of employees—depending on the economic circumstances.

In sum, the ability to deal with people is purchasable only to a limited extent, since its full value cannot be determined prior to purchase. Moreover, its full value depends on the organizational unit as well as the nature of the business.

ISSUE No. 80
Our Saving and Borrowing Habits

Whether an individual saves too little or borrows too much depends on the purpose and extent of either activity. While appropriate and prudent in some circumstances, either can be irresponsible in excess. The evidence suggests that, on balance, people today tend to borrow irresponsibly and are on the brink of saving irresponsibly as well.

Traditionally, saving is viewed as a virtue, while borrowing is considered a vice. However, just the opposite may be true under certain circumstances. Foregoing saving in favor of immediate spending may at times be well justified. A serious hobbyist, for example, may be justified in foregoing saving to spend money on a hobby that provides great joy and fulfillment—whether or not it also generates income. A relatively expensive automobile is justifiable if the additional expense provides added safety for the owner and his family. And foregoing saving is appropriate, and often necessary, for "rainy day" medical emergencies or unanticipated periods of unemployment. Borrowing can also be prudent—if the loan is affordable and applied toward a sound long-term investment.

Were saving and borrowing limited to these types of scenarios, I would aver that people today save and borrow responsibly. However, the evidence suggests otherwise. Americans now purchase on credit far more expensive automobiles, relative to income, than ever before—vehicles that are far more than what is needed for safe transportation. Excessive credit-card debt, another type of unjustifiable borrowing, is at record levels, and rising, among American households. Does the baby-boomers' current penchant for retirement investing compensate for these excesses? Probably not. This trend is fueled by unrealistic expectations of future returns; it may, therefore, escalate to speculation and, at its height, widespread leveraging—i.e., borrowing. Such speculation is more suited to highly sophisticated investors who can well afford to lose their entire investment than to average Americans and their nest eggs.

In conclusion, while people seem to be saving aggressively today, their investment choices and concomitant high spending and borrowing levels call into question the assertion that we are indeed a "nation of savers."

Issue No. 84
Informing Customers About Products and Services

Requiring businesses to provide complete product information to customers promotes various consumer interests but at the same time imposes burdens on businesses, government, and taxpayers. On balance, the burdens outweigh the benefits, at least in most cases.

A threshold problem with disclosure requirements is that of determining what constitutes "complete" information. Admittedly, legislating disclosure requirements clarifies the duties of business and the rights of consumers. Yet determining what requirements are fair in all cases is problematic. Should it suffice to list ingredients, instructions, and intended uses, or should customers also be informed of precise specifications, potential risks, and results of tests measuring a product's effectiveness vis-a-vis competing products?

A closely related problem is that determining and enforcing disclosure standards necessarily involves government regulation, thereby adding to the ultimate cost to the consumer by way of higher taxes. Finally, failure to comply may result in regulatory fines, a cost that may either have a chilling effect on product innovation or be passed on to the customers in the form of higher prices. Either result operates to the detriment of the consumer, the very party whom the regulations are designed to protect.

These burdens must be weighed against the interest in protecting consumers against fraud, and undue health and safety hazards. To assume that businesses will voluntarily disclose negative product information ignores the fact that businesses are motivated by profit, not by public interest concerns. However, consumers today have ready access to many consumer-protection resources and may not need the protection of government regulation. Although health and safety concerns are especially compelling in the case of products that are inherently dangerous—power tools, recreational equipment, and the like—or new and relatively untested products, especially pharmaceuticals, narrow exceptions can always be carved out for these products.

In conclusion, while stringent disclosure requirements may be appropriate for certain products, businesses and consumers alike are generally better off without the burdens imposed by requiring that businesses provide complete product information to all customers.

ISSUE NO. 90
Should Products Be Made to Last?

This topic raises the issue of whether, on balance, consumers are damaged or benefited by quality-cutting production methods. Indisputably, many consumer products today are not made to last. Nevertheless, consumers themselves sanction this practice, and they are its ultimate beneficiaries—in terms of lower prices, more choices, and a stronger economy.

Common sense tells us that sacrificing quality results in a net benefit to consumers and to the overall economy. Cutting production corners not only allows a business to reduce a product's retail price, but it also compels the business to do so, since its competitors will find innovative ways of capturing its market share otherwise. Lower prices stimulate sales, which in turn generate healthy economic activity. Observation also strongly supports this claim. One need only look at successful budget retail stores such as Walmart as evidence that many, and perhaps most, consumers indeed tend to value price over quality.

Do low-quality products waste natural resources? On balance, probably not. Admittedly, to the extent that a product wears out sooner, more materials are needed for replacement units. Yet cheaper materials are often synthetics, which conserve natural resources, as in the case of synthetic clothing, dyes and inks, and wood substitutes and composites. Moreover, many synthetics and composites are now actually safer and more durable than their natural counterparts—especially in the area of construction materials.

Do lower-quality products waste human resources? If by "waste" we mean "use up unnecessarily," the answer is no. Many lower-quality products are machine-made ones that conserve, not waste, human labor—for example, machine-stitched or dyed clothing and machine-tooled furniture. Moreover, other machine-made products are actually higher in quality than their man-made counterparts, such as those requiring a precision and consistency that only machines can provide. Finally, many cheaply made products are manufactured and assembled by the lower-cost Asian and Central American labor force—a legion for whom the alternative is unemployment and poverty. In these cases, producing lower-quality products does not "waste" human resources; to the contrary, it creates productive jobs.

In the final analysis, cost-cutting production methods benefit consumers, both in the short term through lower prices and in the long run by way of economic vitality and increased competition. The claim that producing low-quality products wastes natural and human resources is specious at best.

ISSUE No. 110
Ethical Standards and Successful Business Leadership

In asserting that the most successful business leaders are the ones that follow the highest ethical standards, the speaker raises some very complex questions—about a business leader's fiduciary duties to the firm's stakeholders vis-a-vis the leader's social obligations. Ultimately, however, the answer turns on whether a business leader can recognize when self-interest aligns with social welfare, as discussed below.

One way to define the success of a business leader is simply in terms of the profits (or losses) of the leader's firm. Proponents of this definition also tend to believe that by maximizing profits, at least within legal and regulatory boundaries, a business leader fulfills his or her highest ethical obligation *per se*. However, if we accept these simple notions of business success and ethics, as many people do, then the speaker's assertion amounts to a meaningless tautology. Besides, a certain contrary view suggests that both notions rely on overly narrow ideas about business "success" and how to achieve it.

According to this broader, contrary view, business leaders, by virtue of the power they enjoy, owe certain social obligations to the community and the society that grants them that power in the first place. Such obligations often go beyond legal ones and include, among other duties, a duty to conduct business in a manner that avoids undue risk to the health and safety of customers as well as the public at large. In order to discharge obligations such as these, a firm might voluntarily provide certain product-safety features or take certain pollution-control measures—even if it means foregoing a portion of its profits. Some advocates of this contrary view go even further—to impose on business leaders an affirmative obligation to protect consumers, preserve the natural environment, promote education, and otherwise take steps to help alleviate society's problems.

The most successful business leader is the one who not only strikes the best balance between social obligation and the profit-maximization imperative, but also recognizes and exploits areas where the two objectives are actually in accord, rather than in conflict. For example, a firm's insensitivity to environmental or safety concerns might tarnish its public image and ultimately serve to reduce profits—or vice versa. Indeed, the increasingly close scrutiny of business leaders by media, politicians, and activists—as the recent Enron/Anderson accounting scandal aptly illustrates—suggests that corporate profits and scruples are more likely to go hand in hand in the future.

In sum, although it is wrongheaded to equate profitability with virtue, the two are not necessarily mutually exclusive. The most effective business leader is the one who not only understands this paradox, but also can exploit it to the society's best socioeconomic advantage.

Issue No. 125

Should Education Continue Beyond College?

I strongly agree that education should not end at college graduation and that people should enroll in courses throughout their lifetime. Otherwise, we ultimately risk our careers, our economy, and even our very humanity.

One reason why education should continue beyond college is that specific knowledge and skills needed for most jobs change continually. Workers who neglect to update their knowledge and skills jeopardize not only their jobs and careers but also the opportunity to contribute meaningfully to society—an opportunity that only sufficient mastery of one's chosen profession can afford. Admittedly, some workers can learn what they need to know while on the job. However, in my observation, most workers barely find enough time during a typical workday to accomplish their basic jobs, let alone to stay abreast of the dizzying array of new developments that bear on those jobs.

Moreover, workers should not limit their career-related education to course work in their own fields. Mastery of any profession or field requires some knowledge about a variety of others. For example, an anthropologist cannot excel without understanding the social and political events that shape cultures and without some knowledge of chemistry and geology. Even computer engineering is intrinsically tied to other fields, even non-technical ones such as business, communications, and media. Few people can reasonably expect to learn, either in college or through independent study after college, all that they need to know about other fields in order to master their own field.

Aside from the sorts of post-college course work that further careers, varied educational pursuits throughout life serve to bring to fruition no less than the learner's own humanity. Continued course work in psychology, sociology, and anthropology helps adult learners to synthesize their life experiences—thereby gaining a richer understanding of themselves and their place in community and society. Courses in political science, philosophy, theology, and natural sciences help the adult learner gain fresh insight and perspective on humankind's place in the physical and metaphysical worlds. And no person can become truly human without developing, then nurturing through continued study, an aesthetic appreciation of literature, the fine arts, and the performing arts.

Thus, even the broadest and deepest college education is merely a primer for adult life, vocational and otherwise. We should continue to learn new job-related skills and information, in the interest of advancing the society. But we should also complement those efforts through course work in the sciences, humanities, and arts. We thereby gain the capacity to succeed in career, to find its purpose and meaning, and to understand and appreciate life. To gain these capacities is to become fully human, which, in my view, should be our ultimate end.

Part 8

SAMPLE ESSAYS FOR 20 OFFICIAL GMAT ARGUMENTS

Part 8 contains my responses to 20 of the Arguments in the test maker's official pool. You can obtain the entire list of official Arguments via my GMAT Analytical Writing Web site (www.west.net/~stewart/awa). As you study the responses here in Part 8, keep in mind the following:

- I did not compose these essays under timed conditions. Also, I did quite a bit of fine-tuning to make them better models for you to study. So, don't be concerned if your essays aren't as polished as mine. Be realistic about what *you* can produce in 30 minutes.

- In the first paragraph of each essay I've recapitulated the official Argument, for your reference. Keep in mind, however, that the readers do not expect you to restate the Argument in your essay.

- These essays are intended to provide you with substantive, organizational, and style ideas for composing your GMAT Argument essay; but they are not for copying word-for-word. Be forewarned: GMAT readers will be on the lookout for plagiarism.

> **IMPORTANT!** From time to time, the test maker might change the sequence of Arguments in the official pool; so be sure to check my online updates (www.west.net/~stewart/ws) for the current sequence. Preceding each essay here in Part 8 is a brief phrase that describes the Argument's topic; this description should help you match the essay to the corresponding Argument in the official pool.

ARGUMENT NO. 8

Interest in Management Issues Among Workers

According to this editorial, the common view of workers as generally apathetic about management issues is false, or at least outdated. To support this assertion, the editorial cites a recently published survey in which 79 percent of the 1,200 workers responding to a questionnaire indicated great interest in corporate-restructuring and benefits-redesign issues. Careful scrutiny of the editorial reveals numerous potential problems with it—problems that render its author's position untenable.

A threshold problem is that the editorial neglects to indicate how recently the survey was actually conducted. All we know is that the survey was recently published. The less recent the survey itself, the less reliable the results to indicate current interest levels in management issues among workers, regardless of when the results were published.

Two more potential problems have to do with the survey's methodology. First, unless the surveyors sampled a sufficient number of workers and did so randomly across the entire workforce spectrum, the survey results are not reliable to gauge the interests of workers generally. The number of respondents (1,200) in itself does not ensure representative-ness. For example, if the sample included only managers, then the results would no doubt suggest a much higher level of interest than the average level among all workers.

A second possible methodological problem is that of bias. Perhaps workers who were interested in management issues were more likely than other workers to respond to the questionnaire—possibly because they found the questionnaire more interesting. Or perhaps a significant number of respondents feigned interest in management issues because they believed they might gain favor with their company by doing so. In either event, the survey results would be virtually useless in drawing reliable conclusions about the actual level of interest in management issues among workers generally.

A final problem with the editorial involves the possibility of additional results from the survey—results that the editorial neglects to mention. For example, maybe the questionnaire listed many management issues and the results showed keen interest among workers in only the two particular ones that the editorial mentions. In fact, for all we know, the survey respondents indicated that they were completely apathetic toward all other issues, in which case the common notion that the editorial seeks to dispel would appear to be correct after all.

In sum, the editorial has not succeeded in disproving that workers are apathetic about management issues. To make at least a colorable argument based on the survey, the editorial's author must show that the survey respondents as a group accurately reflect the entire worker population in terms of their interest in management issues generally—not just the two issues listed. To accomplish this, the author must supply detailed information about the survey's methodology—especially about the subject-selection process, what the subjects were told about the survey, and whether or not responses were mandatory.

ARGUMENT NO. 23

Does Einstein High School Require More Funding?

In this speech, a city-council member argues that a substantial increase in funding for Einstein High School is unnecessary. To support this conclusion, the speaker points out that today two thirds of Einstein's graduates go on to college, whereas twenty years ago, only one half did so. From these statistics, the speaker reasons that Einstein must have grown in educational effectiveness over that twenty-year period—despite the fact that the school's funding, adjusted for inflation, has not increased over that period. The speaker's argument suffers from several reasoning flaws, which together render the argument unconvincing.

First of all, percentages from only the first and final years of a twenty-year period hardly suffice to prove a clear trend. One, or perhaps both, of these two years might have been unusual in terms of the percentage of new Einstein graduates proceeding to college. In fact, there might be no clear trend, or the overall trend might be a decline in this percentage. Since the statistics provided are insufficient to show a clear trend, the speaker cannot reasonably conclude based on them that Einstein has grown in educational effectiveness, let alone that it does not need additional funding.

Secondly, the speaker's argument depends on the poor assumption that improvement in educational effectiveness is the only possible explanation for an increase in the college-matriculation rate among new Einstein graduates. The speaker neglects to consider and rule out other possible explanations—for instance, an influx of new residents for whom college education is either more affordable or a higher priority. Without eliminating other possible reasons for the trend, the speaker cannot convince me that the trend is attributable to improved educational effectiveness or that Einstein has in fact improved in this respect.

Thirdly, even if in the past Einstein has grown more effective without inflation-adjusted funding increases, it will not necessarily be able to do so, or even remain as effective as it is today, in the future. A substantial funding increase might now be required for the first time, for any number of possible reasons. For example, perhaps Einstein's facilities have been deteriorating and are now considered dangerously unsafe to the point that significant funding is needed to repair or replace them. Or perhaps a flurry of new developments in educational technology have rendered Einstein's teaching tools obsolete, even though the same tools have been adequate for the past twenty years.

Finally, the speaker's argument assumes that college matriculation rates are the only reliable indicator of a high school's level of educational effectiveness. Yet the mere fact that a high school student does not proceed to college does not necessarily mean that the high school was ineffective in educating that student. Thus, the speaker unfairly equates "educational effectiveness" with college-matriculation rates.

In conclusion, the scant statistical evidence provided in the speech fails to convince me that Einstein can increase, or even maintain, its level of educational effectiveness without increased funding. Instead of relying on a potentially irrelevant statistic from two decades ago, the speaker should have provided Einstein's college-matriculation rates for many consecutive years, up to the present time. To fully prove her case, the speaker should have also provided evidence that substantiates her two crucial assumptions: (1) that college-matriculation rates depend primarily on a high school's educational effectiveness and (2) that college-matriculation rates are the best indicator of that effectiveness.

ARGUMENT No. 28

Shuttle-Bus Service to Local Subway Stations

This editorial points out that commuter use of the new subway train has exceeded projections, while commuter use of shuttle buses that transport people to subway stations is below projections. According to the editorial, in order for a greater number of commuters to shuttle rather than drive to the stations, the city must either decrease shuttle fares or raise parking fees at the stations. For several reasons, this claim is a dubious one at best.

To begin with, the reason for the unexpectedly low shuttle-bus usage might have nothing to do with either shuttle-bus fares or station-parking fees. For instance, commuter awareness of the shuttle-bus option might be growing more slowly than anticipated. For that matter, many commuters might be wary of riding the buses due to a recent shuttle-bus accident. Without ruling out these and other alternative explanations for the low shuttle-bus usage, the author cannot reasonably conclude that adjusting shuttle fares or station-parking fees will have any effect on that usage.

Admitting for the sake of argument that shuttle-bus fares and/or parking fees are responsible for the lower-than-expected shuttle-bus usage, the editorial nevertheless overlooks other ways (besides adjusting shuttle fares or parking fees) to increase shuttle-bus usage. For example, if the shuttles ran more frequently, perhaps more people could, and would, use the buses instead of driving. Or perhaps larger or more comfortable shuttles would achieve the same result. In short, unless the editorial's author explores and eliminates all other options, I remain unconvinced that the only way for the city to attain the stated objective is to either decrease shuttle fares or increase parking fees.

Along a similar vein, the editorial neglects to acknowledge extrinsic conditions, beyond the transit system's control, that might impact shuttle-bus usage. Such conditions might include local demographic shifts, gasoline prices, and road- or highway-construction projects. Should conditions such as these change so that taking shuttle buses to subway stations instead of driving to them becomes more attractive, then the proposed fee adjustments might not be needed to see an increase in shuttle-bus usage.

Finally, the editorial implies that lowering shuttle fares and/or raising parking fees would in fact help change the behavior of commuters who currently drive to the stations. However, the editorial provides no evidence to support this implication. In fact, for all we are told, these commuters can easily afford high fares and fees, and some other factor—such as total commuting time—is the only real concern among these commuters. If so, then the editorial's proposed course of action might very will be totally ineffectual.

In the final analysis, the editorial fails to make a convincing case that the proposed fare or fee adjustments are either necessary or sufficient to modify commuter behavior in the desired way. To strengthen her case, the editorial's author must supply good evidence that commuters have a realistic choice between driving and shuttling to the stations and that their choice is based on how shuttle-bus fares compare to parking fees—rather than on some other factor. A reliable survey of local subway commuters might serve this purpose.

ARGUMENT No. 37

Why Has a Foreign-Made Copy of Motorcycle X Failed to Attract Buyers?

The author of this article first points out that a certain foreign company has failed to attract customers of Motorcycle X, a long-established American motorcycle, with its copy of X. The author then attempts to refute the assertion that the copy's failure is due to the fact that its engine is not as noisy as X's engine. To refute the assertion, the author simply cites two facts: (1) foreign cars are generally quieter than, but sell just as well as, American cars; and (2) television ads for X focus on its appearance while the viewer listens to rock music, not X's engine noise. Unfortunately, these facts accomplish little toward refuting the assertion that the copy's comparatively quiet engine is the reason for the copy's failure to attract Motorcycle X customers.

With respect to the first of the two facts, the author attempts here to draw what might amount to a false analogy between car buyers and motorcycle buyers. The former group might generally prefer quiet engines, while the latter prefer noisy ones. Even if the two groups are largely the same, the same person might very well prefer different features, such as a quiet engine, in a car than in a motorcycle. In either event, it would be unreasonable to draw any conclusions about why people choose one motorcycle over another based on sales of quiet cars vis-a-vis noisier ones.

As for the second fact—about the television ads—the author seems to assume that a significant portion of people who might be interested in buying motorcycles watch the ads enough times to be influenced by them. While this might be the case, the author must provide clear evidence to substantiate this assumption. Otherwise, I cannot accept the author's inference that the ads have any bearing whatsoever on consumer motorcycle-buying decisions.

In citing the ads, the author also seems to assume that X's visual features, which the ads tout, actually influence motorcycle-buying decisions of people viewing the ads. Yet it is entirely possible that these people don't like or don't care about X's appearance but that the ad's raucous music reminds them of Motorcycle X's most appealing feature—its noisy engine. The fact that X has been manufactured for more than seventy years strongly suggests that people are already familiar with the sound of X's engine and therefore that the ads might serve to remind them of that sound.

In conclusion, the author has not provided convincing reasons to reject the assertion that the foreign-made copy's failure to attract X customers is due to its comparatively quiet engine. To bolster his position, instead of relying on potentially irrelevant statistics about car sales, the author should provide better evidence—perhaps in the form of worldwide survey results—that motorcycle buyers have rejected the foreign copy for reasons having nothing to do with engine noise. To further bolster his position, the author might look for a reliable television viewer survey showing that the ads for Motorcycle X entice potential buyers primarily because of the ads' focus on the bike's visual features—or for other reasons having nothing to do with engine noise.

ARGUMENT No. 42

Should the Postal Service Raise Postage-Stamp Prices?

The author of this opinion article claims that raising postage-stamp prices would increase the postal service's revenue while decreasing its mail volume, both of which in turn the author claims would eliminate strain on the postal system and improve morale among postal workers. Based on these claims, the author recommends raising stamp prices in order to reverse what the author calls "deterioration" of the postal service. This argument depends on a series of four cause-and-effect relationships, none of which the article's author has established. Thus, I find the argument wholly unpersuasive.

First of all, raising stamp prices would not necessarily result in a net increase in revenue. If the price raise results in a decrease in mail volume, as the article claims it would, then revenue lost due to decreased volume might exceed revenue gained by selling stamps at higher prices. With less revenue, it would seem less likely that the postal service could take steps to improve morale or reduce system strain, let alone eliminate it—especially if those steps require additional expenses.

Secondly, a net increase in revenue would not necessarily eliminate, or even reduce, system strain or improve morale. The service would actually need to apply the additional revenue toward these ends—for example, by improving system efficiency or enhancing employee benefits. Otherwise, any reduction in strain or improvement in morale could not be attributed to an increase in net revenue.

Thirdly, even if the service applies additional net revenue toward eliminating strain and improving morale, the sort of means I've just described might very well not suffice to achieve those objectives. It might be impossible to fully eliminate system strain, no matter how much money is invested in attempting to do so. And morale problems might be due to the current social or political climate throughout the country, in which case the postal service would be powerless to improve morale regardless of how much money is at its disposal.

Finally, the deterioration to which the author refers might very well involve more than system strain and employee morale. If so, then eliminating these two problems might not suffice to reverse the deterioration.

To recapitulate, before the author can convince me that the proposed price increase will reverse the service's deterioration, the author must establish each of the four causal relationships discussed above. To accomplish this, the author should obtain reliable marginal-revenue projections—perhaps through a survey that gauges how the public will respond to stamp-price increases. The author should also determine, by means of efficiency studies and postal-employee surveys, the extent to which additional revenues could alleviate system strain and morale problems. Finally, the author must investigate all possible contributing causes of the deterioration—and confidently rule out all except system strain and worker morale.

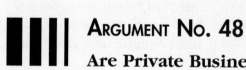

Argument No. 48

Are Private Businesses More Profitable than Public Ones?

This editorial cites the profitability of Croesus Company (CC), recently restored to private ownership, as clear proof that businesses "fare better"—by which I assume the editorial means "are more profitable"—under private than public ownership. This argument relies on several crucial but unsubstantiated assumptions and is therefore unconvincing as it stands.

As a threshold matter, presumably CC was once a publicly owned business. However, the editorial's author must be more explicit that this is the case. Otherwise, any generalizations about the merits of private businesses vis-a-vis public ones based on the profitability of a single private business amounts to shear conjecture, and the argument can be dismissed out of hand.

Turning to the argument's unproven assumptions, the first such assumption is that CC owes its profitability to its newly restored private status. CC's profitability might be due instead to factors such as the economic or regulatory environment—to name just a few possibilities. Moreover, just as a political office-holder might unfairly receive credit for a predecessor's accomplishments, CC's current profitability might be due to policies and actions at CC while it was a public company. In fact, it is entirely possible that CC was more profitable as a public business and that its profitability is in decline—due to its return to private status. In either case, it would be more reasonable to conclude that public businesses are likely to fare better than private ones, rather than the other way around.

Another of the argument's unsubstantiated assumptions is that CC is typical of businesses recently restored to private status. It is entirely possible that, to the contrary, CC's profitability is highly unusual under its circumstances and that in most cases, profits suffer when a business returns from public to private status. Thus, before I can accept the editorial's conclusion, the author must show that CC is representative of most businesses that return to private status.

Even if most businesses that return from public to private status improve their profitability ("fare better") as a result, the author's conclusion that private businesses as an entire group fare better than public ones is far too broad. Perhaps the most profitable businesses are the ones that remain public ones forever. If so, then the author would need to narrow his conclusion accordingly.

In sum, this argument suffers from two classic reasoning flaws: (1) a correlation between two things (in this case, private ownership and profitability) suffices to prove a cause-and-effect relationship and (2) what is true for one member of a group (in this case, businesses restored to private ownership) is also true for that group as a whole. If the author wishes to convince me of his sweeping conclusion, rather than relying on vague and scant information about one potentially unrepresentative business, the author should compare the profitability of public businesses as a group with that of private businesses as a group.

ARGUMENT No. 53

Avoiding a Shortage of Trained Engineers

This editorial points out that in the past, the majority of engineers in this country have come from universities but that the number of university-aged people in this country is beginning to decrease—a trend that the editorial's author believes will continue for the rest of the decade due to a current decline in high school enrollment. The author reasons that the nation will soon be short of trained engineers, then concludes that education funding must increase quickly if this nation is to remain economically competitive in the world. Unfortunately, this argument is dependant on a series of poorly supported inferences and is therefore specious at best.

First, the author has not proven that the current decline in high school enrollment necessarily portends a continued decrease in the number of this nation's college-aged people. The enrollment decline might reverse itself. Or the number of college-aged people might level off, or even increase, despite declining high school enrollment—due perhaps to an influx of college-aged immigrants or a trend in college reentry among older people. Without considering and ruling out possibilities such as these, the author cannot convince me that a future decline in the number of this nation's college-aged people, let alone trained engineers, is likely.

Secondly, the author has not substantiated her inference that a decrease in the number of this nation's college-aged people will result in a decrease in the number of trained engineers. The author ignores the possibility of an influx of trained engineers from other nations, of a trend in retraining older people for engineering jobs, and of a relaxing of the formal education requirements for becoming a trained engineer. In short, for various reasons, the number of this nation's trained engineers might very well remain stable, or even increase, despite a decline in our college-aged population. Accordingly, the author's contention that this nation must increase education funding in order to assure an adequate future supply of trained engineers is questionable at best.

Thirdly, even if the author can prove that increased education funding is needed to ensure an adequate future supply of trained engineers, the author must also establish a clear cause-and-effect relationship between the level of this nation's education funding and its viability in the world marketplace. Otherwise, I remain skeptical of the author's final conclusion that the former is a necessary condition for the latter.

In sum, the author's plea for increased education funding in the interest of this nation's viability in the world marketplace appears groundless. To bolster her argument, the author must provide better evidence that the number of this nation's trained engineers will decline going forward, that this decline portends trouble for the nation's economic competitiveness among nations, and that the decline can be avoided only by increasing education funding.

Argument No. 59

Day Care for Children of Scientists

In this excerpt, the author points out that scientists must work 60 to 80 hours per week in order to further their careers. Based on this fact, the author then makes two assertions: (1) in order for scientists, male and female alike, to further their careers, they must have access to good, affordable, all-day child care; and (2) requirements for career advancement must be made more flexible so that children of pre-school age can spend a significant portion of each day with at least one parent. Neither assertion is particularly convincing, and considered together, they are even less persuasive, as discussed below.

A threshold problem with the argument is that it fails to distinguish between scientists with children and those without children. A scientist with no young children obviously has no need for day-care services or for career-advancement requirements that accommodate the special interests of parents. Thus, the author must narrow both conclusions so that they apply only to scientists with children.

Considering the author's first assertion apart from the second one, the author fails to consider and rule out other options for ensuring proper care for scientists' children during the workday. For instance, a scientist whose spouse (or partner) has time during each day to spend with their child might very well require no professional day care. Besides, many scientist-parents, including single-parent scientists, might have friends or relatives who can provide child care. Thus, to the extent that scientists have other options to ensure day care for their children, the author's first conclusion is unwarranted.

As for the author's second assertion, considered separately from the first one, the author fails to explain why it is important for children generally, let alone children of scientists in particular, to spend a significant portion of each day with a parent. Lacking a convincing explanation, I cannot accept the author's assertion that career-advancement requirements must be made more flexible merely for the sake of allowing significant parent-child contact each workday.

Considering the two assertions together, however, the argument becomes even less convincing. In essence, the second assertion serves to undermine the first one. If the children of scientists spend significant time each day with a parent, without compromise to the scientist-parent's career, then all-day child care would seem unnecessary—in direct contradiction to the author's first assertion. Thus, the author must either reconcile the two assertions or choose one assertion over the other.

In a nutshell, the argument is not only poorly supported but also paradoxical. Before I can either agree or disagree with the author's first assertion, I would need to know what percentage of scientists have pre-school children and what portion of that group have partners or other trusted relatives/friends who are available to care for those children. As for the second assertion, the author seems to rely on certain normative assumptions about parent-child relationships, assumptions that the author doesn't begin to address but must do so before I can agree with the assertion. Moreover, the argument as a whole is illogical on its face. Before I can begin to take it seriously, the author must either abandon one or the other assertion or explain why scientists as a group cannot advance their careers unless they can spend significant time each day with their pre-school children and at the same time have ready access to all-day child care.

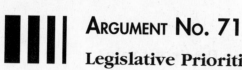

ARGUMENT No. 71

Legislative Priorities and the Problem of Petty Vandalism

The author of this editorial points out that in response to petitions from area farmers and landowners, the legislature has spent valuable time and effort to enact severe laws to deter motorists from picking fruit, stealing samples and foliage, and trampling fields of regional growers. The author claims that these problems are trivial and thus do not merit the legislature's valuable time. To support this claim, the author cites a current plague of crime and violence in this nation's cities. At first glance, this argument might sound appealing; closer scrutiny, however, reveals numerous flaws that, considered together, completely undermine the argument.

To begin with, the argument relies on the unlikely assumption that the plague of crime and violence in cities also poses a problem in this legislature's region. Based on the editorial, this region appears to be largely rural. To the extent that it is, urban-type crimes are unlikely to pose a problem in this region, and the author cannot reasonably rely merely on urban crime statistics to support his position.

Assuming for the moment that this region is in fact plagued by urban-type crime and violence, why shouldn't the legislature also address other, less serious problems, such as fruit vandalism? The author supplies no evidence that the legislature has insufficient time to address both types of problems. Until the author supplies this sort of evidence, he cannot convince me that the legislature's attention to fruit vandalism comes at the expense of its attention to more serious problems.

Besides, the author supplies no proof that the fruit stealing and vandalism problem is "trivial." Even if the problem technically involves incidents of mere "petty vandalism," as the author suggests, the problem might be so pervasive that it poses a serious threat to the livelihood of regional farmers and landowners. Also, the vandalism and stealing might incite more serious crimes, including violent ones. In either case, the legislature would seem well justified in devoting considerable time and effort to respond to the petitions of regional farmers and landowners.

In sum, the editorial fails to convince that fruit stealing and vandalism do not merit the legislature's considerable attention. To better evaluate the author's position on this issue, I would need to know the extent of the problem and its social and economic consequences throughout the region. I would also need to know what other problems the legislature faces and what portion of the legislature's time is needed to address these other problems. Only armed with this information could I make an informed judgment about the proper priorities of the legislature and, in turn, about the editorial's merit.

ARGUMENT No. 74

Will the Sequel to a Vista Studios Movie Be Profitable?

This magazine article predicts that the sequel to a certain Vista Studios movie will be profitable. The article's author bases this prediction on the fact that a series of books based on characters from the first movie are consistent bestsellers in local bookstores. I find this prediction dubious for several reasons.

To begin with, Vista presumably plans to release the sequel to a wide audience, not just to members of this locality. If so, it seems foolhardy to make any predictions about the sequel's general popularity based on the apparent interests of one community.

In addition, the argument depends on the assumption that the books' popularity is due to their characters. Yet the argument does not rule out other possible reasons for their popularity, such as plot lines, illustrations, or even price. If it turns out that their popularity is due to some feature lacking in the two movies, then the author's prediction would amount to little more than conjecture.

Even assuming that the books' popularity is due to their characters, I would remain skeptical about the author's prediction. The movie sequel might contain different characters, in which case it may very well disappoint at the box-office, despite the success of the books and the first movie. Even if the sequel contains the same characters, this feature in itself might not suffice to draw large audiences. Consumer interest in these characters might already be satiated, or the sequel might simply not be as good as the first movie and the books. In either event, the author's prediction might very well not come to pass.

Finally, in predicting that the sequel well be profitable because the books are popular, the author assumes that a popular movie necessarily turns a profit. However, common sense and observation tell me that movie profits depend not only on box-office attendance and video sales (that is, popularity) but also on costs as well. Thus, the sequel might turn out to be popular but unprofitable.

In sum, the prediction is based on scant evidence and unproven assumptions and is therefore tantamount to mere speculation. Before agreeing that the sequel will be popular, let alone profitable, I would require better proof that whatever features account for the books' popularity would also draw large crowds to see the movie sequel. To obtain this sort of proof, I would need to survey readers of the book to determine the book's appeal and of course screen the sequel to see whether or not it holds similar appeal.

ARGUMENT NO. 79

The Problem with Adopting a Company Code of Ethics

The author of this company memorandum concludes that the company should conduct a publicity campaign stressing the importance of protecting the environment and assisting charities, instead of adopting an official code of ethics. To support this conclusion, the author points out that a competing company attracted additional media attention as a result of unfavorable publicity about a violation of its own code. Based on this evidence, the author reasons that by adopting a code of ethics, this company may do more long-term harm than good to its public image. The argument suffers from several reasoning flaws and is therefore unconvincing as it stands.

To begin with, the author has not shown that the competitor's code violation and resulting publicity and media attention actually harmed that company's pubic image. For all we know, the public ignored the publicity, or the media viewed the unfavorable publicity as unfair and rallied to defend that company. In either case, the author's caveat about adopting a code of ethics would seem unwarranted.

Nor has the author shown that this company will violate its code as well or that any such violation would result in harm to its public image. Certain key differences between the two companies might render the analogy a poor one. For instance, this company might take its self-imposed ethical standards more seriously or choose to adopt a more realistic code. In either case, a code violation would seem less likely for this company. Or perhaps the public would be more forgiving of a code violation by this company than by its competitor, for whatever reason.

Nor has the author shown that any such violation would necessarily result in a tarnished image over the longer term. The public may soon forget about the violation, especially if the public shifts its scrutiny to subsequent, more egregious ones by some other company. Besides, the author ignores the possibility that this company can remedy the damage to its image resulting from a code violation.

Two final problems involve the memo's recommended publicity campaign. First, the memo's author assumes without justification that the campaign would serve to bolster the company's public image. In fact, the campaign might have no impact or even backfire—if it makes the company appear hypocritical or disingenuous or if the values that its public holds dear conflict with the ones that the company espouses. Second, in recommending the publicity campaign "rather than" a code of ethics, the memo's author overlooks the possibility of pursuing both courses or some other course that might be more effective than these two in enhancing the company's public image.

In the final analysis, the recommendation is indefensible, at least based on the information the memo provides. To bolster the argument, the memo's author must provide clear evidence —perhaps by way of a public survey—that the competitor's code violation in fact served to tarnish its long-term public image. The author must also show that this company is likely to violate its own code and that the violation would be likely to do long-term harm to its public image. To more fully determine the likelihood of such harm, I would need to compare this company's prospective code with the other company's code. I would also need to assess the integrity of this company's key decision makers. Finally, a public-opinion survey would help me determine what types of policies, or combination of policies, would most likely enhance this company's public image.

ARGUMENT No. 84

The Impending Failure of Company A

The author of this article predicts the failure of Company A, which currently enjoys a large share of the international video-game market. To justify this prediction, the author cites the collapse of Company B, a pioneer and former giant in this field, when children grew tired of its products. In further support of this prediction, the author reasons that demand for Company A's products must be nearly exhausted because its products appear in "so many" American homes. I find this argument unpersuasive, for several reasons.

To begin with, the author ignores other possible causes of B's collapse. Just because the collapse coincided with a waning interest among children in Company B's products, it is unfair to infer that the former is attributable solely to the latter. There are a myriad of other possible contributing causes of B's collapse—ranging from management problems to regulatory changes to increasing competition. If it turns out that Company B's collapse was not due entirely to the waning interest among children in B's products, then it would be hasty to assume that Company A will necessarily fail should it face similar waning demand.

Turning next to the information about demand for Company A's games, the mere fact that Company A's products appear in "so many" American homes accomplishes little toward showing waning demand for its products, let alone toward showing that the company will fail. To begin with, the term "so many" is too vague to be statistically meaningful. Even if by "so many" the author means "nearly all," perhaps among Americans, the demand for more new Company A games is strong. Moreover, the author ignores foreign markets, which might account for a significant portion of Company A's sales. The greater the demand outside America, the less likely Company A will fail.

Even assuming, for the sake of argument, that demand for Company A's products is nearly exhausted, this fact would not necessarily spell the demise of Company A—even if it did for Company B. For all we know, Company A has many other lines of products and/or services, whose profitability ensures the company's survival despite the failure of its video-game line. For that matter, perhaps Company A has an exceptionally talented management team or surplus of cash, either of which might allow the company to respond quickly and effectively in order to save itself.

To recapitulate, the author has failed to convince me that future demand for Company A's products will be insufficiently low for the company to survive. Nor has the author convinced me that Company B's failure portends problems for Company A; to the contrary, with one less competitor, Company A might be more likely to survive. To strengthen the claim that Company A will fail, rather than relying on what might amount to a poor analogy between companies A and B, the author should supply detailed information about worldwide trends in video-game demand and show that A is poorly positioned vis-a-vis its competitors to take advantage of these trends going forward.

ARGUMENT NO. 89

The Escalating Price of Lemons

The author of this editorial points out that at Megamart, lemon prices have increased more than six-fold over the past decade, but in only one of the past eleven years has the weather been unfavorable for growing citrus crops. Based on these facts, the author reasons that citrus-fruit price increases have been excessive and that citrus-fruit growers are responsible for the price inflation. The editorial concludes that "strict pricing regulations"—by which I assume the author means regulations on prices that growers charge—are needed in order to curb this problem. I find the author's argument unconvincing in several respects.

First of all, the argument relies on the unproven assumption that Megamart's lemon prices are representative of citrus-fruit prices generally. For all we know, prices of other citrus fruits, or of other stores' lemons, have remained relatively stable (or even declined) over the past decade. Thus, unless Megamart's lemons account for a very large portion of all citrus fruit sold at market, or for some other reason fairly represent all citrus fruits in price, a widespread pricing problem might not even exist.

Secondly, the author too hastily assumes that it is citrus growers who are responsible for the escalating lemon prices. Perhaps retailers such as Megamart, or wholesalers, are instead responsible for the price inflation. Without eliminating this possibility, the author cannot convince me that regulating prices that growers charge would curb the price trend.

Thirdly, even if the price increases can be traced to the growers, the editorial unjustifiably implies that the growers are profiting unfairly as a result of those increases. Although ruling out poor weather conditions as a possible justification for the price increases, the author overlooks others possibilities. For example, perhaps the growers' costs—for land, equipment, and so forth—have increased commensurately over the past decade. If so, then the growers would have profited little, if at all, by charging higher prices for citrus fruit. Thus, limiting the prices growers can charge might result in forcing them out of business—a result that is clearly at odds with the goal of ensuring stable citrus prices for consumers.

Finally, in claiming that the proposed regulations are necessary to curb price increases, the author ignores other possible means, such as farm subsidies, of achieving the same objective. Until the author rules out all other options, I simply cannot accept that strict pricing regulations are necessary.

In a nutshell, the editorial is wholly unconvincing as it stands. To bolster the argument for strict pricing regulations on growers, the author must supply better proof of an upward trend in all citrus-fruit prices, of the growers' accountability for that trend, and of a truly excessive profit for the growers as a result of that trend. A proper assessment of the author's recommendation would require a reliable statistical study comparing citrus growers' costs with the prices they have charged over the last decade and comparing those statistics with citrus-fruit pricing by retailers as a group. Only then could I determine whether widespread price inflation exists and, if so, which group is responsible for it—and thereby determine whether or not the proposed regulations make sense.

ARGUMENT No. 93

Reversing a Decline in Advertising Applications to KMTV

The author of this editorial concludes that local television channel KMTV should shift its programming focus to farming issues in order to stimulate KMTV advertising applications, which declined in number last year. The author bases this conclusion on a report by a nearby town's television station, KOOP, that advertising applications to KOOP increased in number when KOOP took similar action. Assuming that KOOP's report is true and accurate, I nevertheless find the author's argument unconvincing in several respects.

To begin with, the surge in applications to KOOP was not necessarily due to KOOP's programming change. Perhaps KOOP also lowered its advertising fees around the same time; or perhaps a competing television station increased theirs or went out of business. Any one of a host of possible events such as these might explain the surge in applications. Thus, the author should not assume that KMTV can attain its objective by simply emulating KOOP's programming.

Aside from whether KOOP's programming change was in fact responsible for the increase in number of applications to KOOP, the editorial's author assumes without justification that KMTV viewers would be interested in programs about farming issues. If it turns out that, as a group, they are less interested in farming than in KMTV's current programming, KMTV's viewership might diminish in size and, as a result, the number of applications to KMTV might actually decrease.

Yet another problem with the argument is its implication that the proposed change is the only way KMTV can stimulate advertising applications. Common sense tells me that there are other such ways—reducing advertising rates, improving programming quality, or extending broadcast range, to list a few. The author must explain either why none of these options are available or why they would fail to stimulate applications. Otherwise, I cannot accept that the proposed change is necessary.

Finally, the author seems to assume that the proposed programming change would suffice to bring about the desired increase. However, if it turns out that last year's decline was due to a combination of factors, some of which remain unchanged in the future, a mere programming shift might have no stimulating impact on applications.

In essence, then, the editorial relies on a series of poor assumptions and is therefore unpersuasive. In order to convince me that the recommended change would serve to increase advertising applications to KMTV, the editorial's author must at the very least rule out all possible explanations, other than programming focus, for the increase at KOOP and decline at KMTV. To fully persuade me, the author must also explain why KMTV has no other viable means of bringing about the desired increase.

ARGUMENT No. 98

Boosting Sales by Brewing Low-Calorie Beer

The author of this article indicates that, according to a Magic Hat Brewery (MHB) survey, the majority of MHB's tasting-room visitors last year asked to taste MHB's low-calorie beer. The author then concludes that in order to boost beer sales, other small breweries should also brew low-calorie beer. This argument relies on a number of questionable assumptions and is therefore unpersuasive.

One such assumption is that the survey respondents reported their requests accurately. This may or may not be the case. Many survey respondents might have forgotten what they had requested earlier in their visit, especially if they had consumed a significant amount of alcohol. If the survey results turn out to be unreliable as a result, then any conclusion based on those results must be deemed unreliable as well.

Another such assumption is that, as a group, the MHB visitors who asked to taste MHB's low-calorie beer would actually prefer to purchase low-calorie beer over other beers. However, for all we know, visitors can ask to taste more than one beer, and an even greater majority of visitors requested other beers. For that matter, low-calorie beer might be the only type MHB offered for free, or offered at all, at its tasting room last year, and visitors were informed of this before making their requests. In any event, perhaps visitors who tried MHB's low-calorie beer generally disliked it. If one or more of these scenarios turn out to be true, then the survey results would amount to scant evidence at best that any brewery, including MHB, would actually sell enough low-calorie beer to justify brewing it.

Assuming for the moment that MHB's visitors as a group would prefer to purchase low-calorie beer over other beers, this group might not be representative of beer-drinkers generally, especially if the group constitutes a small portion of the beer-drinking population. Yet the author's conclusion relies on the assumption that they are. If it turns out, for example, that MHB visitors are especially calorie-conscious, or especially loyal to MHB products, then other breweries might be very disappointed with sales levels of their own low-calorie beers.

In the final analysis, the author cannot defend her recommendation based solely on the survey results. The author must also show that the survey results are reliable and that they accurately reflect the beer preferences not just of MHB visitors but also of beer-drinking consumers generally. In conclusion, to determine whether or not they should brew low-calorie beer, other breweries should not rely on the dubious results of a single, problematic survey. Instead, they should compare the total market demand for low-calorie beer with the current supply and try to assess the extent of brand loyalty among low-calorie beer drinkers.

ARGUMENT No. 105

Should Bayview High Students Wear Uniforms?

In this editorial, the author recommends that Bayview High require its students to wear school uniforms. To support this recommendation, the author compares Bayview to Acorn Academy, a local private school that has adopted this policy. Specifically, the author points out that Acorn students earn higher grades and are more likely to attend college and that Acorn reports less absenteeism and tardiness as well as fewer discipline problems. This argument suffers from several reasoning flaws, which together render the editorial wholly unconvincing.

To begin with, the editorial does not indicate how long Acorn's current school-uniform policy has been in effect. If the policy is new, then Acorn's various successes (listed in the editorial) cannot be attributed to the policy, and the author's recommendation is completely groundless.

Assuming that Acorn's school-uniform policy is well established, Acorn's comparatively high student GPA and college-matriculation rate might still be due to other factors, such as higher student intelligence levels, higher-quality instruction, or greater support (financial or otherwise) from parents. Without considering and eliminating these and all other feasible explanations for the comparative academic success of Acorn students, the author cannot persuade me that Acorn's school-uniform policy is responsible for, or even contributed to, that success.

Similarly, the author fails to consider other possible reasons for Acorn's reportedly lower incidence of absenteeism, tardiness, and discipline problems. To begin with, perhaps these sorts of problems are simply not reported as often at Acorn as at Bayview; if so, the reports would provide scant support at best for the author's argument. Even if they are reported as often at Acorn, perhaps Acorn students have readier access to health care, psychologists, and counselors; live in safer neighborhoods or more stable households; or have more reliable transportation to school. Any of these conditions might explain less absenteeism, tardiness, and delinquency. Moreover, the author has not considered and ruled out the possibility that students who are forced to wear uniforms are actually more likely than other students to act in a rebellious and delinquent manner. If this is the case, then the author's implicit claim that Acorn's school-uniform policy has contributed to its low incidence of absenteeism and delinquency problems would be very weak indeed.

Even if the author can show that Acorn's school-uniform policy has contributed to the various successes listed in the editorial, a similar policy at Bayview would not necessarily carry similar results. Perhaps Acorn students are generally far less recalcitrant than most, and Bayview students as a group would resent the new policy and rebel by refusing to study or attend classes or by exhibiting disruptive behavior at school. If so, then the author's recommendation might turn out to be counterproductive.

To sum up, as it stands, the editorial fails to establish either (1) a clear cause-and-effect relationship between Acorn's school-uniform policy and the cited successes at Acorn or (2) that a similar policy would result in similar successes at Bayview. Instead of relying on questionable reports from a single school, which might very well serve as a poor point of comparison for Bayview, the editorial's author should supply credible evidence—perhaps from a reliable scientific study—about the psychological effects of school-uniform requirements on the academic performance and other behavior of students similar to the ones at Bayview.

ARGUMENT No. 117

A New Parking Garage for River City

The author of this editorial asserts that in order to strengthen the economy of the area around River City's Dock Street, the city should approve the proposed construction of a multilevel parking garage on Dock Street, a course of action that would require demolishing most buildings on the block. To support the plan, the author claims that the buildings that would be demolished to make way for the garage are of no economic value because they are among the city's oldest. In defending the plan against concerns of historic preservationists, the author points out that even in ancient cities such as Jerusalem and Athens, old buildings are demolished to make way for new ones that improve the local economy. I find the author's argument unconvincing on several grounds.

To begin with, the author seems to assume that the buildings that would be demolished have no economic value simply because they are relatively old. Yet the author provides no evidence to substantiate this assumption. For all we know, there might be other possible uses for those buildings that would provide net economic benefits to the city exceeding those of the proposed plan. Perhaps these buildings, which the author implies are historic, would be moneymaking tourist attractions or upscale office buildings or loft-style condominiums that would bolster the city's tax base. In short, without weighing the net economic benefits of various alternatives for the old buildings, the author cannot justify the proposed plan based on the fact that the buildings are old.

As for the author's defense against concerns for historic preservation, the author's analogy to Athens and Jerusalem is dubious at best. In all likelihood, those two cities boast a great number of very old buildings, whereas River City might not. Accordingly, demolishing some old buildings around Dock Street might be deemed a great historic loss for that city, while in Athens or Jerusalem, it might not—especially if the demolished buildings have less historic value than others in these cities. Also, it is possible that in Athens and Jerusalem, old buildings are demolished only when they are shown to provide no marginal economic value or if they pose a significant public safety threat and that neither condition is true of the old Dock Street buildings. Finally, perhaps space is more scarce in those cities than in River City, in which case the demolition might be justifiable in those cities but not in River City.

Finally, the author's claim that in order to strengthen its economy, River City should approve the proposal rests on the assumption that there are no viable alternative means of achieving this end. Yet the author fails to substantiate this assumption. Common sense tells me that there are a host of other ways River City might strengthen its economy. Perhaps one of those ways would be just as, or even more, effective than the proposed plan—in which case, the proposal would not seem compelling at all.

In the final analysis, the author's argument rests precariously on faulty reasoning and scant evidence. Instead of relying on a poor analogy between River City and two ancient cities, the author should show—by comparing all possible means of strengthening River City's economy (including saving the old buildings and putting them to productive use)—that the proposed plan is in fact necessary.

ARGUMENT No. 122

Maximizing Employee Productivity at Diversified Manufacturing

In this memo, the human resources department of Diversified Manufacturing (DM) claims that DM could help counteract its declining market share by changing its paid-vacation policy for its professional staff. The new policy, like the current one, would provide four vacation weeks per year; but the new policy would limit any vacation to one week.

According to the memo, DM's central-office managers report that their employees are most productive just before vacations. Based on these reports, the department reasons that under the new policy, DM's professional staff would give DM more days of maximum productivity. The department's argument suffers from four serious reasoning flaws, which together serve to completely undermine it.

First, the memo provides no evidence that the reports from the managers are reliable. The managers might have fabricated the reports so that the company would adopt vacation policies that they would prefer for themselves. The memo's author must first convince me that the reports are not biased; not until then could I begin to consider the department's recommendation.

Secondly, for all we know based on the memo, DM's professional staff, as a group, already limit their own vacations to one week each. If so, then implementing the recommended policy would have absolutely no effect on productivity, let alone market share.

Thirdly, while the reports involved employees of DM's central-office managers, the new policy would apply to DM's "professional staff." It is unfair to assume that the productivity patterns of the former group are similar to those of the latter—unless of course the managers' employees as a group are considered to be professional staff.

Finally, the memo fails to consider possible productivity losses resulting from the new policy. Single-week vacations might not afford employees sufficient time to fully rejuvenate themselves, and burn-out might result. Moreover, it might be impracticable for staff members to interrupt their jobs for a vacation more than once a year, in which case burn-out would be even more likely. On the other hand, if employees do take full advantage of the new policy, their more frequent vacations might serve to stanch organizational workflow, especially with respect to projects requiring sustained, uninterrupted effort and progress.

In a nutshell, the department's argument depends on potentially unreliable and irrelevant reports from central-office managers and on an overly simple analysis of how vacation policies impact worker productivity. Thus, lacking certain additional information, I find the argument dubious at best. In order to properly evaluate it, at a minimum, I would want to know whether or not the central-office managers and their employees are professional staff, and I would want to survey DM's professional staff about how they would respond to the proposed policy. I would also want to study the impact of this sort of policy on organizational efficiency among similar firms.

ARGUMENT No. 124

How Exeunt Theater Company Can Increase Profits

In this memo, the director of Exeunt Theater Company (ETC) anticipates an increase in revenues from ticket sales because ETC has moved to a larger theater. The director then recommends two courses of action in order "to further increase profits": (1) producing plays that have been most successful in the nation's largest cities and (2) hiring Adlib Theater Company's fundraising director, on the basis that corporate contributions to Adlib have increased dramatically during the three years she has worked for Adlib. I find the director's argument unconvincing because it rests on numerous unsubstantiated assumptions, as discussed below.

As a threshold matter, the director's expectation of increased revenues due to an increase in seating capacity assumes that there is pent-up, unfulfilled demand for seating at ETC's productions. Unless the director can provide clear evidence to substantiate this assumption, I cannot be convinced that ETC's revenue, let alone its profits, will increase as a result of moving to the larger theater—especially if the cost of renting the larger theater exceeds the cost of renting a smaller one.

Turning to the first prescription for enhancing profits, the director's rationale for it rests on the assumption that the tastes and interests of theatergoers in the city where ETC's theater is located are similar to those of theatergoers in large cities. However, the director provides no evidence that this is the case. Therefore, I remain unconvinced that ETC will increase profits by producing the plays that are the most successful ones in large cities.

Turning next to the second profit prescription, here the director might very well confuse cause and effect with mere correlation. Specifically, just because Adlib's fundraising director has worked for Adlib during the same time period that corporate contributions to Adlib have increased, it is unfair to conclude that the latter is attributable to the former. Until ETC's director establishes a clear causal connection between the two, I remain skeptical of the recommendation to hire Adlib's director—at least on this basis.

Even if ETC's director can convince me that the two prescriptions are likely to increase ETC's profits, the director concludes too hastily that these prescriptions are the best means of achieving ETC's desired profit goals. Perhaps one or more other courses of action would be as effective or more effective in maximizing ETC's profits. Without weighing all of ETC's options, the director simply cannot convince me that ETC should adopt the director's recommendation.

In the final analysis, the recommendation is unjustified as it stands. To bolster it, the director might conduct a scientific survey of area theatergoers to determine the sorts of ETC productions area residents are most likely to attend, and if ETC's current theater is more expensive to rent than a smaller one, whether or not the demand for those productions warrants ETC's recent move to the larger theater. To better evaluate the argument, I would need to investigate the circumstances surrounding the increase in corporate contributions to Adlib, to determine their true cause. I would also need to know what other means for increasing profits are at ETC's disposal—to determine whether or not the director's proposed course of action is in fact the optimal one.

ARGUMENT No. 131

Omega University's Music-Therapy Program

In this memo, the music department chair at Omega University argues that in order to improve its financial status, Omega should aim to increase enrollment in its music-therapy degree program. To support this argument, the chair reasons that Omega graduates will easily find jobs in the field because (1) group music therapy has been shown to be beneficial to mental-illness patients, and (2) the number of music-therapy job openings has increased during the past year. For several reasons, I find the director's argument unpersuasive.

With respect to the argument's penultimate conclusion—that Omega's graduates will easily find music-therapy jobs—the chair assumes that in the future, there will continue to be sufficient job openings in music therapy for Omega graduates. However, a recent one-year increase is insufficient evidence in itself to convince me that this trend will continue, providing a ready job supply for new Omega graduates. Moreover, should this trend actually reverse, then adopting the chair's proposal might result in a decrease in Omega's job-placement rate, which might very well have a negative impact on the school's overall reputation and, in turn, financial status.

Even assuming a continuing ready supply of music-therapy jobs, the validity of the chair's penultimate conclusion depends on the additional assumption that Omega graduates will be able and willing to accept those jobs. However, employers in this field might favor graduates of other schools over Omega graduates, for whatever reason. Or new jobs might open predominantly in geographic areas where Omega graduates are unable or unwilling to live and work. In either case, by increasing enrollment in its music-therapy program, Omega might actually reduce its job-placement rate, which, as explained earlier, might serve to diminish Omega's financial status.

Turning to the chair's ultimate conclusion—that the proposed course of action will improve Omega's financial status—here the chair fails to establish a clear cause-and-effect relationship. Perhaps the chair reasons that if Omega's job-placement rate for its music-therapy graduates improves, then Omega will command higher tuition or attract greater financial support from alumni, governments, or corporations. However, with no solid evidence to support this reasoning, the chair's claim amounts to little more than pure conjecture.

By the same token, the chair fails to consider the costs of expanding Omega's music-therapy program. Accommodating additional students might require additional equipment, faculty members, and even facilities. Such costs might very well outweigh marginal revenue, in which case the chair's proposal would turn to be poor financial advice.

To sum up, neither the argument's penultimate nor ultimate conclusion is born out by the evidence provided in the memo. A proper evaluation of the former conclusion (i.e., that Omega graduates will easily find music-therapy jobs) would require (1) more information about the reputation of Omega's music-therapy program among employers of music therapists and (2) reliable music-therapy employment projections for recent college graduates, especially in the vicinity of Omega. To fully assess the chair's ultimate claim (i.e., that an expanded music-therapy program will improve Omega's financial status), I would need reliable, detailed projections of Omega's marginal costs and revenues should it follow the chair's recommendation.

Your online ticket to educational and professional success!

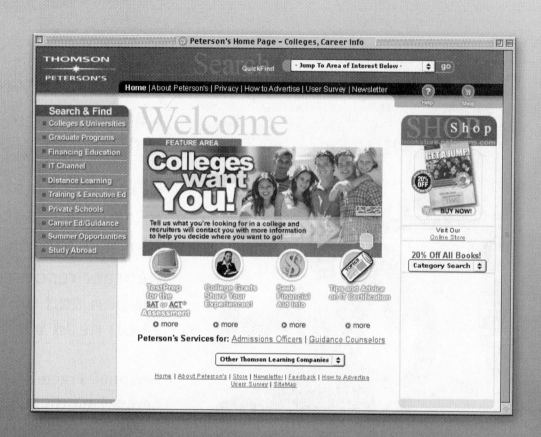

At **petersons.com**, *you can explore thousands of colleges, graduate programs, and distance learning programs; take online practice tests; and search the Internet's largest scholarship database and you'll find career advice you can use—tips on resumes, job-search strategies, interviewing techniques and more.*

www.petersons.com ■ tel: 800.338.3282

THOMSON

PETERSON'S